# England's
# MEDIEVAL
# NAVY

# *England's* MEDIEVAL NAVY

## 1066–1509

*Ships, Men & Warfare*

SUSAN ROSE

**Seaforth**
PUBLISHING

*For the Principal and Fellows of Lady Margaret Hall,*
*Where my love of history was nourished and encouraged*

First published in Great Britain in 2013 by
Seaforth Publishing,
Pen & Sword Books Ltd,
47 Church Street,
Barnsley S70 2AS

www.seaforthpublishing.com

*British Library Cataloguing in Publication Data*
A catalogue record for this book is available from the British Library

ISBN 978 1 84832 137 3

Maps by Peter Wilkinson
Typeset and designed by Roger Daniels
Printed and bound in China by 1010 Printing International Ltd

HALF TITLE PAGE
This picture from a chronicle written in Flanders depicts England as a sea-girt nation. The prospect is from Flanders, possibly Bruges, and is, of course, imaginary. The ships shown are early fifteenth century vessels.

(BRITISH LIBRARY)

TITLE PAGE
A romanticised version of the Battle of Damme by a nineteenth-century artist. It does convey the way sea battles were fought at very close quarters in this period. Most of the other images in the book are from medieval illuminated manuscripts.

(© NATIONAL MARITIME MUSEUM, GREENWICH, LONDON)

# CONTENTS

A general map of England and France showing the major medieval ports in each realm.

England and France 1000–1500

IRELAND

*Irish Sea*

ENGLAND

*North Sea*

Kinsale

London

Sandwich · *The Downs*

Antwerp

Southampton · Winchelsea · Dover

FLANDERS

Portsmouth · Calais

*Isle of Wight* · Boulogne

Plymouth · Montreuil

Dartmouth · Crécy

Kingsbridge

St Michaels Mount · Dieppe

PONTHIEU

PICARDY

Guernsey

*Bay of the Seine* · Harfleur

Jersey · Rouen

Caen · *River Seine* · Paris

NORTH ATLANTIC OCEAN

NORMANDY

Brest · St Malo

BRITTANY

FRANCE

MAINE

*River Loire*

*Bay of Bourgneuf*

ANJOU

POITOU

Ile de Ré · La Rochelle

Ile D'Oléron

Gironde · *River Charente*

Bordeaux · *River Dordogne*

*Bay of Biscay*

*River Lot*

*River Garonne*

Bayonne

NAVARRE

CASTILLE

The Narrow Seas East: the area between England and the Low Countries where many of the most important encounters between English and enemy shipping took place is shown in some detail.

The Narrow Seas West: the waters between the south of England and the north of France, which for the majority of the period after 1213 constituted the frontier between the two kingdoms.

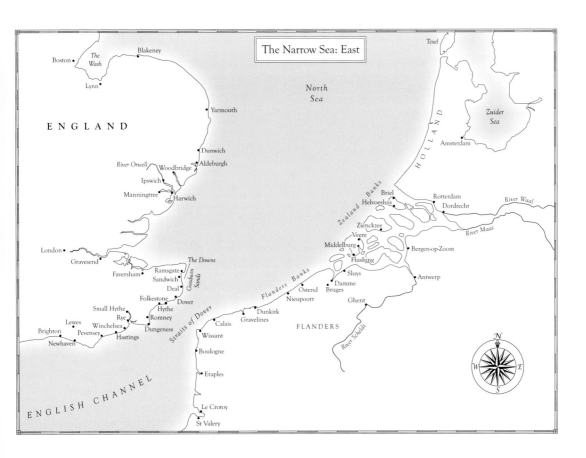

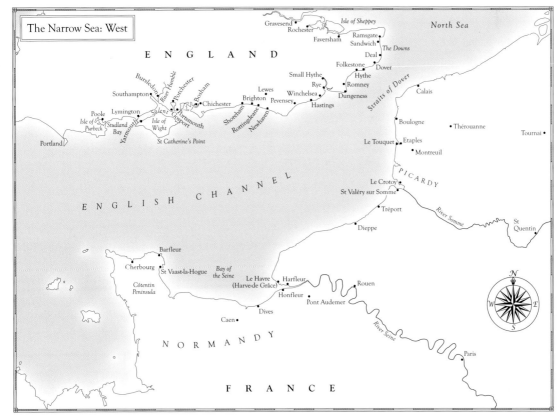

# The Realm of England and its Neighbours

Shakespeare's image of the realm of England as:

> a precious stone set in a silver sea,
> which serves it in the office of a wall
> Or as a moat defensive to a house
> Against the envy of less happier lands[1]

has bitten deep into the English imagination. It is linked to ideas of naval strength and the notion that England has always resisted invaders, safe behind its watery ramparts. To the English people of an earlier period, from around the end of the eighth to the middle of the eleventh centuries, such an idea might well have appeared ridiculous. The sea, rather than being a defensive wall, was the highway by which successive waves of invaders arrived bringing destruction, insecurity and fear in their wake.

In 787 a local official or reeve in a coastal village in Mercian territory, who had gone to find out who were the strangers who had come ashore from three unknown ships, was slain by the intruders. The *Anglo-Saxon Chronicle* then stated, 'these were the first ships of the Danes to come to England.'[2] Six years later it recorded that on 8 January 793, 'the harrying of the heathen miserably destroyed God's church on Lindisfarne by rapine and slaughter.'[3] The years that followed were marked by more frequent, bolder, and more serious incursions which gradually changed from expeditions for plunder to attempts at conquest and colonisation by the seafaring peoples of the north. Whether called Norsemen, Danes or Vikings, all arrived by sea in well-armed groups which usually had little difficulty in overcoming any resistance offered at the coast and moved rapidly inland. Despite Alfred's defeat of the Danish invaders at the end of the ninth century and his efforts at building up a defensive force of ships, until the middle of the eleventh century England continued to be on the periphery of a northern world centred on Scandinavia. From 1016–42, England was, in fact, ruled as part of the northern empire established by Cnut of Denmark.

The accession of Edward, usually known as 'the Confessor', returned the crown to a dynasty of Anglo-Saxon origin, but to many in England the situation in 1066 following his death must have seemed familiar, threatening a repeat of earlier raids and invasions. While an Englishman, Harold Godwinson, had acceded to the throne, he was confronted

by rival claimants: William in Normandy and Harald Hardrada from Norway. What was completely unexpected was the result of the events of September/October 1066.

On 25 September 1066 Harold utterly routed the combined forces of Harald Hardrada and his own rebellious brother Tostig at Stamford Bridge outside York. Twenty-four vessels sufficed to transport home the defeated Norsemen who had originally landed from more than three hundred ships. Just under three weeks later, on 14 October outside Hastings – 'at the grey apple tree' in the words of the *Chronicle* – Harold himself and the great majority of his thanes and housecarls were themselves slain by the victorious army of William, Duke of Normandy. The rapid establishment of the new Norman dynasty, supported by a new aristocracy with for the most part the same origins, served to alter the strategic imperatives of English monarchs. Nicholas Rodger has gone so far as to state 'that it is a striking paradox that the Norman Conquest made possible by an impressive fleet caused the rapid decline of English sea power.' England was now part of a state which occupied both sides of the English Channel, but which had much less interest in the realms to the north, and 'exercised only feeble and intermittent power over the nearer parts of the Celtic world':[4] Wales, Scotland and Ireland.

Both the King/Duke and many of his most important noble followers held lands on both sides of the Channel. It was inevitable that, from this time on, one of the main

This is a photograph of the replica of the Viking ship known as Skudelev 2 under sail. This was one of the ships excavated from the Roskilde Fjord in Denmark where a number of ships were sunk in the eleventh century to block access to the harbour. This ship was clearly a warship and the vessels of the Danish invaders of England in the ninth and tenth centuries would have resembled this ship.

(WERNER KARRASCH, THE VIKING SHIP MUSEUM, DENMARK)

preoccupations of English rulers would be their relationships with the various counties and duchies to the south and the east which made up the realm of France and the Low Countries. The likelihood of coastal raids or more serious incursions mounted by rulers from Scandinavia diminished as these areas were torn by internal conflict, but within the British Isles there was also a continual possibility of war with the Scots, the Welsh and the Irish.

While English monarchs remained Dukes of Normandy, the whole stretch of the Channel coast fronting England was usually in friendly hands. The rulers of Flanders and Brittany were normally well disposed to the English, while ties with Normandy were naturally very close. The Crown's main need for shipping was for swift transit across the Channel between the two sections of the royal dominions. There was an even greater need for this after Henry of Anjou (later Henry II) had become Duke of Aquitaine and the ruler of large tracts of southwest France, following his marriage in 1152 to Eleanor, the heiress of Aquitaine. Two years later he had also been crowned King of England. The so-called Angevin Empire stretched from the border with Scotland to the foothills of the Pyrenees.

His sons and successors, Richard I and John, were, however, confronted with a resurgent French monarchy forever aiming to extend its power over the lands of its 'over-mighty' vassals like the Angevins. John lost control of Normandy following the Battle of Bouvines in 1214. The frontiers of the remaining English domains in France were frequently under attack and fluctuated considerably as the fortunes of war varied between the two rival powers. Once he had seized control of Normandy, the French king had excellent ports on the Channel coast under his direct rule. English rulers from the reign of John had much greater need of naval power: not only vessels which could maintain communications with their more distant dominions, but which were also capable of both offensive and defensive action at sea against a determined adversary. Commercial rivalries between the merchants and mariners of both realms added another cause of tension, which was often increased by the activities of sea rovers of various kinds. Some merely took advantage of the opportunity to enrich themselves by robbery at sea; others claimed some sort of justification, whether acting in reprisal for losses already suffered or against the enemies of the Crown. Piracy, to use the modern term, was, of course, not a new problem. It had long been a hazard of seaborne trade but, as trade increased in quantity and value in the thirteenth and early fourteenth centuries, it became more widespread, and was particularly associated with the mariners of the west of England and the Brittany coast.

William the Conqueror had successfully asserted his rule only over the kingdom of the English within the British Isles, but his successors had ambitions to extend their rule over all the peoples of the islands. In the west lay the Welsh principalities and over the sea were the lands of the Irish. In the north, Scotland's border with England was not clearly defined and the scene of frequent conflict which easily escalated to bitterly fought warfare. More or less any military activity against the Welsh, the Scots or the Irish necessitated the use of ships. Because of the difficulties in travelling overland in the rough

terrain of both Wales and Scotland and the adjoining parts of England, the prime need was for naval transports of all kinds, taking men and provisions, horses and war machines, and all other kinds of war materiel to the scene of conflict. The need for warships as usually understood was limited in these campaigns. The wars with neighbours across the Channel, well able to create their own naval forces, were more likely to involve both transports and vessels with an offensive capacity.

Whether the main theatre of war was in the British Isles or across the Channel was determined by the inclinations and ability of individual monarchs and the situation in which they found themselves in relation to their adversaries. John faced a French invasion from across the Channel. His son Henry III faced problems in his remaining French territories, Gascony and Poitou, as well as troubles in Wales. Edward I, the conqueror of Wales and the 'Hammer of the Scots', was in dire need of naval transports for his armies and their supplies for most of his reign while fighting these campaigns, but also needed to be on his guard against the French king.

From the early years of the fourteenth century, the military strategy of English kings, whether on land or by sea, was driven by two imperatives. On the one hand their relations with Scotland were of continuing importance and met with varying success; the Scots triumphed at Bannockburn in 1314, while David II of Scotland was a captive in England from 1346–57. On the other hand, relations with France continued to dominate much English policy. A series of limited campaigns in the first half of the fourteenth century merged into the long-term conflict known to later historians as the Hundred Years War. This formally began when Edward III claimed to be the rightful king of France in October 1337 and only finally drew to a close in 1453, by which time the English had lost all their French lands except the town and Pale of Calais. Warfare was not, of course, continuous throughout this whole period. The advantage shifted from one combatant

A vessel depicted in the Bayeux Tapestry, a record of the Norman invasion of 1066 made probably by nuns in Canterbury shortly after the events depicted. The side rudder is clearly shown and the almost identical stem- and sternposts decorated with animal heads. The row of shields along the side of the ship protected the crew. The ship is shown under sail but probably carried oars as well.

(AUTHOR'S COLLECTION)

to the other, and open conflict was interrupted by some lengthy periods of truce. At sea, the logistical support of royal armies continued to be of great importance. The possibility of encounters at sea between enemy fleets leading to something that could be called a naval battle increased, perhaps made more likely by developments in ship design.

Commerce-raiding continued to be a continual hazard, principally in the Channel and on the routes taken by traders in wine from Bordeaux and its region, and in salt from the Bay of Bourgneuf. During the second half of the fifteenth century, even if the Crown initiated little in the way of naval activity as the country became embroiled in the civil wars known as the Wars of the Roses, there were advances in navigation and ship-handling which would underpin the achievements of the navy of the Tudor monarchs. Perhaps it was in this relatively quiet period as far as overseas military expeditions by the English Crown are concerned, and when the French Crown, having driven the English from virtually all French territory, had become more interested in the politics of the Italian states than its old enemy across the Channel, the myth of English invulnerability to seaborne invasion began to grow. During the reign of Elizabeth, this myth was reinforced by English successes in the conflict with Spain and was put into Shakespeare's ringing and evocative words. Certainly to the English people of the period with which we are concerned (1066–1509), his picture of the sea as England's wall and 'moat defensive' might well have seemed an overly optimistic view of both the distant past and more recent history. Many coastal towns could look back at raids on their territory, and the fear of invasion remained.

This is a somewhat fanciful image of the battle of Hastings from a fifteenth-century chronicle. This is depicted as a contemporary land battle. The Norman fleet can, however, be seen in the background. Seaborne invasions were greatly feared by the English at this period.

**(BRITISH LIBRARY)**

The Tower of London showing the King conferring with his Council. London Bridge is shown in the background with the Pool of London and merchant ships. River craft are shown in the foreground. The picture emphasises the importance of ships and mariners to the kingdom.

(BRITISH LIBRARY)

In the chapters which follow, the way in which English kings after the Conquest learnt to use the navy of England to increase the safety and prosperity of the kingdom will be described and analysed. At this period, the word 'navy' was used for any general body of ships. To contemporaries, therefore, the navy of England included all vessels in the realm whether owned by the monarch or by private individuals, not just fighting ships. The design of ships and harbour facilities and fortifications, the development of navigation and what is known of the lives of mariners will also be discussed, along with some comparisons with the navies of England's closest neighbours. The unspoken aim of successive monarchs was perhaps to begin to build 'the wall of England', its naval defences, with a success which became apparent in later centuries.

## CHAPTER I

# The Sources for Medieval Maritime History

SIR NICHOLAS HARRIS NICOLAS, writing in the first half of the nineteenth century in the Preface of his *History of the Royal Navy*, declared that 'it is from the Chroniclers that the narratives of expeditions and sea fights have been derived', but went on to explain how 'all the details which afford accurate and complete information of Naval matters' have been taken from royal writs and accounts.[1] Any modern writer will be forced to follow much the same approach. For most of the period from 1066–1500 official legal and financial records are by far the most plentiful written documents. These were compiled by the clerks in the Chancery and Exchequer, the basic organs of royal government. It is not until the late fourteenth and fifteenth centuries that more personal and private documents can be found which give some limited impression of individual personalities. Another possible source, especially with regard to ship design, is visual material of various kinds including illustrations in manuscripts and town seals. There are also, of course, material survivals from the period which cast light on maritime history and the people who made their living from the sea. While excavated wrecks from our period in British waters are few and far between, and contain little in the way of surviving equipment or personal possessions, we can also learn from the layout of harbours and coastal towns and their fortifications. All these will be discussed below.

This picture comes from the margin of a manuscript. The vessels shown are probably intended to be cogs. The ferocity of sea warfare is conveyed, along with the fact that the taking of prisoners for ransom was seldom practised at sea, although usual in land battles.

(BRITISH LIBRARY)

## Chronicles and narratives

Medieval England is in general well served by chroniclers, who often provide a careful and thoughtful narrative of events. While the earliest writers were churchmen, by the second half of the fourteenth century chronicles were also kept by laymen, most notably in the City of London, and had become in some cases more deliberately literary creations rather than mere annals. Chronicles dating from after the Conquest were usually in Latin, until either English or occasionally French became more common in the late fourteenth and fifteenth centuries. While most chroniclers have a reasonably good understanding of their own society and the way it was organised, a particular problem can be encountered when they are writing about maritime affairs. It is more or less impossible to know if any individual writer had any direct experience of the sea or had ever himself been on board a vessel, no matter what the circumstances. The details of sea fights tend to be glossed over in standard phrases with, not surprisingly, most emphasis laid on the result. There was also little acceptance of the modern belief that writers should not copy the works of their predecessors without acknowledgement. It was very easy for a standardised stereotypical account of a battle to become part of a chronicler's 'toolbox', as it were, to be produced in the appropriate place when needed.

This is an early picture of a sea battle from a copy of *De Re Militaris*, a Latin handbook of good practice for commanders that has a short section on naval warfare. The weapons used in war at sea are shown, including longbows, crossbows and pikes. There is little sign of tactics particular to a sea battle.

(SOURCE?)

The account of the battle of Dover in 1217 between the French and the supporters of the young King Henry III in a contemporary verse biography of William the Marshal is dramatic, but says little of the way the two fleets were handled. The author lays more emphasis on statements like 'When they captured a ship they [the English] did not fail to kill all they found aboard and threw them to the fishes leaving only one or two and occasionally three alive.'[2] Describing the same event, Matthew Paris, the highly regarded chronicler based at St Albans Abbey, mentions the English fleet changing course in response to a wind shift which was to their advantage, but says little else about the course of the battle.[3] After describing a conventional boarding action, he was clearly most interested in the grisly execution of Eustace the Monk, a Flemish sea rover who became something of a folk hero. Neither writer was present at the battle and it is hard to discover whether they had access to any participants, or were merely relying on common reports of the encounter.

In the few cases where it is clear that the writer was well versed in maritime matters and was present at a sea battle, more reliable detailed information can sometimes be included. The life of a Spanish nobleman adventurer, Dom Pero Niño, by his standard bearer, Gutierre Diaz de Gamez, known as *El Victorial* includes valuable information about the tactics used at sea by experienced commanders.[4] The author had much to say about galley warfare in the Mediterranean where he had sailed with his master. In 1406, Niño was supporting the French Crown in the Channel and the waters off Cornwall. One story concerns an encounter in the Channel not far from Calais between the Spanish galleys assisted by some French balingers (small swift ships equipped with both oars and sails) and an English fleet of sailing ships. The author explains how the galley crews were given courage by a ration of wine handed out before the battle commenced. He lays emphasis on the wind direction and its strength, and how a fire ship was allowed to drift towards the enemy at the beginning of the battle. Finally, he describes how one of the leading galleys was saved from capture by the English by a French balinger suddenly altering course in the midst of the fray and ramming an English ship.[5] This incident does not appear in contemporary English chronicles and may perhaps over-emphasise the skills and bravery of Niño and his galleymen, but it also casts light on fighting at sea, which is often dismissed as little more than hand-to-hand fighting on the decks of vessels grappled together.

Despite these problems, however, chronicles are invaluable for their accounts of events. It must be remembered that not only those originating in England itself can be helpful but also those written in France, the Low Countries, and elsewhere. The accounts of

This is a short extract from a naval account from around 1350 in The National Archives and gives some idea of the usual layout. All sums of money on the right of the image are in Roman figures and refer to 'money of account' pounds, l (libri), s (solidi or shillings), and d (denarii or pence). This bore little relation to the actual coinage in people's pockets. The title 'Recepta' (receipts) is in the right-hand margin.

**(THE NATIONAL ARCHIVES)**

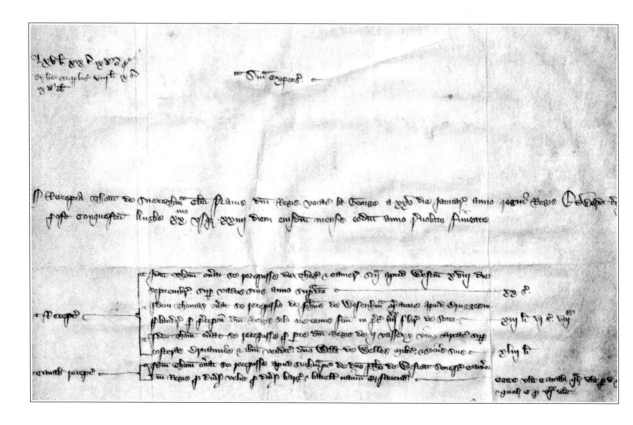

campaigns and battles in chapter 7 will make clear how much information about English maritime affairs is found in narrative sources from a wide range of European countries, as well as from England itself.

## Royal documents: accounts, writs and legal documents

The earliest payments to shipmasters are recorded among the final section, the so-called 'foreign accounts', of the Pipe Rolls, which were kept separate from the bulk of the rolls which relate to the dues and fees of county sheriffs. The purpose of these rolls was to record the accounts of sheriffs and all other officials who received or expended royal funds. The rolls constitute the main audited accounts of the Exchequer and run in a continuous series from 2 Henry II (December 1155/December 1156) till 1810. By 1358, in the reign of Edward III, an official with the title of Clerk of the King's Ships existed, with separate audited accounts in this part of the Pipe Rolls. These rolls had, however, finally

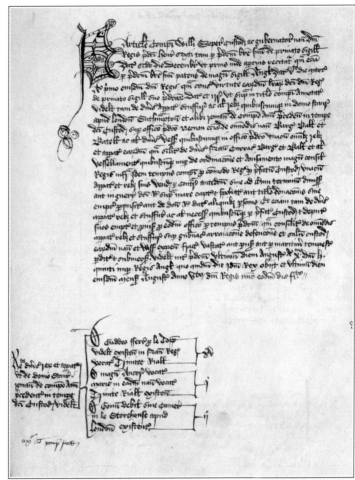

This the opening page of the Account Book of William Soper, Clerk of the King's Ships 1421–27. It sets out the basis on which he held the office and then lists equipment in store belonging to a royal ship called the *Trinity Royal*, including an anchor called Marie.

(© NATIONAL MARITIME MUSEUM, GREENWICH, LONDON)

become so bulky and awkward to handle that from 42 Edward III (1368/9) certain accounts were enrolled on separate Rolls of Foreign Accounts. The Accounts of the Clerks of the King's Ships were included in this group and can be found on the Foreign Account Rolls from 1371 till 1452, when no new appointments were made to this office till the reign of Henry VII.[6] Between 1233 and 1426/7 the Pipe Rolls also contain a few scattered 'special' accounts for the building of galleys and other ships for the Crown.

A great deal of very useful financial and other material concerning the use made of ships by the Crown can also be found among what is known at The National Archives as Exchequer Accounts Various.[7] This is a vast collection of accounts, writs, indentures, and other documents on many topics, but a great deal is usefully indexed under the heading of Army Navy and Ordnance, beginning with items from the reign of John. Many of the documents are particulars of account: that is, the accounts kept by an individual officer concerning his income and expenditure which were delivered to the Exchequer, often at the end of a term of office, and used by the Exchequer clerks to make up the audited accounts. Their survival is much more patchy and sporadic than that of the audited rolls;

This picture well illustrates the problems in using pictures from medieval manuscripts as evidence for ship design; here it is easy to see that the waves have been depicted schematically. It is not so easy to interpret the way the hull of the ship has been shown.

many officials probably took them back to their homes once the tedious auditing process had been completed. The particulars of account of William Soper for 1422–27, for example, can be found in the collection of the National Maritime Museum, having formerly been part of the Phillipps collection, rather than at Kew in The National Archives.[8] If they did remain at the Exchequer the clerks do not seem to have regarded their safe keeping as much of a priority. There are also accounts relating to individual royal campaigns or directed to particular ships' masters for repairs, mariners' wages, or for victualling ships. For certain periods, particularly in the fourteenth century when the monarchs were using the Chamber rather than the Exchequer as the royal office in charge of the finances of a war campaign, the details of payments to ships and their crews can be found in the Wardrobe Books. Details of accounts relating to shipbuilding and repairs from the reigns of Henry VII, when the office of Clerk of the King's Ships was resuscitated, can be found in ledgers in the series called Exchequer Books.[9]

Many other classes of documents also contain information about naval and maritime affairs. The most useful are probably the Patent and Close Rolls, which contain the text of writs and other royal orders directed by the King to individuals or corporations. These documents can be used to trace the careers of shipmasters or royal officials, or to find details of the gathering together of royal fleets. Complaints of robbery at sea may also appear here, along with the appointment of commissions of inquiry. Town archives, particularly those of London, Exeter and Southampton, also contain material about maritime matters, but most documents are more concerned with trading vessels and their cargoes rather than the use of ships by the Crown.

Documents coming from private sources are not plentiful, and date entirely from the fifteenth century. One or two of the Paston Letters provide a small amount of important

This image of a Mediterranean galley comes from the earliest known manuscript which contains technical shipbuilding material, including some attempt to depict sections through a hull. Here the image is most informative about the design of the sail and provides little extra information about hull design. This was still largely a matter of the experience of the shipwright in the early fifteenth century.

(BOOK OF MICHAEL OF RHODES)

information.[10] The Cely Papers include accounts relating to the purchase and operation of a merchant ship by the London wool merchants George and Richard Cely in the 1480s.[11] In much the same period, the Howard Household Books have references to the small fleet operated by the Duke of Norfolk, which was sometimes used on royal business.[12] There are also a small number of polemical writings which discuss naval and maritime matters. Of these the best known is probably the *Libelle of Englyshe Polycye* which, *c.*1436, used the metaphor for the Channel as a defensive wall taken up by Shakespeare over a century later. In the words of the poem, 'England was likened to a cite/ And the wall environ was the sea.'[13]

### Visual and material sources

Faced with the restricted nature of some documentary sources and the doubtful reliability of others, images of ships in all kinds of media can provide valuable evidence. The same can be said of material survivals like the remains of wrecked vessels and contemporary model ships. All can provide evidence not easily come by elsewhere.

*Images in illuminated manuscripts and other sources*

There are many beautiful illustrations in manuscripts from our period which include ships of all kinds involved in all kinds of activities. There are also carvings in wood and in stone, graffiti, and images on seals and coins. There are, however, some major difficulties in using these images as evidence, whether for the design of a ship or the way it was handled, or for any other purpose. There are issues to do with the artistic conventions of the day, the limitations of the medium involved and, as with chroniclers, the level of first-hand knowledge of maritime matters which the maker may or may not have possessed. Virtually none of these images was originally created with the intention of conveying technical information to the viewer.

The vivid images of building William the Conqueror's invasion fleet found in the Bayeux Tapestry were not only created in embroidery on linen, but were intended to be a small part of a visual endorsement of William's right to claim the throne of England. Many of the striking and often reproduced images of incidents in the Hundred Years War, including the battle of Sluys and the battle of La Rochelle, were originally made for a particularly fine and costly copy of *Froissart's Chronicle*, illuminated in the fifteenth century about a hundred years after the events depicted.[14] *The Beauchamp Pageant*, which includes important drawings of the use of ships in warfare, was produced between around 1483 and 1492, as a celebration of the life of Richard Beauchamp, Earl of Warwick, who died in 1439.[15] The problems associated with the use of medieval illustrations of ships and shipping as historical evidence have been fully discussed by Joe Flatman in a recent book. He emphasises that, despite the problems and if used with caution, medieval illustrations can 'enrich technological analyses of vessel traditions, materials and components.' He is also inclined to see the artists as often depicting 'genuine experiments in maritime technology'.[16] His conclusion that 'medieval illuminated manuscripts are no more likely to present technologically unrealistic arcane or archaic images than is modern advertising' seems reasonable, but holds good for the period in which the image was produced, not for the period it may be ostensibly representing.

Another problem with these illustrations also needs consideration. This relates to the interpretation of the images when they depict, for example, hull planking. A schematic way of representing waves, quite common in these images, causes us no problem; we are well aware of what is being represented. With particular hull types we do not have certain information from other sources of the precise way in which a hull was designed and built, of the model which the artist was using. It is here that attempted interpretations may, in fact, be misleading without very careful and critical consideration. What, for example are we to make of the extreme curvature of the two topmost strakes, or planks, of the hull which can be seen in many illuminations of ships from the thirteenth and early fourteenth centuries? Could such a hull design have been seaworthy or practical?[17] To what extent are images on seals or coins distorted to fit the circular space available? The earliest drawings which have some pretensions to being based on up-to-date technology – that is, the methods used by those building galleys in the Arsenale of Venice – are those in the book put together by a Venetian galleyman, Michael of Rhodes, dating from 1434.[18] The first true technical drawings with measurements made in England are those in the treatise dating from c.1580, probably by Matthew Baker, an Elizabethan royal shipwright, known as *Fragments of Ancient English Shipwrightry*.[19] Medieval artists depicting ships never had any intention of producing technically accurate drawings.

### Carvings and coins

Images in other media, carvings in wood or stone, suffer from many of the same difficulties. There is often also the additional problem that where they were originally placed was exposed to the weather, so that details have become eroded and are no longer visible. This erosion is very noticeable in the carvings on the outside of the Greenway Chapel in St Peter's Church, Tiverton; photographs from the early part of the twentieth century are preferable to those taken more recently.[20] Even so, the images are vigorous and striking. Much has also been made of the images on seals, coins and medals. Probably the best known is Edward III's gold noble which shows him triumphant after his victory at Sluys, on board his own ship the *Cog Thomas*. The seal of New Shoreham in Sussex is often cited as the most powerful iconographic evidence for the design of the ship type known as the hulk. The image is of a vessel with a very pronounced bow-shaped hull, with the planking coming right up to the fore and aft castles, where it seems to be held in position with either some sort of block or even ropes. No stem- or sternposts are visible. The weight given to this image is largely derived from the inscription on the seal which reads in Latin '*hoc hulci segno vocor os sic nomine digno*'. The translation, 'by the sign of a hulk I am called Mouth which is a worthy name', begins to make sense when it is remembered that Shoreham's original name was Hulksmouth.[21]

### Evidence from wrecks

The reliability of many of our speculations regarding the design of medieval ships would,

This is a photograph taken at the time of the excavation of the site of the wreck of Henry V's *Gracedieu* in the Hamble River in the 1930s.

(© **NATIONAL MARITIME MUSEUM, GREENWICH, LONDON**)

The Gokstad ship; this magnificent vessel built *c.*890–900 AD was unearthed from a burial mound in the Oslo fjord in 1880. This view shows the remains of the mast, and the ribs supporting the clinker planking. The vessels shown were found in the ship and were probably equipment for cooking on shore or for storing food.

**(WIKIMEDIA)**

of course, be tested if there was a good body of evidence from excavated ships, whether found underwater, or buried on the shore. Unfortunately, however, although more archaeological evidence has been made available in recent years than ever before, it is still scanty, with much weight being given to a handful of prominent examples. In British waters, the most significant known wrecks are those of the *Gracedieu*, built by order of Henry V and launched in 1418, now lying underwater in a bend of the Hamble river above Bursledon, and the Newport ship. This was found buried in the mud on the foreshore of the river Usk at Newport in June 2002, when foundations were being dug for a new arts centre. Fragments of ships' timbers turn up much more frequently, often having been reused to repair wharves and the like; this is particularly the case along the Thames in London, where planking from ships has been found quite often, on both the Southwark and the City sides of the river.[22]

Further afield, close study of the Bremen cog, discovered in the river Weser in 1962, has provided much detailed information of the hull design of this very widespread type of vessel. Other cogs have also been found; for example, one wrecked off Kampen, a

This picture shows English ships approaching Lisbon on their way to join the Crusades; it is not a realistic image. It gives a good idea of the conventional way in which ships were depicted in the elaborately illuminated versions of chronicles and stories produced for kings and nobles, particularly in the fifteenth century. In these illustrations the ships shown are those of the period of the artist not of the event.

**(BRITISH LIBRARY)**

port on the Zuider Zee, and another found in 1997 near the island of Poel in the Baltic. Much of our knowledge of northern ships from an earlier period comes not only from the astonishing vessels excavated from burial mounds, especially the Gokstad ship dating from the end of the ninth century, but also from the group of five ships dating from the eleventh century recovered from the Roskilde fjord in Denmark from 1962. These vessels, known as the Skuldelev ships, were filled with stones and scuppered some two hundred years later than their original construction to form an underwater barrier to prevent other ships entering the fjord. After careful excavation and investigation five ships were identified. Those numbered 2 and 5 were longships or warships; number 1 was a beamy robust cargo ship. All the wrecks, although incomplete and with badly distorted hulls from the weight of the stones placed in them, provided a great deal of information about the techniques and materials used in shipbuilding at this time.[23]

All these wrecks, however, are usually lacking the upper works of the ships. Also, of course, virtually nothing survives of the rigging or the sails; one tiny fragment, less than a couple of inches long, which may be from some hempen cord, was found on the Newport ship. It is nevertheless a unique survival. Replicas of cog ships and of all five of the Skuldelev ships have been constructed in an endeavour to establish their sailing characteristics and to solve some of these problems with regard to upper works, rigging and sails. This form of 'experimental archaeology' has its critics, but if conducted with care and rigour, following a set of clearly defined aims, can add much to our knowledge of vessels of which only incomplete technical information survives.[24]

### Model ships

Another possible source of information about the design and techniques of shipbuilders in our period is model ships. Medieval seafarers or travellers, if they survived a fierce storm or some other terrifying incident at sea, were often moved to record their gratitude at their escape from certain death by donations to a church, or the shrine of the saint whose intervention had saved them. They might also commission an *ex voto* in the form of a ship model to be displayed in the church as a memento of their gratitude. Some of those which have survived to the present day seem to have been made by craftsmen with knowledge of shipbuilding, and provide more evidence of ship construction. The best known of these models, the Mataro model from Portugal, generally thought to date from *c*.1450 and to be that of a carrack, still has much of its rigging, a particularly valuable feature. This model has been frequently described and is presently in a museum in Rotterdam. Another was found in the collegiate church at Ebersdorf, now a suburb of Chemnitz, a place a considerable distance from the sea.

To build up a picture of England's medieval navy, evidence from all these different sources is needed, much in the manner of solving a jigsaw puzzle. There are, of course, still some areas where firm conclusions are difficult, but in the main the combination of all kinds of documentary and material evidence can produce a reasonable understanding of the world of the medieval mariner, particularly those in the service of the Crown. It is to these mariners and their ships we will now turn.

## CHAPTER 2

# Strategic Imperatives

## The Norman invasion

IN THE OPENING SECTIONS of the Bayeux Tapestry there are many images of ships: Harold sets out from Bosham before being captured by Count Guy; William prepares an invasion fleet which then sets out across the Channel laden with armed men and their horses. These familiar pictures seem to suggest that from the very beginning of Norman England its rulers perceived their new realm as a maritime nation: a nation where a successful monarch would perforce have to have an appreciation of the way ships should be used to ensure the safety of the kingdom and its people, and to boost its power. Since the tapestry depicts a devastatingly successful invasion by seaborne forces, defence against an enemy following the same approach might well have been the prime strategic imperative for an English king in the years after 1066.

The tapestry, however, does not depict any naval action. The vessels are transports or passenger vessels. It is still not entirely clear why Harold and his companions embarked at Bosham in 1063 or 1064 on what was to be a fateful voyage; one suggestion is that it was a mere pleasure trip. Other Norman chroniclers rather implausibly state that Harold was on his way to Normandy, sent by Edward the Confessor to confirm the latter's promise to William that he would indeed be Edward's successor on the English throne.[1] There was clearly no warlike intent in the voyage. As they board the ships Harold's companions are shown carrying a hunting dog and a hawk. They had also previously enjoyed a convivial feast. None of the Englishmen seem to be carrying weapons even in the episode which shows Harold's capture by Count Guy.[2]

Similarly, the great fleet which William assembled to bring his forces to England was not intended to fight the English at sea, nor would it have been capable of doing so. Many of the ships (which were apparently not decked) were carrying horses; the ships were laden with arms including chain mail, but none of the men depicted are wearing this for the crossing from Normandy.[3] The nature of the source may lead us to treat it with some caution. Its aim is to glorify the Norman achievement; the medium used also clearly has limitations. There is, however, good evidence from the *Anglo-Saxon Chronicle* and Norse sagas that engagements between fleets were more or less invariably fought in a bay, estuary, or other landing place in close proximity to the shore, not on the high sea. This is not surprising given the design of the longships apparently used by both the Norsemen and the Anglo-Saxons which are shown in the tapestry. These were not only undecked but also had a low freeboard. Despite their inherent seaworthiness, this design feature would have made them very vulnerable to capsize in any sort of boarding action on the open sea.[4] Experience with sailing the replicas of the Skuldelev ships, two of which (Skuldelev 2 and Skuldelev 5) were longships probably built just over twenty years before the Norman invasion, has demonstrated that in favourable conditions both could, nevertheless, travel fast. The replica of Skuldelev 5, *Helge Ask*, recorded a top speed of 15 knots under sail in good weather conditions.[5] The possible speed of ships like these would have compounded the difficulties of defenders with few means of collecting detailed up-to-date intelligence about the enemy's whereabouts. An encounter on the open sea between two opposing fleets would have been largely a matter of chance and the outcome very uncertain. It was much more likely that once the enemy had reached land the defenders' vessels could come up and bar the invaders' retreat to the open sea, or that they might find, and hope to destroy, vessels beached on the foreshore.[6]

From the late ninth century, Anglo-Saxon rulers had had relatively easy access to ships; some were royal vessels, others served for pay, while the bulk of any fleet would be raised from a specifically maritime variant of the duty incumbent on all men to defend the realm. This took the form of an obligation on some landholders to provide a ship, or the cost of a ship in money, and to man it with a local crew.[7] The fact that William had set about collecting a fleet and an army to invade England would have been impossible to hide from merchants and seafarers visiting the Norman coast, and would have relatively quickly reached the ears of Harold Godwinson. In response to this threat, he assembled both land and sea forces at Sandwich in the early summer of 1066 and then, in the words of the *Anglo-Saxon Chronicle*, 'sailed to the Isle of Wight and lay there the whole summer and autumn'. Levies were also stationed all along the coast. The problems in successfully defending his new realm, however, became starkly clear by September. His naval forces

A section of the Bayeux Tapestry showing Harold Godwinson and his companions setting out from Bosham in Sussex with hunting dogs and a hawk. This voyage ended disastrously in the incident in which Harold swore fealty to William of Normandy on holy relics, an incident which provided the justification for the invasion of 1066.

(AUTHOR'S COLLECTION)

ran out of supplies, 'no-one could keep them any longer', so the fleet sailed to London before dispersing.[8]

At that very moment news reached Harold of the arrival in the Tyne of a force of more than three hundred ships under the command of Harald Hardrada of Norway, and then of the fall of York to the invaders. Godwinson had no alternative but to march north to deal with this invasion. This he did triumphantly, winning a spectacular victory at Stamford Bridge outside York. Three days later (28 September) William's forces set sail from St Valéry-sur-Somme and landed at Pevensey the following morning. Even if Harold's fleet had still been at sea somewhere near the Isle of Wight, its chances of successfully intercepting the Norman ships and interrupting the disembarkation of William's forces would have been very low.[9] As had been the case since the first Norse raids on England at the end of the eighth century, the successful defence of England depended on the fighting abilities of land-based forces and the skills of their leaders. The slaughter of the King and most of his supporters at Hastings meant that on this fateful occasion there was little prospect of successful resistance to the Norman invasion.

## After the Conquest

The new rulers had a different strategic perspective from that of their predecessors. The new combined domain of England and Normandy looked to the south across the Channel. The threat from the north was of less concern. This reorientation of England's understanding of her rightful place among neighbouring realms became even more noticeable after the accession of the Angevin dynasty in 1154. The main attention of Henry II and his sons was focused on their lands in southwest France and their rivalry with the King of France. This almost led to a virtual partition of the British Isles, as the outlying Celtic areas were less in awe of the new rulers in England than earlier Saxon and Danish monarchs.[10] The desire to conquer or reassert control over the Welsh, the Irish and the Scots, however, eventually also became an important influence on the strategy of English rulers after the Conquest.

Strategic imperatives regarding the situation across the Channel changed radically in the reign of John. After he had lost control of Normandy around 1204, the Channel once more marked the frontier between England and France, although the English crown still had lands in Gascony. The need to protect England, especially the southern coasts, against attack from the sea became more pressing. In 1213, the battle of Damme led to the destruction of the ships of an enemy threatening invasion, even though it happened almost certainly by lucky chance. English naval forces came upon the French fleet, with some of its vessels beached and some riding at anchor, at Damme in the estuary of the river Zwyn in Flanders. Fighting took place both in the waters of the estuary and on the foreshore. The English destruction of many French ships and the taking of a great deal of booty ensured that Philip III of France abandoned his immediate intention to invade England. The tactics used, however, were little different from those used by King Alfred against the Danes over three hundred years earlier.[11]

A much more significant development in the use of ships to defend the realm occurred in 1217. The regime of the ten-year-old King Henry III was faced with the fact that Louis, the Dauphin of France, had already successfully invaded England and was supported by the barons who had rebelled against Henry's father, John. Much of the east of the country was in Louis' power. In May 1217, the rebel land forces were defeated at Lincoln by Henry's supporters. A French fleet bringing reinforcements and fresh supplies was assembled and set sail from Calais on 24 August. We do not know how news that this fleet had put to sea reached the English, but on this occasion the English ships encountered the enemy off Dover on the high seas. The ensuing action depended on good ship-handling by the English, who defeated the French, taking and executing the commander of the French fleet.[12] There would be no similar engagement on the high seas until Edward III fought the battle known both as *Les Espagnols sur Mer* and the battle of Winchelsea in August 1350.[13] This was an English victory, but had little immediate strategic importance. Much more effective in saving England from invasion was the battle of Sluys, fought a little earlier in 1340, amid the sandbanks of the estuary of the river Zwyn with, if some chroniclers are to be believed, the French ships chained together.[14] The overwhelming English victory ensured that the would-be invader's forces no longer had the means to cross the Channel, and mount an invasion.

Was, however, a fleet necessary to achieve this desirable end? Sometimes political negotiations and the building of alliances could be as effective; sometimes the uncertain weather in the Channel made the sea in truth the 'wall of England' by confining an invasion fleet to port until the time was no longer propitious for such an action. In 1264, an invasion fleet gathered again at Damme during the civil war between Henry III and the baronial opposition. Strenuous efforts were made in the name of the Crown to put together defensive forces of both ships and of men. The invasion, however, never materialised because the invasion fleet was delayed so long by contrary winds that supplies were exhausted and the force dispersed.

In both 1385 and 1386 the great efforts made by the French King Charles VI to mount an invasion of England equally came to naught. In 1385 the French strategy of encouraging the Scots to attack northern England while they invaded in the south failed because of weather damage to the French fleet on its passage up the North Sea, and discord among the supposed allies. The French king himself could not sail from Sluys because of the capture of Damme, his base, by Flemish rebels in July 1385. As Jonathan Sumption puts it, 'the French learned that it was unsafe to attempt the invasion of England without first securing complete control over Flanders.'[15] The following year Froissart provides a vivid account of French preparations; enormous quantities of supplies, 'wines, salted meat, hay, oats ... onions, wine, vinegar, biscuits, flour ... beaten egg yolks in barrels', were assembled at Sluys. So many ships were gathered in the harbour that as one stood at Sluys looking out to sea one saw a 'whole forest of masts'. Strikingly, however, the English plan of defence, again according to Froissart, did not depend on ships or any intervention against the French fleet at sea, but on allowing the French to land and march inland for three or four days: 'Then first, before attacking him they [the English] would attack and capture the ships and take or destroy all the supplies.' Since the countryside would have been laid waste, 'they [the French] would be starved and in a desperate position.'[16] The French, however, delayed their departure. By mid November, few of the shipmasters wanted to attempt the crossing in the likelihood of foul weather; on 16 November 1386 it was announced to the assembled host that the invasion had been deferred until further notice. [17]

## Coastal raids

By the fifteenth century the likelihood of an invasion from France had lessened. In many ways a much greater problem was presented to the rulers of England by sudden rapid coastal raids by the French, or mercenaries in their pay. These were often a source of fear in coastal counties. They could be extremely damaging locally, and also undermined the confidence of people living near the sea in the Crown, and its officers. From the point of view of the maritime community, the loss of vessels burnt or captured in harbour and the destruction of wharves or warehouses and their contents was very serious. These were important and expensive assets which could not be replaced easily or swiftly, while the goods looted might represent much of a merchant's capital. Protection against such raids was not easy, since accurate advance intelligence was hard to come by. Once a raid was in progress, local land forces could be gathered to put the enemy to flight, but only after some delay, by which time a port and its people had already suffered greatly. Fortifications, town walls, bulwarks and bastions were

These two images show the fortifications built around Southampton after the town was sacked by the French in 1338 and badly damaged. The walls were built along the quayside, but land reclamation since that date has ensured that they are now some distance from the water's edge. The walls were financed by a royal grant and kept in repair by a levy on all householders in the town. The ship shown is a modern reconstruction embedded in the roadway.

(AUTHOR'S COLLECTION)

improved in the fourteenth century as one means of defence against these incursions. Southampton's experience is a good example. The castle dated from the middle of the twelfth century, but being in the north of the town was not in a good position to defend the main quays in the south by the Water Gate; by the beginning of the fourteenth century it was also in poor repair. There were simple barriers at the harbour end of the main streets, French Street and English Street, but these were not fortified. The only other defensive work was a barbican, 'towards the sea', which the burgesses had intended to clad in stone in 1336.[18]

Whether this work had been completed or not, it proved to be useless against the French raid of October 1338. Froissart, in a passage written some time after the events, described how a fleet with more than a thousand fighting men 'came into Southampton harbour one Sunday morning when the people were at mass.'[19] The town was pillaged with the King himself losing a large quantity of both wool for export, and also wine for the royal household which was stored in the town. Many buildings were set on fire and women were raped. The invaders then retreated to their ships and 'with a good wind' put in at Dieppe, 'where they shared out their booty'. In the spring of the following year, work started on enclosing walls, while a garrison was stationed in the town and at the priory of St Denys on the Itchen.[20]

Other towns along the south coast suffered similar attacks in 1338/9, and also later

Carrickfergus Castle in Northern Ireland. Carrickfergus was the centre of English administration in the north from the reign of Edward I to that of Henry IV. Fleets were mustered here to transport men, horses and war materials to assist Edward's campaigns in the west of Scotland.

(AUTHOR'S COLLECTION)

in the 1370s and 1380s. In 1377, shortly after the death of Edward III, a fleet composed of the ships of the French and their mercenary allies caused mayhem all along the south coast, attacking Rye, Rottingdean, Lewes, Folkestone, Portsmouth, Dartmouth and Plymouth.[21] As late as 1457, Sandwich was severely damaged during a daring raid by the French, despite extensions to the fortifications earlier in the fifteenth century.[22] The distress caused by the spate of raids in 1377 was brought to the Crown's attention in the parliament which met in October of the same year. The Commons complained of the 'great disruption and damage which there has been on many coasts of the sea', caused by the 'coming of the said enemies'.[23] The following year the MPs from Cornwall requested help, because of the 'burning of all the ships, boats and towns which are in the ports and along the coast of the sea'.[24] Land forces bore the responsibility of driving the raiders away; ships had an important but minor role in attempting to provide protection from raids of this kind. In an effective counter tactic, English mariners from the south coast ports and from Jersey and Guernsey frequently mounted retaliatory raids on ports in French territory, taking as much delight in pillage and destruction in, for example, Harfleur and the Ile de Ré, as the French did in England. The Cotentin peninsula also suffered badly, as did Boulogne, which was raided in 1340, 1347, 1351 and 1377.[25]

## The protection of trade

The idea of the 'safeguard of the sea', which was of so much concern to coastal dwellers, also preoccupied the merchant community, which suffered from attacks on commercial shipping. Sometimes this was out and out robbery on the high seas, or piracy, sometimes

Conway Castle in North Wales. This magnificent castle was built on the coast so that it could be supplied by sea and was one of a group of similarly located castles built by Edward I to ensure his control of Wales. These castles have been called 'white elephants' since more mobile forces might have been more effective in defeating Welsh resistance than castle garrisons.

(WIKIMEDIA)

it was under some sort of official sanction by a ruler, a form of *guerre de course*, or privateering. The exact status of the robbers who had stolen his goods while in transit probably was of little immediate concern to a merchant, but it became of vital importance when trying either to recover the goods or get compensation for their loss from the authorities or via the courts. Mariners of all nations with access to the trade routes which criss-crossed the North Sea, the Channel, the Bay of Biscay and the sea near the Atlantic coasts of Spain and Portugal might be involved in this activity. In England, individuals of standing in their own community, who held positions of trust under the Crown, might also be guilty of acting as corsairs.

One of the most prominent examples is the well-known Dartmouth family, the Hawleys. John Hawley senior was mayor of Dartmouth fourteen times, an MP, held public office as an escheator for Devon and in the customs, and served the Crown on official voyages to 'keep the seas'.[26] At the same time, both he and ships' masters in his employ had apparently no compunction in robbing cargoes from ships in the Channel when it suited them. One ship coming from Lisbon to Sluys with a cargo mainly of oil, honey and hides was forcibly taken into Dartmouth by Hawley's men in 1402. Hawley was compelled by the King to release the ship and its crew, but hung on to the cargo. His son, John Hawley the younger, had a very similar career, in fact, on one occasion continuing his father's action against an Italian, Richard Garner. Garner complained bitterly in a Chancery writ that Hawley the younger had tried to bar his action maliciously. This action was connected with the occasion when John Hawley the elder's mariners had taken a cargo of La Rochelle wine in Garner's possession out of a Breton vessel, and had also assaulted Garner's factor on the ship, threatening him that if Garner had been there, 'they would have beaten his eyes out of his head'.[27]

In the climate of violence which existed on the high seas for most of our period, it was hard for the Crown to formulate and implement an effective strategy. On the one hand, merchants and their allies in Parliament complained vigorously and called for measures to keep the seas. On the other hand, at times these very same merchants might be robbing other seafarers. The defence frequently put forward when such incidents came to court or were brought before the King's Council was the vexed question of truces, often of relatively short duration. It was generally agreed that the vessels or cargoes of the King's enemies were 'fair game'; it was not, however, always clear, at least to seamen, precisely who were 'the King's enemies' at any particular time. It was also the case that, for example, a French merchant could ship 'enemy' goods in a Flemish vessel, or Italian merchants might ship goods in a Breton ship as in the case above; detailed discussions regarding the ownership of a desirable cargo or the status of a ship were not likely to be undertaken for long on a heaving deck with a crew of armed men in attendance. A further complication was that at certain times, particularly during the reign of Henry IV, for example, the taking of French cargoes at sea was being tacitly encouraged by the Crown as a low-level (and of course inexpensive) way of continuing the war against the French.[28]

The fear caused by the threat of coastal attacks and the prevalence of robbery at sea could even be manipulated to the advantage of the Crown. One of the stated purposes of the tax on imports known as tonnage and poundage, which was granted regularly by parliaments from the time of Henry IV was to 'safeguard the sea', although no method was specified in the statutes granting the tax, and there is little evidence that much money was ever eventually expended for this purpose. The anger of trading interests at the lack of security at sea was at times forcibly expressed. In the parliament of March 1406, at a time when attacks on trading vessels had soared, the speaker, Sir John Tiptoft, put forward, together with a whole series of other complaints on the conduct of royal government, the urgent need to provide protection for English shipping. This was so pressing that it could not wait until after the Easter adjournment of parliament. An ordinance was worked out which placed the responsibility for protecting shipping on the 'merchants, mariners and ship owners of England'. They would be funded by a grant of money from the tonnage and poundage duties and a quarter of the subsidy on wool exports to provide, for seventeen months from 1 May 1406, ships, mariners, and a force of two thousand fighting men to patrol the seas. The scheme rapidly collapsed in acrimony. By December of the same year the merchants had relinquished their responsibility, with the strong suspicion that the money supposedly specially assigned to pay for their forces was finding its way instead into the general funds of the Exchequer.[29]

The situation did not improve markedly until the accession of Henry V saw the resumption of the Hundred Years War and the capture of much of northern France by the English. In 1416–20 the King also initiated Channel patrols by groups of ships under royal command, which had some success in dealing with warships hired by the French Crown and also, of course, made the 'freelance' activities of sea robbers much more risky.[30] The reign of Henry V and the success of his naval policy was looked back on with nostalgic pride by the author of the rhymed pamphlet, the *Libelle of Englysshe Polycye*, written *c.*1436. He declared that the aim of any ruler of England should be to encourage trade and make sure that the English were 'maysteres of the narowe see'. The writer then goes into detail about the different merchants and their wares who frequent English shores and the goods taken over seas by the English. His main point, however, comes near the end of the poem:

> Kepe than the see abought in special
> Which of England is the rounde wall,
> As thoughe England was likened to a cite
> And this wall environ was the see.
> Kepe than the see, that is the wall of Englond,
> And than is Englond kepte by Goddes sonde.

The writer praises both Edward III in whose reign, 'the see was kepte and thereof he was lorde', and Henry V who built the great ships. He did this because 'it was not ellis but that he caste to be/ Lorde round aboute environ of the see.' This will was lacking in his time as the writer lamented:[31]

> Set many wittes wythouten variaunce
> To one acorde and unanimitie
> Put to gode wylle for to kepe the see ...
> Thus shall richesse and worship to us longe[32]

It was, in fact, notable that, as English power in France declined in the 1430s and control of some French Channel ports (Dieppe in October 1435, Harfleur in November of the same year) was lost, that security on the Channel declined. The friendship of both Flanders and Brittany could also no longer be taken for granted. This change of circumstances is reflected in the Commons petition presented to the parliament of 1442. 'From one day to the next', they claimed:

> your poor merchants of this your realm are robbed of their ships goods and merchandise of great value ... and your poor lieges dwelling near the sea coasts are taken on land from their own houses with their chattels and their children ...which mischief happens because your said merchants are discouraged from having force and power of ships and fighting men to guard the sea and its coasts.

This is because enemies have obtained forged safe-conducts, charter parties and letters of marque, so that such robberies go unpunished. As well as requesting changes to the system of safe-conducts, the Commons put forward a bill setting out the minimum forces required to keep the seas. This required a force of eight large ships each attended by a barge and a balinger with four pinnaces, probably to be available to maintain communications. These vessels would be manned by 2260 mariners with twenty-four shipmasters and pursers. Including an allowance for victuals, the cost of this force for eight months would be £6090 13s 4d, to be largely met from tonnage and poundage.

The ships themselves would be privately owned and would come from ports all round the country from Newcastle to Bristol. Only one officer on each of the large ships would be a royal appointment. These '8 knights and worthy squires chosen and named of the west, south and north so that no county be disparaged' would act as the captains of the squadron.[33] The King seems to have given his assent to the scheme but there is no trace in the records that any squadron of this nature was ever in fact assembled or put to sea.

Sea rovers acting under letters of marque could be stripped of this justification for their activities by a royal command; the 'freelance' pirate was much harder to control. It could be done, perhaps, only when a group of sea robbers had no support from any authorities in the area in which they operated, and no advantage accrued to these authorities from the activities of the sea-rovers. This is demonstrated by the fate of the *Vitalienbrüder*; this group of violent pirates had been used initially as a weapon in the conflict in the Baltic between Sweden and Denmark, with some involvement of the Hanse towns of Rostock and Wismar. Disputes over trading rights had also led to bad relations between the Hanseatic League and England in the 1380s, and attacks on each other's shipping, in which the *Vitalienbrüder* were involved. Their attacks, however, became indiscriminate, being directed against any vessels trading in the North Sea or Baltic. Their former protectors turned against them, and in this instance the leaders were taken and executed, leading to the extinction of the group. The problems between the Hanse towns and England which led to continuing violence against each other's shipping were finally resolved in 1475 by negotiation and the signing of a treaty, not by naval action of any kind.[34]

## The logistical support of land forces

For the English Crown during the whole of our period, a much simpler and in the end probably more important strategic use of naval forces was to provide transport for royal armies fighting either across the Channel or in those regions of the British Isles not directly controlled by the English Crown. All English rulers in our period acted, as we have seen, in the knowledge that they had the power to compel any vessel in English waters to take part in the service of the Crown; this might on occasion involve some risk of fighting at sea – much more frequently it meant that vessels were required to transport men, horses, all kinds of supplies and victuals to assist military expeditions of all kinds.

In the eleventh and twelfth centuries precise details of the way in which the Crown made use of its powers of requisition over English shipping are hard to come by. It is obvious that Norman kings, their nobility and their followers crossed the Channel frequently, since all had business in both England and Normandy. Chroniclers, however, either focus on 'good stories': for example, the well-known incident of the drowning of William, heir to Henry I, in 1120 when the *White Ship* was wrecked off the coast of Normandy on the reef of the Ras de Catteville,[35] or include no information about the administration or organisation of naval matters. Thus when Roger of Hoveden described Henry II's invasion of Ireland in 1171, he merely stated somewhat enigmatically that Henry collected 'together a large fleet of ships', which consisted of 'four hundred ships laden with warriors horses armour and provisions'.[36] It is very probable that the King used his powers to arrest shipping to serve the Crown to assemble the fleet, but no further details have survived. The chroniclers similarly devote much space to Richard I's expedition to the Holy Land on crusade in 1190, but again have little interest in precisely how he gathered a fleet.[37]

In the reign of John, as the amount of surviving documentary evidence increases, it becomes much more possible to get a clear idea of how the Crown used its naval resources to support military operations and the importance it attached to this use of shipping. John had three possible sources of shipping to use in this way: his own vessels, those from the Cinque Ports owing service to the Crown under their charter, and arrested shipping. From these diverse sources he was able to put together considerable fleets which transported his forces to France as he strove to recover the lost Angevin lands. The administration of these fleets was in the hands of royal clerks, most notably William of Wrotham, the Archdeacon of Taunton, and Reginald of Cornhill. The method of arresting shipping in aid of the defence of the realm, which is revealed in Exchequer documents from this period, was based on the issue of writs ordering these and other officials to arrest shipping in the ports; this included 'alien' vessels , that is, those from foreign ports.[38] It has been suggested that John had little idea of how to deploy the vessels at his command, but clearly the logistical support of this probably ill-co-ordinated collection of miscellaneous ships was an essential first step in any campaign across the Channel.[39]

The reign of his son Henry III saw the continuation of this use of the 'navy of England' in the widest sense. Henry's attempts to regain lost territory in Poitou and to defend the remnants of Gascony which were still loyal to the English Crown were not very effective or successful, but each expedition necessitated the gathering of a fleet to transport his forces to France, or to supply them once they had arrived. The fleets were made up of the King's own ships, the Cinque Port levies, and arrested ships, as before. In 1242, for example, orders requiring the despatch of shipping to aid Henry's expedition to Gascony were issued to ports in Ireland, Dunwich, and other east coast ports in July; this was repeated in September. By February of the following year Henry was urged to return to England from Bordeaux, having achieved nothing of note. He did not in fact disembark at Portsmouth until September 1243, even though royal orders requiring ships to return the King to his kingdom were first issued in April.[40] Even the most inglorious of campaigns could not be undertaken without access to adequate naval support.

Edward I, however, in his wars against Wales, Scotland and France used the maritime resources of his kingdom to great effect. His success, it can be argued, largely depended

Caerlaverock Castle; this castle on the Solway Firth was besieged by the English in the early thirteenth century. The siege was successful because ships were deployed to bring in reinforcements including siege machines although the castle was inaccessible for heavy materials by land.

(WIKIMEDIA)

Scotland

Stirling
Kirkcaldy
Dunfermline
Kinghorn
Leith
Dunbar
Falkirk
Edinburgh
Firth of Forth

SCOTLAND
River Dee
Aberdeen
Dunnottar Castle
Inverlochy
Brechin
ARDNAMURCHAN
Tobermory
Cairn-Na-Burgh
Mull
River Tay
Broughty
Dundee
Arbroath
Perth
St Andrews
Cupar
Fife Ness
North Sea
Forth River
Dumbarton
Firth of Forth
LOTHIANS
Islay
Bute
Largs
Berwick
Kelso
Norham
Dunivaig Castle
Arran
Firth of Clyde
Roxburgh
Alnwick
North Channel
Kintyre
Rathlin I
NORTHUMBERLAND
Lough Foyle
Dunaverty Castle
Morpeth
Annandale
River Tweed
Shields
ANTRIM
GALLOWAY
Caerlaverock Castle
River Tyne
Hexham
Newcastle
Larne
Carrickfergus
Kirkcudbright
Carlisle
Skimburness
ULSTER
CUMBERLAND
Isle of Man
ENGLAND
Drogheda
Irish Sea

N W E S

This map shows those areas in the north of Great Britain and Ireland which were most affected by Edward I's campaigns in Scotland.

(PETER WILKINSON)

on his ability to support and supply his land forces by sea. His early Welsh campaigns in 1277 and 1282 owed some of their success to his use of ships to bring in supplies to the north Welsh coast using both Chester on the one hand, and Anglesey on the other, as bases. In 1294, when the Welsh rebelled against English rule, his policy of establishing castles on the coast with a harbour incorporated in the castle works made it easy to bring in food and other materials to the garrisons. The garrisons, however, were of little use against the swiftly moving forces of the rebels who were able to bring Edward almost to the point of losing his hard-won conquest. It has been forcefully argued that the need for shipping in Wales to supply the 'King's white elephants' was to the detriment of the more urgent and more important campaign in Gascony being carried on at the same time.[41]

Edward's use of shipping for logistical purposes for his campaigns in Scotland between 1297 and his death in 1307 perhaps reveals a more successful strategic approach.[42] The greatest need was for vessels to carry supplies to his forces once the campaign was under way, since it was not possible for an army to 'live off the country' in the relatively inhospitable surroundings of the Border country or the west coast of Scotland. The need for a secure base for the delivery of supplies underlines the importance of the good harbour at Berwick to both the English and the Scots, while in 1303 when Edward I penetrated as far north up the east coast of Scotland as the Moray Firth, he took care to take both Montrose and Aberdeen, two of the only reasonably sheltered anchorages on a generally harsh and difficult coastline.[43] For his campaigns on the west coast of Scotland in 1296, 1299, 1301 and 1303, ships were used not only to bring in supplies, but also to transport both men and horses from Ireland – generally to Skinburness, the English base on the Solway Firth. In 1303, the Earl of Ulster, in charge of this aspect of the campaign, ordered the fleet to gather at Dublin, Drogheda or Carrickfergus. Some of these vessels had to be specially adapted to carry horses. A total of 179 ships was involved, coming from thirty-one English and Irish ports; these stretched all the way along the English and Welsh coasts from Lynn and Harwich in the east to Caernarvon, while Ireland contributed ships from Youghal, Cork, Ross, Dublin and Drogheda.[44]

A close look at the fleet which revictualled Berwick in 1301 reveals that fifty-four ships were arrested for this purpose, including at least three which were said to be Flemish. The others came from thirty-three different ports and havens, mostly on the east coast of England. As well as victuals for the army, these ships also carried items like the King's own pavilion, or carts to transport the supplies once disembarked.[45]

In addition to these essential general supply fleets, other ships were also needed in special situations. In 1300, Caerlaverock Castle on the northern shores of the Solway Firth was besieged by Edward's forces. Its site was so well protected by mudflats, marshes and dykes that it was very difficult for an army to bring up the heavy siege engines needed. The English were on the verge of defeat when their ships arrived with both supplies and the engines needed to bombard the fortifications.[46] Similarly, in 1304 the mayor and bailiffs of Newcastle were ordered to build a barge for the King as quickly as possible, since this type of vessel was urgently needed at Perth. It therefore had to be capable of navigating the Tay to the town.[47]

The havoc that could be caused by the failure to ensure that enough shipping was available to supply the royal armies was only too clear in 1322. Contrary winds made it impossible for supply ships to reach Edward II and his army, forcing him to retreat in ignominy to the English border. The misery of an army caught in this situation was well described by Froissart writing of an unsuccessful English raid into Scotland in 1327:

Some were so famished that they snatched the food from their comrades' hands which gave rise to serious brawls among the men. As an added misery it never stopped raining the whole week and consequently their saddles, saddle-cloths and girths became sodden and most of the horses developed sores on their backs ... They themselves had nothing to keep out the wet and the cold except their tunics and their armour and nothing to make fires with except green wood which will not stay alight under the rain.[48]

Edward III, therefore, was well aware of this aspect of the strategic use of England's naval resources from the earliest days of his reign. The fiasco of the campaign of 1327 occurred when power was still in the hands of his formidable mother, Isabella, but from 1330 onwards he was his own master and there is ample evidence of the way in which ships were deployed to support his expeditions north of the border. Much of this evidence has been subjected to detailed analysis, allowing a clear appreciation of the scale on which Edward III used the maritime resources of his kingdom in support of his campaigns in Scotland, and after 1337 across the Channel during the Hundred Years War. For his campaign in 1333 in Scotland the King paid for 228 vessels manned by around five thousand mariners. As well as other supplies these ships carried 7,886 tuns of cereals (wheat, barley and oats) and 532 tuns of wine to the north.[49] The initial fleet for the campaign in 1346/7, which culminated in the spectacular English victory at Crécy and the siege of Calais, involved no fewer than 747 ships manned by over fifteen thousand mariners.

An attempt to provide an overall total for all ships used by the Crown for logistical purposes between 1324 and 1360 has come up with the figure of 3,099 ships apparently manned by over sixty-six thousand sailors.[50] These figures do raise some problems. Identifying individual ships can be very difficult, and it is impossible as far as mariners are concerned. It is probably best to regard the totals as reflecting the number of recorded voyages undertaken in the pay of the Crown and the size of crews, not precise numbers of individual vessels or crewmen. Nevertheless, it is plain that the Crown made great demands on the maritime community of England, and would have been unable to pursue its aggressive strategy against both Scotland and France without this logistical support.

The need for very large fleets like those raised in the 1340s and 1350s was perhaps not so evident in the later years of the fourteenth century, when the pace of the wars slackened considerably. The most notable fleet was perhaps that put together in 1386 to transport John of Gaunt's army to northern Spain to advance his claims to the throne. This consisted of around eighty-six ships paid for by the Crown together with some vessels of the Portuguese allies of England. On this occasion crews receiving pay totalled 2,765 seamen.[51] The ships collected for the Agincourt campaign by Henry V in 1415 constituted perhaps the last of the enormous fleets setting forth from England to invade France in the medieval period. The author of the *Gesta Henrici Quinti* describes the scene:

He himself [the King] went down by barge from his castle of Porchester to the sea going aboard his ship called the *Trinity* between the port of Southampton and Portsmouth. And at once he had the yard of her sail hoisted half-way up the mast to indicate his readiness to set sail and at the same time to serve as a signal to the ships of the fleet which were dispersed in various places along the coast to make haste to join him as soon as they could. And when on the following Saturday almost all of them has arrived seeing the wind blowing in his favour he spreads his sails to the breeze in company with about fifteen hundred vessels not including those who stayed behind of which there were about a hundred.[52]

Henry's success in this campaign and in that of 1417, consolidated in the Treaty of Troyes in 1420, restored the strategic situation to that of the time of William the Conqueror. Once more the Channel no longer marked the frontier between two warring kingdoms, but a barrier between two parts of the same realm. There was a continuing need for men and supplies to pass from one to the other, often in considerable quantities, but this had perhaps more the characteristics of a regular 'ferry service', than that of specially assembled invasion fleets.

The deteriorating situation in northern France as Charles VII's campaign to restore the French monarchy became more and more successful is reflected in documents like the *Instructions concerning the management of the War in France under the Duke of York* issued in 1440. These included the clause which required the King to order those appointed to keep the seas to 'entende diligently to the keeping of the mouthe of the sayne as well for letting and empeschement of the vitailing of Hareflewe [by this time in French hands] as for the secure going of vessel and vitaillers unto Rouen.' It was also set down that if York should in fact lay siege to any coastal town in French hands that the King would order 'and pourveie an arme of ii m men upon the see to kepe any of the said sieges' to support 'and acompaignie and strenghte hym as the necessitie shulde or myghte require.'[53]

Similarly, in 1450 when the situation in Normandy for the English forces was desperate, the commanders of a force intended to send much-needed relief to the Duke of Somerset, who was besieged in Caen, asked that seakeeping should be a priority so that 'the soudeours may have sure conveieng at alle tymes, aswelle for passage and comeyng over as for conveyance of vitaile.'[54] In the same year, a fleet was also assembled to bring succour to the English facing an equally difficult situation in Gascony. This consisted of eighty-three ships, with over a quarter being of more than 200 tuns burden, a considerable size for the period.[55]

## Conclusion

Many commentators have accused medieval English kings of having little or no appreciation of the role of sea-power in the defence of an island kingdom. Norman and Angevin kings have been castigated for apparently forgetting 'the application of ships for directly military purposes'; 'They were used as auxiliaries to essentially land-based campaigns not as weapons of war in their own right.'[56] In the context of Gaunt's campaign in Spain it has been claimed that 'there was little understanding of sea-power

and some dislike of the naval weapon among the generals who controlled English government at this time.'[57] The most recent assessment of Edward III's maritime policy, on the other hand, has accepted some of the praise heaped on his head by nineteenth-century historians, and has argued that 'in terms of naval innovation Edward III must be considered England's most important king.' It has, however, also been asserted that his reliance on merchant shipping, arrested for warlike purposes, 'ensured that success could never be sustained indefinitely.'[58]

All these views, although based on the available evidence, perhaps overlook the limitations of resources and technology within which English medieval monarchs had to work. Their maritime strategy was intended to support the aims of their war policies which, as we have seen, were concerned primarily with the defence of their realm, and after that with their desire to control or conquer the northern and western fringes of the British Isles, and to compete successfully with their neighbours across the Channel, principally the French monarchy. In all these scenarios the use of shipping as logistical support was obviously essential. To regard this, as some writers have done, as a misunderstanding of the possible use of sea-power is a mistake.

It is also the case that in order to transport an army and its baggage train across the Channel in medieval times it was not necessary to have 'control' of the sea crossing (as was the case in the time of the Armada or Napoleon's abortive invasion plans). The lack of up-to-date reliable intelligence, the design of ships, the weapons to hand, the expense

This is a later engraving of a sixteenth-century sketch of Calais and its harbour. It shows the port itself, the shipping and the quays and the Tower on the Rysban, an important feature of the defences of the town. Once in English hands after 1347 it was essential to maintain the supply route with England, usually from the port of Sandwich.

(AUTHOR'S COLLECTION)

and difficulty of maintaining a 'standing' navy: all made the interception of a fleet at sea impractical and more or less never attempted. Defence against invasion was concentrated on land forces and fortifications, and had been since before the Conquest. One reason why the battle of Sluys was so celebrated was because it was so unusual, and even in that case it has been argued that its strategic importance was in the end negligible. Henry V was perhaps more aware of the battle-winning potential of warships, but his victories in Normandy removed the justification for his building of a squadron of very large vessels and his institution of regular Channel patrols. The need for transports, however, did not diminish.

After the loss of all the French territories, with the exception of Calais, by the English in 1453, there was a gradually growing perception of the need for a more developed strategy with respect to maritime forces. This was perhaps best expressed by Sir John Fortescue, a judge and jurist, who, in his *Governance of England*, wrote:

> And though we are not always at war upon the seas, yet it is necessary that the King always has some fleet for the repressing of pirates to protect our merchants our fisheries and the dwellers upon our coasts and also that the King always keeps some great and mighty vessels for the defeat of an army when any shall be made against him upon the sea. For then it shall be too late to have such vessels made. And yet without them all the king's navy shall not suffice to assail carracks and other great vessels nor yet to be able to break up a mighty fleet gathered purposely.[59]

This was written during the second period of Edward IV's reign, probably not long after his recovery of the throne from Henry VI in 1471, a time when the English Crown possessed no ships of its own, as had been the case since the late 1430s. Fortescue was concerned to point out the perils which arose if the King had insufficient resources to govern wisely, and it is therefore remarkable that he should lay emphasis on the need for 'mighty vessels', about the most expensive contemporary items of 'military hardware'. He may well have been aware that advances in ship design and ship-handling, together with developments in shipboard artillery, were beginning to make it impractical and unwise for a monarch to rely on arrested shipping. In making the case for a 'royal navy', Fortescue was anticipating the way the maritime strategy of English monarchs would change in the last year so of the fifteenth century and the first decades of the sixteenth.

In our period there were very few sea battles, but this does not mean that the contribution of ships and seamen to the policies of English kings was of little importance. In his *Governance*, Fortescue neatly summarised some of the purposes for which a royal fleet was needed but omitted the most essential, the transport of men and supplies. The provision of logistical support to land armies was the task on which ships were most frequently engaged and one that was essential to the success of royal armies, wherever they were operating. It is this truth which is perhaps represented in the frames of the Bayeux Tapestry with which this chapter began.

## CHAPTER 3

# The 'navy of England': Understanding the Naval Resources of the Crown

TO A MEDIEVAL ENGLISH RULER, the justification of using the term 'the navy of England' to refer to all vessels in English waters in English ownership was plain. These ships were at the disposal of the monarch for the defence of the realm in times of need; the idea of a distinction between the navy, as commonly understood nowadays, and the merchant marine did not exist. This did not mean, however, that there were no 'King's ships' and no organisation to support and maintain them. During our period, it was not unusual for the Crown to own ships which might be used for commercial purposes as well as warlike ones. These vessels, however, varied greatly in number from time to time. The bulk of any fleet which put to sea in the service of the King would be made up of arrested ships: ships which had been requisitioned on behalf of the monarch by royal officials for a particular voyage. Also present in many fleets were the ships of the Cinque Ports. The charters granted to this ancient confederation of towns on the coasts of Sussex and Kent laid down that the barons or citizens of these towns were under an obligation to provide fifty-seven ships each manned by twenty-one men to serve the King at sea for two weeks without pay. Most royal fleets would contain contributions from these three different sources of shipping, the whole being worthy of the description 'the navy of England'.

## The King's ships

There is little evidence regarding ships in the ownership of English kings from the Conquest to the early thirteenth century. The Pipe Rolls from the later years of Henry II include payments to mariners of what seem to be vessels hired for a particular purpose among the entries for the county of Hampshire. The names of certain individuals recur but the phrase used, for example, *'navis Samsonis Wascelin'*[1] could refer either to an owner or to a shipmaster. There is no clear evidence that these were royal ships. The purpose of these voyages was to perform routine errands for the Crown, often to transport the Treasury and its clerks to Normandy when the King was in his French dominions. The vessels may have been carrying chests of coins or other valuables since an escort was often required, the only defensive action undertaken at this time by ships in the King's pay. The ships themselves seem to have been based at Southampton, or on one occasion,

Bosham. The only vessel which may have been in royal ownership as usually understood, or at least on a long-term 'lease' is the one described as an *esnecca* which was commanded by Alan Trenchemer. In 1187 he requested payment for timber and carpenters' supplies '*in reparando esnecca regis*'.[2] He was also paid for various short sea voyages including one with 'treasure' across the Channel like those undertaken by various other shipmasters.[3]

### The reigns of John and Henry III

As we have already discussed, John's loss of control of Normandy and other territories in France changed the strategic situation. This was quickly reflected in the royal attitude to the ownership of ships. John has been credited with the acquisition and organisation of a fleet of at least fifty ships, a feat which Sir Nicholas Harris Nicolas, the distinguished nineteenth-century historian, claimed gave him the right to be considered the 'actual founder of the Royal Navy of England'.[4] It is the case that on the dorse of a membrane in the Close Roll of 6 John (June 1204/May 1205) there is a list of fifty-two galleys dispersed in groups of between one and five vessels in ports along the English coast from Lynn to Gloucester, with a further group of five in Ireland. They are divided into three squadrons in the charge of Reginald de Cornhill, William de Wrotham and William de Manson and John de la Warr respectively. Cornhill and Wrotham were two of the most experienced servants of the Crown at this period with their activities extending to many other areas of royal business; the fact that the administration of the King's ships was entrusted to them is a measure of the importance with which this task was regarded.[5] Wrotham is addressed in writs dealing specifically with maritime matters by various titles including *custos galliarum* (keeper of the galleys). The amount of naval activity by the Crown is reflected in the many references in the Pipe Rolls[6] to the payments made to shipmasters at this time, and other writs and orders in the Close and Patent rolls.

There is no doubt that John made considerable use of naval forces in his campaigns against Philip Augustus of France. In 1205, for example, he assembled, for what proved to be an abortive expedition, one of the largest fleets of medieval times to which his galleys made a worthwhile contribution.[7] It has also been suggested that there are clear indications that his older brother, Richard I, while on campaign in northern France, had earlier employed a squadron of royal vessels. Richard is credited with building seventy *cursoria* for use in harrying the enemy and bringing up supplies along the river when fighting in the valley of the Seine.[8] This term has been translated as 'swift ships', following the meaning in classical Latin. It is, however, unlikely that these were oceangoing ships, as claimed by a French chronicler,[9] given the winding nature of the Seine at this point and the distance from the sea. They were most probably specialised 'river barges' adapted for rowing or poling upstream. Apart from payments for the fleet collected for his participation in the crusade of 1190, the Pipe Rolls of Richard I's reign record only intermittent payments for the expenses of ships, several involving the same Alan Trenchemer who had served his father in a similar capacity. Thus in 1193 Trenchemer was paid just over 44 marks for 'making the King's ship'[10] and in 1195 received nearly £12 for providing forty leather head-coverings and forty doublets for the crews of the King's three 'long ships'.[11] The task undertaken by these ships included taking the King's harness (armour) and other possessions overseas, transporting the treasury, and also elite passengers like the Queen and the sister of the King of France and other courtiers.[12]

Whether or not John inherited the *cursoria* from his brother, his own squadron of royal ships were seagoing galleys. Some at least were probably still in existence in the reign of his son Henry III, who seems to have maintained them at least in the first years of his reign. A list in the Close Roll for 1229 includes galleys at Dunwich (2), Shoreham (2), Southampton (1), in the Thames (2), in Ireland (6), Bristol (2), Winchelsea (2) and Romney (3).[13] It is hard to be sure how many of these ships belonged to the Crown. References to payment for galleys continue to be scattered through the Pipe Rolls and Close Rolls. Some were certainly often in or near Portsmouth where John had definitely established some kind of naval facility. In 1229, a certain Jeremy, who is given the title of *Custos magne navis et galearum*,[14] was ordered, in conjunction with the authorities in Portsmouth, to provide two good galleys from the royal squadron for a voyage to Gascony by Henry de Trubleville, the seneschal, together with all armaments, anchors, cordage and other necessaries.[15] In 1242 canvas taken out of some captured ships was to be used to make sails for three galleys and the Crown was to be informed if there was insufficient material to finish this work.[16] A little later, in 1243, the sheriff of Sussex was given the task of extending the building at Rye which housed seven galleys and to make sure that these vessels and their equipment were safely stored.[17] These ships were still there five years later when the sheriff was further instructed to make sure all was well with them and that no deterioration had taken place.[18] At the same time the local worthies in Portsmouth were ordered to make sure that hurdles in store in the town were not rotting and to bring them under cover if necessary. These hurdles were essential for the transport of horses by sea when temporary stalls were constructed in the hold of a ship. In 1257 the King was renting storage for the equipment of his galleys and barges at Winchelsea from one Jacob de la Nesse.[19] These materials were still in his custody in 1264.[20]

This bundle of writs still tied together as they were by an Exchequer clerk in the first years of the fourteenth century contains orders sent by King Edward I to local sheriffs and other authorities to arrest ships to support his Scottish campaigns. Ports all along the English coasts are involved. Some ports were reluctant to obey the orders and they are threatened with dire consequences for contempt of a royal order and the possible delay to the campaign.

**(THE NATIONAL ARCHIVES)**

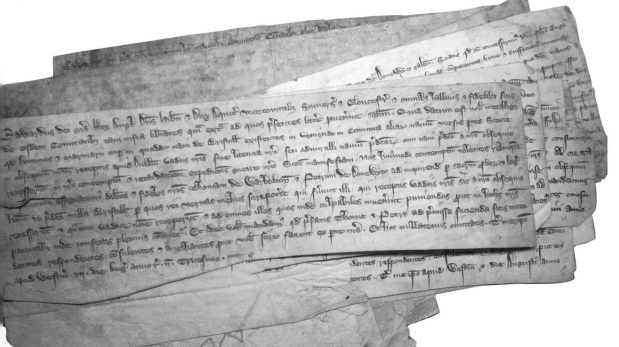

What is lacking from these sources is any clear indication of the use made of these ships, and the existence of any office dedicated to their maintenance. Henry III certainly summoned fleets largely made up of arrested shipping to participate in his campaigns across the Channel, or to deter his enemies during periods of civil unrest, but the role played by his own ships is not made explicit. Some seem to have been used for trading voyages, a practice which continued into the fifteenth century. Others were perhaps treated like personal transport; there are few indications that their role was seen as particularly warlike or necessarily included leading fleets of arrested shipping into battle.

### The campaigns of Edward I and Edward II

It might be expected that the role of the King's ships would begin to change in the reign of Edward I, as an aggressive royal policy, both towards other parts of the British Isles and towards enemies across the Channel, became a dominant feature of the reign. Certainly, fleets were raised on numerous occasions to transport and supply armies to the north and west of the British Isles and across the Channel. The part ships in royal ownership played in these campaigns is, however, obscure. References to royal ships in the records are scant and ambiguous. Can we, for example, consider the barges built at the King's request in Hull and Ravenser (1299), Conway (1301), Great Yarmouth (1304) and Newcastle upon Tyne (also 1304) as royal ships? All were built at the King's expense (sometimes by direct Exchequer grant, sometimes by allowances from the taxes being paid by the town in question), but there is no record of what tasks they were employed on and very little information on why they were commissioned. Those built at Great Yarmouth and Newcastle were intended for use in Scotland, with the Newcastle barge being wanted at Perth with some urgency, but that is all that is known.[21]

Edward I also ordered a much larger shipbuilding campaign in 1294. In November of that year, the King ordered that twenty vessels described as galleys, propelled by 120 oars each, should be built by twenty-six towns, all to be ready by the totally unrealistic date of Christmas in the same year. This was his response not only to the outbreak of hostilities with France over English rule in Gascony, but also to the fact that the French King Philip Augustus had set up a royal shipyard to build galleys at Rouen. The obvious use for any ships built at this French shipyard would be to attack English trade and raid vulnerable coastal towns. Edward's wildly ambitious programme did result in at least eight vessels being built, for which accounts survive; these were constructed at Dunwich, Ipswich, London (two ships), Lyme, Newcastle, Southampton and York. These were all built at the King's expense; the accounts are found either on the Pipe Rolls or in the class of Exchequer Accounts Various at Kew but there is no information as to their subsequent careers or how they were maintained and crewed.[22]

Some may well have survived to form part of the group of royal ships owned by Edward II. References to these can be found in the Calendars of Patent and Close rolls. Many have the description 'of Westminster' after their name, used in much the same way as royal ships in the fifteenth century are often called 'of the Tower'. It seems unlikely that Edward II's ships were based as far up the tidal Thames as Westminster, where there do not appear to have been any facilities for ship repair and the like. This term may have been a signifier of royal ownership. Casual mentions in the rolls reveal that the *Christopher of Westminster* was to be financed out of the fee farm of Great Yarmouth,[23] while this ship and a companion, the *Jonette*, were some time later anchored off Orwell.[24] In 1312, four ships, the *Marie*, the *Jonette*, the *Swalve*, and the *Nicholas*, all said to be 'of Westminster', were ordered to sail to Perth as quickly as possible.[25] This was at the time when Edward II's forces were facing defeat by those of Robert Bruce. Perth, in fact, surrendered to the Scots in early 1313. On this occasion the ships may have been needed for a clear military purpose but much more often Edward's ships were said to be engaged on unspecified matters relating to the 'king's business'.

It is hard to be sure how many ships were at one time or another in Edward II's ownership; there may have been as many as eighteen. At least three are described as cogs[26] and one as a galley.[27] The only indication of some sort of administrative machinery to care for the ships is the naming of one Alexander le Peyntour as keeper of 'our ships' in a quite unrelated action for debt.[28] Standing a little apart from this group of vessels are two others of which a little more is known. These were built at the order of the Crown at Bayonne in the spring of 1320 by Thomas de Driffeld. They sailed to England once completed and appear in English records as the *Galley of St George* and the *Ship of St Edward*. Both were certainly oared ships and were accompanied by a small unnamed galiot or 'spinace'. Their involvement in royal business was on the same lines as the other royal ships mentioned, but they also lived up to the reputation for piracy of seamen and ships from Bayonne, by getting involved in seizing cargoes from the 'king's enemies'. The *St Edward* took 240 tuns of white wine out of a vessel called the *Nostre Dame de Saint Johan* in 1327, and also made the mistake of robbing a Flemish ship laden with the goods of the Bardi of Florence, bankers, merchants and major creditors of the Crown.[29] Nothing more is recorded of either vessel which probably returned to Gascony after these incidents.

*Edward III's ships*

Once Edward III had come to the throne and taken full powers from his mother and Roger Mortimer he began to pursue forward and aggressive policies in Scotland and France. From this time on the role of royal ships becomes much better documented. There are separate accounts presented at the Exchequer for a royal official called the Clerk of the King's Ships for the year 1344 till 1451/2. The earliest accounts up to 1364/5 can be found on the Pipe Rolls, but in a separate section, not jumbled up among sheriff's returns for individual counties. From 1371 they are enrolled on the Foreign Account Rolls. To back up this material, there are a great many particulars of accounts, the detailed returns of individual accountants from which the rolls were compiled, lists of expenses, receipts and writs, in the class of Exchequer documents in The National Archives at Kew called Accounts Various. All this and other administrative documents from Chancery classes allow a clearer view of the way in which royal ships and the 'navy of England' as a whole was used for the benefit of the Crown and the nation.

A list has been compiled from this material of nearly a hundred vessels which, the

author claims, are 'royal ships' because they were 'used by Edward III' at some point in his long reign.[30] This is perhaps a confusing definition, because it is clear that not all these ships, by any manner of means, were owned by the Crown in the usual sense of the word, nor was their maintenance and equipment always a charge on the Exchequer. All are recorded to have served the King on at least one occasion, but the same could be said of any of the arrested ships which made up the body of the fleets transporting Edward's armies overseas. A more precise view of ships in royal ownership can be extracted from the administrative documentation and the accounts. The particulars of account kept by William Clewere, Clerk of the King's Ships in the 1350s, although he had been purser on the *Cog Thomas* from 1344, reveal that he was responsible for a group of from nineteen to twenty-nine vessels. Some were clearly very small, for use on inland waters. Others were large and well-equipped, including the *Cog Thomas*, and at least six other cog ships, as well as the *Jerusalem*, the *Edward*, and the *Nawe Seint Marie*.[31] Confusingly, the enrolled accounts for 1353–58, when the Clerk of the King's Ships is named as Thomas Snetesham, include the names of only around twelve ships.[32] This may be because the duties of the office had been divided between two clerks at this time with Clewere apparently paying for shipkeepers (the crew caring for a ship which was not at sea), and Snetesham dealing with repairs. The accounts kept by John de Haytfeld relating to the years 1369–70, when the war with France had restarted after a period of truce, list no fewer than forty-two vessels. This, however, includes a number of small barges and at least nine ships which were explicitly said not to be in royal ownership.[33]

What is more notable than their numbers, however, is that Edward III's own ships were fighting ships. They could not, of course, entirely escape the bread and butter transport activities which, at one time or another, seem to have involved almost every ship unwise enough to be at anchor in an English port when the royal commissioners came looking for ships to arrest for service to the King. At the battle of Sluys, however, the pride of the King's own squadron, the *Cog Thomas*, was in the van of the attacking fleet, with the King himself on board. At the battle in the Channel off Winchelsea, known to contemporaries as *Les Espagnols sur Mer*, present and in the thick of the engagement were the *Cog Thomas*, the *Bylbawe*, and the *Jerusalem*, and other smaller vessels as well.

*The royal ships in decline*

During the remainder of the reign of Edward III, the King's own ships played a much reduced role in the war with France. The financial problems of the Crown made the maintenance of such a fleet less and less attractive. Of the few new vessels provided for the Crown, one at least, the *Paul*, was provided by the City of London to serve under the King in 1373.[34] The recurrence of epidemics of the plague, notably in 1361/2, 1369 and 1375, ensured that the demographic decline clear after its first arrival in 1348 continued. It is hard to estimate how this might have affected the seafaring population, but there is some evidence of increased difficulties in recruiting mariners. The decline in the number of royal ships became even more obvious in the reigns of Richard II and Henry IV. Those that remained seem to have been regarded more as symbols of royal might than as fighting ships. Thus the ships for which John Chamberleyn was responsible as Clerk of the King's Ships under both kings from 1398–1405 were elaborately and expensively decorated. The total fleet numbered from four to six vessels, with three being especially splendid. These were the *Gracedieu*, a balinger built at Ratcliff, which had a red hull with other colours on the stern and *le celeur*; a golden eagle stood on the bowsprit, while a golden crown ornamented the *beek*. The *Trinity* had a similar colour scheme with gilded images of St George, St Antony, St Katherine and St Margaret on the stern, as well as two escutcheons of the royal arms and two with St George and the Garter in gold; on *le celeur* there were again two eagles. In contrast the *Nicholas* was painted black with white ostrich feathers picked out in gold and escutcheons of the royal arms and St George and the golden image of St Christopher.[35]

By 1409, however, when the Clerk of the King's Ships was one John Elmeton, the royal fleet had dwindled to a ceremonial barge for use on the Thames and the *Trinity* no longer as gorgeous as before.[36] Things continued in much the same way for the remainder of Henry IV's reign. There was very little activity in the office with expenses only totalling £159 2s 7¼d in 1411, of which £125 15s 11¼d was still outstanding when the account was enrolled. The nadir of the fortunes of the King's ships was perhaps reached when the clerk appointed at the beginning of the reign of the new king, Henry V, declared in his accounts running from March to July 1413 that he had neither received nor spent any money.[37]

### Henry V and his great ships

From this low point in the fortunes of the royal ships until the death of Henry V in 1421 there was a sudden and dramatic change. During his reign, William Catton and William Soper, Clerks of the King's Ships respectively from 1413–20 and 1420–42, headed busy, well-organised and relatively well-financed 'departments' of state. Catton's term of office was in some ways the most notable. The change in culture under his clerkship from gentle decline and final total inertia in the first years of the fifteenth century can only have been initiated by a radical change in policy by the King. Catton was appointed in July 1413 but by the following year was already responsible for seven royal ships. The enlargement of the royal naval squadron then proceeded apace; it is reasonable to suppose that Henry V had set in motion preparations for a much more active policy with regard to the use of shipping in the renewed war against France. The first seven ships included two, the *Petit Marie* and the *Gabriel*, which had belonged to Henry IV. Another, the *Cog John*, was probably a prize taken from Prussian traders presented to John, Duke of Bedford. The new approach to the whole concept of royal ships was first seen in the

This image comes from a chronicle written very soon after the events described, the overthrow of Richard II by his cousin Henry IV. The illustration shows the departure of Richard II by sea to Ireland, on the campaign which precipitated his overthrow. On the ships themselves the reef points on the sails are clearly shown.

**(BRITISH LIBRARY)**

building of the *Trinity Royal*, which was to be the first of the group of vessels known as the King's great ships. This ship was of 540 tuns capacity, much larger than most other ships in English ports at this date. Some at least of her timbers were reused from the old *Trinity* of Richard II's reign; she was clinker-built and probably two-masted. She was a successful and admired royal ship, leading the fleet with the King on board as it left Southampton for what became the Agincourt campaign in 1415. She was as gaily painted as earlier royal ships with vermilion, gold, *smarer lake*, *jude fine*, and both Russian and Flemish ochre laid in for the painters.[38] She would have made a brave sight leading the fleet past the Isle of Wight where swans swam among the ships, a good omen according to a chronicler.[39]

She was, moreover, in some ways a prototype. Catton was also in overall charge of the building of the *Jesus* of 1000 tuns capacity at Winchelsea, the supervising shipwright being William Goodey. She was ready for service in 1416, and at very nearly twice the size of the *Trinity Royal* must have been an imposing vessel. She was again clinker-built and two-masted. Catton also oversaw the construction of the *George* of 120 tuns at Dartford. For the building of even more ambitious vessels at Southampton another official was recruited. This was William Soper. Unlike Catton, a 'career' royal servant who had been a royal yeoman to Henry V before his succession to the throne, Soper was primarily a merchant and shipowner. He may, however, have first come to the attention of the court and the officials in London as an MP for Southampton in the parliament of 1413. At the end of this year a ship belonging to Soper was involved in the capture of a Castilian ship, the *Santa Clara*. This was brought into Southampton and although some items on board were returned to the owners (including the ship's dog) the vessel herself was treated as a legitimate prize. By February 1414 Soper was in charge of a complex rebuilding operation which saw this ship transformed into the *Holy Ghost de le Tour* of 740–760 tuns capacity. Exactly how this operation was conducted is not made clear in the accounts but there is no doubt that the *Holy Ghost* was based on this ship. At the same time, he also supervised the repair of a Breton prize, the *St Gabriel de Heybon*, and the building of the balinger *Ane*. This might seem to be a heavy programme, but in addition Soper and one Robert Berde, a master shipwright from Southampton, were put in charge of the biggest shipbuilding operation of all, the construction of the *Gracedieu* and her attendant vessels, the balingers *Valentine* and *Falcon*.[40] The *Gracedieu* was a truly enormous ship of 1400 tuns. In all probability the largest clinker-built vessel ever constructed, she had three masts, and marked an even more dramatic departure from the general run of converted or adapted trading ships that had made up the squadron of royal ships in the previous reigns, than her three fellow 'great ships'. More will be said of her design and the use made of her below but behind this building project undoubtedly lay a new policy for royal ships, with a different view of the use that could be made of them in warfare. These great ships can rightly be called the first true warships owned by the English Crown since the days of the Vikings.[41]

In his last accounts Catton took responsibility for thirty-six ships. Thirteen of these were prizes, an indication of the success of royal policy at sea. Of the remainder, in addition to those newly built, one came as a 'gift' (the ship, the *Craccher*, was originally the property of the West Country shipowner John Hawley, who on occasion operated on the boundaries of the law with regard to piracy), others as purchases, or had been in royal ownership for some time. Soper's responsibilities were initially for a slightly smaller number of vessels. Three had been lost at sea and others had been granted as rewards to royal servants; the *Gracedieu* entered royal service just as Soper became Clerk of the King's Ships, along with the *Valentine*, *Falcon* and the balinger *Roos*, forfeited to the King at Bayonne. After Henry V's unexpected death in August 1422, however, the fortunes of the royal ships changed drastically. These vessels were in law the King's private property; there was, therefore, no legal bar to the sale of the ships to reduce royal debts as required by the King's will.

### The dispersal of Henry V's ships

Soper thus spent the years from 1422–25 organising the dispersal of the greater part of the fleet of royal ships which he had done so much to build up in the first place. Only the four great ships were exempt from this process and, after spending some years at anchor in Southampton or in the Hamble river, were finally laid up in 1429 on the mudflats along the Hamble above Bursledon. The other vessels were either sold or granted to royal officials, so that by 1436 the only seaworthy royal ship was the *Petit Jesus*, originally the follower of the *Jesus*, which was rebuilt at Bursledon in 1435 as a three-masted balinger, probably for use as a swift means of crossing the Channel for royal officials. Henry V's will required the sale of ships to raise the sum of 1000 marks (£666 13s 4d); the proceeds

This is a possible reconstruction of Henry V's great ship, the *Gracedieu*, shown against the background of the precise spot where the remains of the ship lie. The modern vessel at the stern belongs to the group who were diving on the wreck for an investigation carried out by *Time Team*.

(AUTHOR'S COLLECTION)

of the sale in fact amounted to just over £1000. It may well have seemed to the new king's councillors that there was little need for such an expensive item as the royal ships. The old method of using requisitioned merchant ships would surely suffice to control corsairs or provide transports now that both sides of the Channel were firmly in the hands of either the English or their allies.[42]

*Royal ships in the second half of the fifteenth century*
The way in which the tide of war turned against the English in the 1430 pointed up the weakness in this argument and created a case for the need for royal ships. However, although Richard Neville, Earl of Warwick, acquired and deployed with some skill a small squadron of ships capable of giving a good account of themselves in a sea battle in the 1450–60s there were no ships in the ownership of the Crown from c.1436 till the 1470s, when there is evidence that Edward IV had begun to acquire a small squadron of ships including the *Falcon* bought in 1475 and the *Mary of the Tower* bought in 1479.

The first Clerk of the King's Ships to be appointed since 1452 was Thomas Roger, who received his first letters patent in regard of the office in 1480. Rogers was responsible for the repair of the *Mary Ashe* and the other ships bought by the Crown.[43] He continued in office under Richard III, with naval activity at much the same low level, although the Crown apparently owned at least six ships, the *Grace Dieu*, *Mary of the Tower*, *Governor*, *Martin Garsya*, *Fawcon* and *Trinity*. These vessels are all named in the accounts of the Clerk of the King's Ships presented for auditing by Roger's widow in 1488.[44] All these ships, however, with the exception of the *Mary*, had passed out of royal ownership by the time the accounts were made up. Roger, however, was not involved in the major shipbuilding endeavour which began in 1487. This was the building of two large carracks, the *Sovereign* of around 450 tuns at Southampton, and the *Regent* at Reding on the Rother. Together with the *Mary of the Tower* these ships made up a squadron of 'great ships' reminiscent of those of Henry V. By 1495 all three were in the charge of Robert Brygandyne, whose accounts as Clerk of the King's Ships give an impression of well-directed energy. The *Mary of the Tower* does not appear in his records, but the *Regent* and the *Sovereign* were joined by two galleasses built in 1497, the *Sweepstake* and the *Mary Fortune*. All carried a heavy armament of shipboard artillery, and thus could more realistically be called warships than the great majority of their predecessors.[45] All survived to form the nucleus of Henry VIII's much expanded royal fleet.

## The ships of the Cinque Ports
The fortunes of the King's own ships, therefore, waxed and waned in this period as individual monarchs not only pursued or abandoned aggressive foreign policies or faced a real danger of invasion, but also showed signs of possessing some understanding of the possible use of a small core of royal ships in war at sea. What, however, of the vessels of the Cinque Ports, which have often been put forward by historians in this period as the basis of English sea-power and the origin of the Royal Navy?

This confederation of port towns in southeast England probably came into existence before the Conquest, perhaps in the reign of Edward the Confessor. The basis of its privileges and organisation was a series of charters granted and confirmed by English kings on their accession. These laid down that in return for trading and tax privileges and the right to have their own court of law, known as Shepway, the ports would provide the Crown with the service of a total of fifty-seven ships, each manned by twenty-one men for a fortnight without pay. The head ports were Dover, Sandwich, Hythe, Romney, and Hastings; to these were added the so-called 'ancient towns', Rye and Winchelsea.[46] Other smaller coastal and inland villages, including Brightlingsea in Essex, and Grange on the Thames estuary, were allowed some participation in the privileges as 'limbs' of the ports, but the issue of ship service was mainly the concern of the original five and the two ancient towns.

It has been pointed out that the terms of the service demanded by the charters were impractical. Fifteen days' unpaid service was far too little to cover an entire campaign or even a quick cross-Channel expedition. The number of mariners specified was too rigid; at the usual ratio of three or four mariners per tun capacity this implied ships of from 60 to 80 tuns which would exclude both the largest and the very common smaller ships. The terms of the charters also did not change over our whole period, despite the fact that there were changes in ship design, and also that parts of the coast between Dover and Hastings suffered severely from the effects of silting in the harbours and the build-up of shingle banks along the coast. From the end of the fourteenth century this had had the effect of greatly reducing the usefulness of some of the harbours of towns in the confederation and their ability to provide ships for royal expeditions.

There is, however, no doubt that the Cinque Ports were regarded as a somewhat special part of the 'navy of England'. In the thirteenth century the mariners of the ports performed a variety of tasks for the Crown but it soon became apparent that their main value was in the provision of logistical support. When the King wished to raise a fleet for a military purpose, most frequently to transport an army and its supplies to the intended scene of battle, a writ directed to the Lord Warden of the Cinque Ports required him to provide ships. These writs occur frequently in the records, usually in conjunction with more general orders to commissioners to requisition ships in English ports which were not members of this confederation. Frequently, both sections of a fleet raised in this way served on the same terms.

There are only a few instances in the reign of Edward I during his wars in Scotland when the Cinque Port ships are singled out for special treatment. For example, in the Wardrobe Book listing the expenses of the campaigning season of 1299/1300, the clerk has taken care to deduct the fifteen days' free service owed to the Crown by the Cinque Ports from the total period for which these vessels were paid. All were in fact at the disposal of the Crown from 23 July till 2 September 1299. A similar deduction was made in 1306 when twenty-six ships from the Cinque Ports were employed in the Scottish campaign for seventy days in all, but were paid for fifty-five.[47]

Later in the fourteenth century it seems that, just as land armies largely lost their feudal character and were made up of companies of paid soldiers raised by captains according

to the terms of indentures made with the Crown, so payment to the mariners of the Cinque Ports for their whole period of service became the norm when they were summoned to serve the Crown. Apart from an expedition in 1323 when the Crown demanded only twenty-seven ships, but wanted them to be manned by the same number of mariners as would have served in the fifty-seven charter vessels, the charter terms were not a material issue. The Cinque Ports, therefore, contributed a goodly proportion of the ships available to serve the Crown but very frequently did so on the same terms as other ports. The number of vessels involved has been calculated in an attempt to arrive at the total number of Cinque Port ships which served the Crown in the years 1322–60. This has shown that over 115 vessels from Winchelsea, eighty-eight from Sandwich, and thirty-three from each of Dover and Hythe were involved. The great fleet of 1346 which took Edward III and his army to France before the battle of Crécy included sixty-four from these same ports.[48]

Towards the end of the fourteenth century and in the fifteenth century the Cinque

This is a group of photographs of the remaining fortifications of Sandwich and Rye, prominent members of the confederation of the Cinque Ports. *Top left* is the Ypres Tower at Rye that commanded the anchorage on the river Rother. *Bottom left* is the Barbican at Sandwich that opened on the quay by the bridge over the Stour. *Right* is the Fisher Gate that led directly into the town from the quay and was the entry used by the French forces when the town was sacked in 1457 and the mayor killed.

**(AUTHOR'S COLLECTION)**

This series of pictures show the surviving gates of Winchelsea. *Top right* is the Pipewell gate, originally built *c.*1300. It opened on to the road to the ferry to Rye; it was destroyed in an attack by Spanish allies of the French in 1380 and then rebuilt *c.*1400. *Top left* is the Strand Gate that protected the steep road up from the haven at the bottom of the hill on which the town was built. *Bottom left* is the new gate on the road leading inland in a quarter of the town which may never have been fully developed. It was well outside the new fortifications proposed in 1415.

**(AUTHOR'S COLLECTION)**

Ports contingent in any royal fleet declined markedly in number. One reason for this was the severe silting suffered by the ports on the Kentish coast. Sandwich Haven, which had provided a sheltered anchorage for ships behind Deal spit, was becoming more and more difficult of access because of the build-up of sandbanks in the estuary. The Wantsum Channel which divided the Isle of Thanet from the mainland, and allowed vessels to reach the Thames without having to navigate round the North Foreland, was also drastically narrowed by silt deposits and by the draining of the marshes.[49] Further west, the eastward drift of sand and shingle along the Kent coast caused by tidal currents also affected the anchorages at Romney and Hythe. These two ports were threatened with the loss of some of their privileges in 1341 when they could not contribute fully to a royal fleet.[50]

A further danger on the coast on the borders of Sussex and Kent was breaches in the shingle banks which protected the havens and coastal towns in stormy weather. These storms seem to have become more frequent in the thirteenth century, and by 1250 'Old' Winchelsea was suffering badly from inroads by the sea. These culminated in the storms of 1287/8, when the town was finally completely overwhelmed. The decision had already been taken by the King to re-establish a new town on the hill above the Brede estuary at Iham. 'New' Winchelsea overlooked the harbour in the estuary which extended to the Camber anchorage and Rye. The first rent roll of the new town dates from 1292. To some extent the increased tides in the rivers Brede and Rother, which followed the storm damage of the thirteenth century and ran up as far as Appledore, benefited Rye,

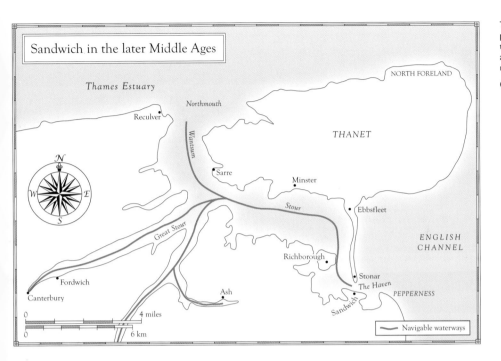

Sandwich in the later Middle Ages

Thames Estuary

NORTH FORELAND

Northmouth

Reculver

Wantsum

THANET

Sarre

Minster

Stour

Ebbsfleet

Great Stour

ENGLISH
CHANNEL

Richborough

Fordwich

Stonar
The Haven

PEPPERNESS

Canterbury

Ash

Sandwich

0        4 miles
0        6 km

Navigable waterways

but both towns had difficulties in keeping their harbours open for large ships by the end of the fifteenth century.[51] It was also the case that the Kentish ports were losing trade and influence to ports further west, from Southampton to Falmouth on the one hand, and competition from London itself on the other hand. Throughout our period, however, kings summoned the ships of the Cinque Ports to serve the Crown, even if by the time of Henry VII this could be seen as a formality or nod at tradition, rather than as a practical means of raising a goodly contribution to a fleet.

### Arrested shipping

This did not apply to the Crown's general power to arrest shipping in English ports, which loomed large in any plans to send armies across the seas. Arrested vessels made up the bulk of any royal fleet, whether its primary purpose was to support or transport royal armies for a land campaign or whether it was intended as a fighting force. Although the Crown had had the right to requisition ships for purposes like these since before the Conquest, all the details of the system can only really be understood from the thirteenth century, when sufficient documents survive, whether accounts, writs or other royal orders.

There was no great practical difficulty in using merchant ships for naval purposes until the very end of the fifteenth century. The idea of a warship of a completely different design from that of one used for trading voyages hardly existed. Largely because of the images of ships in some early thirteenth century manuscripts, and the fact that some ships were described as being 'of castle' round about this date, for a brief period there may have been a minor difference between trading and war vessels. Ships which were conscripted by the King for warlike purposes had, it has been suggested, somewhat flimsy 'fighting platforms' fitted at the bow and the stern. In some manuscript illuminations and early town seals, the 'castles' shown have a decidedly temporary appearance. A particularly good example is the town seal of Winchelsea.[52] The advantages of these so-called aftercastles and forecastles, in providing useful extra accommodation for passengers and the ship's company and for other purposes, seem to have rapidly gained acceptance. From around the first half of the fourteenth century, castles were an integral part of the hull of most sailing vessels and this adaptation for use as a fighting ship was no longer necessary.

### Horse transports

Arrested merchant ships, however, had to be adapted if they were needed to transport horses. This was a necessity in many campaigns undertaken by the English Crown, whether across the Channel or north to Scotland. Particularly in the fifteenth century when mounted archers had become an important element in English land armies along with knights, large numbers of horses were needed. Moreover, a knight's war horse was a highly trained beast; a horse seized from an intimidated peasant or townsman while on the march was not an adequate substitute. Some of the best known frames of the Bayeux tapestry show horses peering nonchalantly over the gunwales of the Norman ships and then being disembarked by leaping over the ship's side.[53] Later royal accounts make clear that something more in the way of preparations were necessary for ships transporting horses. Edward I ordered the shipment of horses from Ireland for his campaign in the west of Scotland in 1303, with the vessels being adapted with hurdles and other necessities.[54] More details can be found in the account of the sheriff of Essex in 1340, who provided wood to make gangways to load the horses, hurdles to make stalls, along with racks (for hay?), canvas for mangers, ropes, rings, and nails for this purpose.[55] It has been suggested that, since the vessels being converted to take horses were decked, some kind of entry port would be cut in the hull to load the animals. There is no mention of the prior existence of a facility like this in ships arrested to transport horses. Neither is it clear how an opening like this would be waterproofed when the vessel was under way, nor are there any supplies provided for this purpose.[56] There is, however, more evidence from the Mediterranean that in those waters at least some kind of opening in the hull did allow horses to be disembarked in a somewhat similar fashion to vehicles from a modern 'roll on-roll off' ferry. The exact nature of the adaptations to vessels to carry horses and the method by which the horses were embarked and disembarked in northern waters must remain speculative.

### The system of arrest

There is much better evidence of the way in which the highly important system for arresting ships to serve the Crown was operated. The first move was the issue of a writ, normally in the form of a letter patent, which appointed commissioners to undertake this task; there might be a requirement that only ships above a certain tonnage should be arrested and usually the ports to be visited might be named, as well as the time and place for the assembly of the fleet. It was not unusual for there to be in fact a considerable time lag between the decision to raise a fleet and the day it set sail. Collecting the ships, crews, armed men, horses, supplies of all kinds including victuals for the men and the

horses, was a complex task. Stormy weather and adverse winds might easily prevent an expedition leaving harbour for weeks. Some muster lists survive which provide details, sometimes including tonnage and crew numbers of the ships which reached the collecting port. Finally, the accounts recording payments to shipmasters record those vessels that certainly took part in a particular expedition. Some can be found in the Wardrobe books kept in the King's Chamber; others are found in various classes of Exchequer documents most often the Accounts Various.

### An Irish fleet

The relatively small fleet assembled in Dublin, Drogheda and Carrickfergus in 1303, to transport the army led by the Earl of Ulster to take part in the campaign led by Edward I in the west of Scotland, gives a good idea of the way such a fleet was brought together. Alexander Byknor was commissioned in the first place to locate sufficient ships. Although this is not made clear in the final accounts, it seems very probable that he used his authority to arrest all suitable ships which were in port in Ireland at the relevant time. His assistants

This representation of a horse disembarking from a vessel through something rather like the bow door of a modern car ferry is not entirely fanciful. Chronicles describing amphibious campaigns in the Mediterranean mention knights riding straight up the beach from transports. It is certain that large numbers of horses were taken by sea to France from England as well as to Scotland from Ireland.

**(BRITISH LIBRARY)**

travelled through all four Irish provinces looking for vessels, and the resulting fleet contained ships from no fewer than thirty-one English and Irish ports, ranging from those based at Harwich to those coming from ports like Caernarvon and Chester. It is probable, but not made explicit in the documents, that the vessels, whether normally based in England or Ireland, were in Irish ports at the time of their arrest. Some ships needed repairs before they could take part in the expedition, and over £37 was spent on the necessary materials in Dublin and Drogheda. There are few details regarding the size of the ships and their crews, since in this instance the totals spent on ships from the same home port are aggregated. Thus the five ships arrested which were based in Conway were manned by a total of forty-eight mariners and four boys; at the usual ratio of four men per tun this would probably imply a group of ships of around 40 tuns each. In all, 145 ships were arrested, not including those used as horse transports.[57]

### A fleet bound for Gascony

This fleet can be contrasted with that raised in 1443 to transport the Duke of Somerset and his company to Gascony. This consisted of ninety-four ships, the great majority of which came from English south-coast ports; nevertheless, no fewer than fifty-one ports were represented, mostly by a single vessel. The greatest contribution came from Dartmouth, which supplied thirteen ships ranging from the enormous 400-tun vessel, the *Mary*, to two small ships of 30 tuns each. The fleet also included twelve ships based outside England; one from Calais and one from the Garonne were certainly from English-held territory, but that did not apply to that from Portugal or the two from Breton ports. Foreign-owned ships were clearly not exempt from the attentions of the royal commissioners on the hunt for shipping. In this fleet, at least a third were large ships in contemporary eyes, of over 100 tuns capacity, but there was also a group of small ships of 24–30 tuns, with crews of from five to six men. These were probably used as victuallers rather than as troop transports.[58]

### The Crécy campaign

Foreign ships were also swept up into some of the major fleets raised by the Crown in the fourteenth century. The fleet which left England in 1346, carrying the army which would win the battle of Crécy and lay siege successfully to Calais, is listed in a number of documents copied at a later date from a lost original, probably the naval section of the accounts kept by the Treasurer for War for the campaign, Walter Wetwang. The fleet consisted of 700 English ships manned by 14,151 mariners, and a further thirty-eight foreign ships, including fifteen from Bayonne (controlled by the English Crown as part of the Duchy of Aquitaine) and fourteen from Flanders. These were manned by 805 mariners. The crew numbers for the contributions of individual ports make it plain that many vessels were small. Twenty-five royal ships were involved along, with forty-seven from Fowey and forty-three from Yarmouth, the two ports with the largest squadrons in the fleet. Eight others sent more than twenty each. In all eighty-three ports were involved in England and Wales.[59]

Organising and collecting a fleet of this size, even if only for a Channel crossing, was a major undertaking. An operation on a similar scale was that undertaken in 1359/60. On this occasion the royal household, the army captains, the soldiers, and their equipment were transported to Calais by a major fleet of around 438 ships and some smaller squadrons of as few as eight ships.[60] With Calais as a secure base for the English forces, its harbour firmly in English hands by this time, it was no longer necessary to bring over the entire force in one group with the establishment of a bridgehead as the first imperative.

Even more impressive in size was the fleet which took Henry V to Harfleur in 1415. Since he had rejected Calais for his entry point, perhaps because it was situated too far to the east, Henry again sailed in one fleet which most chroniclers agree consisted of around 1500 ships.[61] Collecting such an enormous fleet undoubtedly put great pressure on English maritime resources, arousing considerable opposition from some shipowners; royal officials were dispatched in April 1415 to Holland and Zeeland to see if ships could be hired there.[62] This may have been because the response to the orders arresting all ships in English ports sent out in March had clearly revealed that insufficient shipping would be available for the needs of the army being put together. Any shipowner or shipmaster in the whole of this period was well aware that when any warlike activity was in prospect by the Crown, whether in the more remote parts of the British Isles or across the Channel, his vessel might be forcibly recruited for the defence of the realm.

*The economics of ship arrest*

Service in royal fleets, however, was not unpaid. The shipmaster would receive 6d per day, as would the officer known as the constable; ordinary seamen received 3d and boys 1½d, also per day. These rates of pay remained unchanged throughout the fourteenth and fifteenth centuries and were the same as those paid to mariners and masters in royal ships, except a small elite group of shipmasters who had been granted annuities by the Crown. They also seem to be very much in line with those paid to craftsmen working in shipyards, where the most skilled men also often received 6d a day, with proportionally less for labourers. For mariners on arrested ships, the notion of receiving a daily wage might have seemed strange. On trading voyages the crew might be paid in one of three different ways; one (*a deniers*) involved a cash payment. More frequently, the crew were offered the chance of participating in the success of the voyage. This could be by using their assigned portage or cargo space to load their own goods for trade, or by the arrangement known as *au fret de la nef* whereby the crewman gave up his own portage space for a chance to share in the profit of the voyage as a whole.[63] There was also a system known as *regardum* or *de regard*, which especially on impressed ships was a ration allowance. The victuals provided are known from the accounts of royal ships, and were a basic diet of bread, salt meat, salt fish and occasionally cheese, washed down with beer, cider or wine if available.[64]

The person whose interests seem to have been ignored in this system was the shipowner who might or might not have been identical with the shipmaster. His trading profits were forfeited for the entire period of the arrest, and there was no established method for compensation in the case of loss or damage, unlike the situation with war horses where a system for valuation and compensation existed. A ship has been called 'the single most expensive piece of capital investment in the medieval money economy', but this did not incline the Crown to act with generosity to shipowners.[65] There are few instances in the records of claims for the loss of a ship on royal service being met. In one case the unfortunate mariners of Dunwich lost four ships on a voyage to Gascony in the winter of 1295/6. They appealed to the King for compensation; a report on the incident did not appear until twenty-three years later, and they did not finally receive any money for the lost ships and unpaid wages of mariners on the same expedition until 1327. Perhaps a little more fortunate was Robert de Paris of London, who in 1387 was granted a captured cog to replace the loss of a newly-built barge.[66]

Shipowners, in fact, very frequently attempted to evade or ignore the royal demands for their shipping. During Edward I's later campaigns in Scotland when the demand for shipping must have seemed almost unceasing, writs under the privy seal were despatched threatening punishments on shipowners whose promised vessels had not joined a royal expedition, or who had left a fleet without permission, even though they had received royal wages.[67] The writs thundered about the contempt shown to the Crown, and the delay caused to the expedition by the non-appearance of promised ships, but the reluctance of the mariners concerned to obey the Crown is understandable. Deserters from royal fleets, whether ships and their crews or parties of mariners, were a continual worry for those charged with arraying a fleet. There was a particular problem, for example in 1342, when a large group of English ships abandoned the royal campaign in Brittany in favour of continuing to Bordeaux to load wine. No fewer than 230 ships were listed as deserting the King's service in the Close Rolls. The detailed accounts in the Wardrobe Book show that the crews of 142 vessels lost pay because of failure to do their full duty. The crews of eighty-eight ships forfeited all their pay and were threatened with dire punishments.[68]

*Parliamentary petitions*

Later in the fourteenth century much of the frustration of shipowners at the burdens placed on them by the arrest of their shipping by the Crown found expression in petitions presented to the Commons in Parliament, a forum where merchant and trading interests were well represented. Claims were being made in the Commons in 1348 that the 'fleet is almost destroyed throughout the land', because of the demands made by service to the Crown and the subsequent loss of shipping.[69] In 1371 the main issue was the inordinate amount of time arrested ships had to wait in harbour before an expedition set forth; the crews were unprovided for in this situation, and many 'abandoned their ships to rot and waste.' Shipmasters, it was claimed, were also being driven into royal service to the grave detriment of merchants trying to organise trading voyages. To these petitions the royal answer tended to be cautious and non-committal, often that an remedy would be sought by the advice of the Council.[70]

In the following years, the complaints of shipowners and mariners represented in the Commons grew ever louder. There were requests for payment from the moment of arrest and for compensation for the use of the ships by the Crown and for equipment used in the same service. King Richard II finally gave way in 1385 when, after further petitions stating that the navy was enfeebled and wasted by royal demands, it was agreed that every ship 'armed on the sea for the safeguard of merchants and in defence of the realm' should receive '2s for each ton-weight per quarter'. This was less than the 3s 4d per ton that had been demanded, but certainly better than nothing.[71] In both 1404 and 1416 in the succeeding reigns, shipowners again requested the payment of 3s 4d per ton weight. Henry IV's response was that the 'good ancient ordinance in this matter be upheld and preserved.'[72] Henry V's reply was more evasive merely stating that the 'king wishes to do that which right and reason require in this matter'.[73] There is little evidence that the payment was made and it was not requested by the Commons after 1416.

There is little doubt that the way in which any English naval expedition was put together, from diverse sources using different methods, made it hard to control the fleet. The small core of royal vessels had commanders who may have had some previous experience of war at sea, or of the complex task of transporting an army. Others from the arrested ships may have never been involved in anything similar; the masters of foreign vessels who were caught up in these fleets may have had little English. Communication problems must have been formidable. Yet large armies and all their equipment, including the horses and bulky and unwieldy artillery, were on many occasions taken across the Channel, south to Gascony or north to Scotland. Gathering a fleet together took many hours of work from royal clerks, sometimes expected to travel widely from port to port, but usually also having the help of local worthies. The rewards for this kind of service were paid erratically and were never very great. It seems undeniable that arresting ships, especially on the scale that happened during the reign of Edward III, could disrupt trade, but the same could be said of war itself, or the endemic robbery at sea which also tended to flourish in times of war.

The King relied heavily on his ability to arrest shipping at need; the role of royal ships was as much as symbols of royal might and authority as fighting vessels. These ships were never more than a small minority in any fleet. Nevertheless the somewhat ramshackle collections of ships of all sizes and from all along the English coasts which made up what contemporaries called 'the navy of England' was an essential tool for any English medieval monarch with warfare on his mind. In most circumstances they filled their role competently, even if not always with alacrity.

## CHAPTER 4

# Ships and Ship Types

WE NOW NEED TO LOOK IN SOME DETAIL, as far as this is possible, at the design of the vessels which made up this all embracing 'navy of England'. Though change came slowly and in an evolutionary way in response to influences from many directions, there are significant and obvious differences between the ships of the era of the Conquest, and those which are so beautifully illustrated in the Antony Roll of Henry VIII's navy.[1] It is not always easy to track these changes or to date them precisely. One reason for this is the nature of the evidence, much of which comes from sources which were never intended to convey technical information of the kind which is easily available in later periods. There are no treatises in English on shipbuilding before the reign of Elizabeth, and no models of hulls or complete vessels like those produced in dockyards in the seventeenth century. A standard for the way in which a ship's size was described, however, did come into general use in this period. A ship's capacity was measured in most of Northern Europe including England by the number of Bordeaux wine barrels or 'tuns' it could carry. A tun was a standard measure containing about 210 gallons. There was a formula for calculating this – there was no need for a 'test loading' as it were; there are cases of ships arriving at port carrying more wine than their normal tunnage would have permitted.[2] The system was apparently well understood, but has no direct connection with the later 'tonnage' relating to weight. Italian shipwrights used a similar approach based on the Italian wine 'but' or *botte*, which was about half the size of a Bordeaux tun.

## A review of the evidence

If we seek out material evidence for ships in our period, we are faced, as was mentioned in chapter 1, with a scant few examples. There is little evidence from shipwrecks, whether discovered on foreshores or excavated underwater. Wrecks, from their very nature, will more or less never consist of a complete ship including both hull and upper works, or be in good condition. In the case of medieval ships, fragments are more commonly found than anything approaching a complete hull. The most common finds are sections of planking reused to buttress the sides of quays or other waterside erections. The catalogue of archaeological finds relating to ships, boats and their fittings from the period 1050–1500 excavated in Britain and the Channel Islands (before 1994, the date of the publication of the book in which it can be found) has far more entries for this kind of fragment than anything else.[3] Those which refer to more substantial finds tend to be frustrating: remains of a clinker-built vessel were found, for example at Eastbourne in 1963, but were destroyed during pipe-laying. The remains of other ships in Rye, which may have been from the sixteenth century, are inaccessible under a road and the railway.[4] The mid fourteenth-century ship found in Sandwich on the site of the former Sandown Creek was ripped apart by mechanical diggers and men with chainsaws who were laying new sewer pipes.[5]

The most important piece of archaeological evidence from this period in England is the remains of Henry V's *Gracedieu*. After she had been laid up on the mudflats in the river Hamble in 1434 and stripped of most of her gear, she was struck by lightning on 9 January 1439 and caught fire. Most of the ironwork on board was then removed from the wreck, and what remained was left to moulder away on a quiet bend in the river. At extreme low water on equinoctial spring tides some of her

The excavation of the Newport ship in process behind a coffer dam on the shores of the river Usk. This is a very rare discovery of a mid-fifteenth-century vessel with the structure of the hull clearly visible.

(FRIENDS OF THE NEWPORT SHIP)

beams protruded from the mud, and gave rise in later years to the belief that a Danish ship burnt by the Saxons about 877 lay in the river. A local landowner undertook some investigations in the 1870s, recovering some timbers but causing damage to what remained. The first serious attempts to examine the wreck occurred in 1933 and 1936, with a preliminary account published in the *Mariner's Mirror*. This helped to establish the identity of the vessel as the *Gracedieu*. Further investigations have since been carried out by the University of Southampton, to which the wreck now belongs.[6] This survival of an identified medieval ship for which there is a body of documentary evidence about her building and her career has no parallel elsewhere.

The so-called Newport ship came to light much more recently in 2002. She had been completely forgotten until her remains emerged from the mud on the banks of the river Usk, where builders were excavating the orchestra pit for a new Arts Centre for Newport. The vessel had been laid up in a muddy inlet, or pill, probably for repairs to take place, and then for some reason abandoned. She cannot be certainly identified as a named vessel but has been dated to the mid fifteenth century since a coin with the date *c.*1446–51 was found under the mast step, placed there by her builders as a good luck token. Most of the forward part of the ship has been recovered, although the stern was inaccessible beyond the coffer dam which enclosed the excavation. She was clearly a merchant ship, and of a type common in northern waters at the time. As much as possible of her remains were removed from the original site for study and conservation and, it is hoped, will eventually be exhibited in a dedicated museum.[7]

Vessels excavated outside Great Britain have also provided important information about the design of medieval ships in northern waters. These include the Roskilde 'Viking' ships and the Bremen cog, both found in 1962, and other cog ships found mainly in the Baltic or during the creation of polders in the former Zuider Zee. Replicas of the Roskilde ships and the Bremen cog have been constructed so that their sailing and handling characteristics can be studied, further increasing the knowledge of medieval ships.[8]

Another kind of material evidence comes from votive ships presented to churches or other religious foundations in gratitude for the salvation of the donor from some peril encountered at sea. The best known of these which has relevance for our period is the Mataro ship, which came originally from a small fishing village near Barcelona. It was put on the market in 1929 in New York and eventually came into the possession of the Prins Hendrik maritime museum in Rotterdam, where it still remains. Although there has been much discussion of its features, it is accepted that this is a carefully made model of a ship from the early part of the fifteenth century, from which much can be learnt of hull design in a vessel from southern waters.[9]

Another votive model has even more recently (c.1979) come to light. This is the Ebersdorf ship, originally presented to the church dedicated to the Virgin in the little town of Ebersdorf, near Chemnitz. This is, of course, a long way from the sea, but the model is connected with a legend well known in the district. A knight from a local noble family was returning from a pilgrimage to the Holy Land, bringing a fortune for his bride who awaited him. A terrible storm arose on the voyage home, and the knight pledged to donate a ship filled with gold to the church if disaster was averted. Fortunately the winds dropped, the sea calmed, and he made port in safety. He fulfilled his vow and the model was made and filled with gold as he had promised. The model has suffered some damage over the years and is now preserved in Dresden. A careful examination has confirmed a date of c.1400, and that the model was made by a shipwright as an accurate representation of a northern European ship of that date, with resemblances both to the Mataro model and to the Bremen cog.[10]

The Ebersdorf ship: a votive model presented to a church near Chemnitz in Germany a long way from the sea. The hull was skilfully made by a shipwright and shows details of the fitting of the stem- and sternposts.

(HORST OERTEL, CHEMNITZ-EBERSDORF)

### Illustrative evidence

Illustrations, whether in illuminated manuscripts or in larger scale paintings and murals, can also be a source for the design of medieval ships. The problems of interpretations presented by these images are, as mentioned earlier, formidable. If the illustration comes from a manuscript this will never be a technical manual of any kind but maybe the life of a saint, a chronicle, a romance or a devotional work. In larger paintings, the depiction of ships will usually be subsidiary to the main subject of the painting, which again may often be religious. The story of St Ursula and her one thousand accompanying virgins, for example, as shown on a reliquary in Bruges, includes lively scenes of the waterfront at Cologne. The sequence of paintings in the Accademia Gallery in Venice by Carpaccio, also devoted to the legend of St Ursula, has clear depictions of fifteenth-century ships in the painting, in the sequence ostensibly devoted to the arrival of important persons at a port and called 'The Return of the Ambassadors'. It is impossible to know how much knowledge any of the artists had of the sea and ships, especially when they were monks in religious houses some way from the sea. Another set of problems are associated with the artistic conventions under which any particular artist worked. It is reasonable to suppose that artists did not deliberately portray ships in a misleading way, but this also supposes that the artists or illuminators understood what they were portraying.

Edward III's gold noble issued after the battle of Sluys. In an inspired example of medieval 'spin' it shows him on board the *Cog Thomas*.

(© NATIONAL MARITIME MUSEUM, GREENWICH, LONDON)

There was much discussion in early volumes of the *Mariner's Mirror* as to precisely what feature of ship design, of around 1300, artists were representing in a collection of images which seem to show the stemposts of vessels bound round with thick ropes. This corresponds with no known method of ship construction, though it has been associated with the ships known as hulks. To complicate matters further, the viewer also needs to have some visual conception of what the medieval artist is representing. This is not always the case with some features of medieval images of ships. Thus van Nouhuys when discussing the Mataro model points out that the little model has been made with what we might call scuppers: holes bored through the planking to drain the deck, which come out just below the level of the deck itself. He links these with what appear in illustrations as square holes with dark spots in the middle, at a similar level on a ship's side. These have been interpreted as gun ports, even though the pictures date from a time long before broadside firing had been developed.[11] Scuppers of this type were not known to exist before the model was carefully examined. The images on the seals of port towns, and also occasionally coins, have similar problems aggravated by the need to accommodate the image on a circular base.

*Documents*

Visual evidence clearly has to be treated with caution if one is looking for answers to questions of ship design. The documents which might provide this information are also disappointing in some respects. Almost all are accounts of shipbuilding for the Crown. They provide a great deal of information about matters like the cost and provenance of materials, and about wage rates and the numbers of men employed. They say little or nothing about design or the structure of a vessel. Some of the technical terms used are also still not certainly defined, or precisely linked to elements in the later, better-documented technology of wooden shipbuilding. The total amount of wood, cordage, ironwork and the like purchased may be recorded, but not how this was used in building and fitting out a vessel. Another complication is the fact that medieval Exchequer clerks and the writers of chronicles often use the names of ship types somewhat loosely. The same ship can be described as both a barge and a balinger, while there are other less common terms for ship types in the documents, about which very little is known. In Edward III's reign the accounts of Clerks of the King's Ships include references to vessels called 'flunes'; these were clearly small and probably not unlike barges, but there is little further information beyond their name.[12] There are areas of uncertainty in documentary evidence just as there are with visual and material evidence.

## Oared vessels

Ships carrying a large number of oars were built and widely used throughout our period. Generally speaking, the largest carried about one hundred oars, although many could be much smaller. These vessels, which were also equipped with masts and sails, used oars for the increased ability this conferred to manoeuvre in restricted areas or adverse winds. This would very often be when approaching a haven or when on a river or estuary, especially when the channel was narrow and winding and obstructed by sandbanks. It

A full rigged ship from the Antony Roll of 1546. The vessel shown, the *Matthew*, was launched in 1545 and was typical of ships derived from Henry V's great ships. The hull is carvel built. The gun ports on the side and stern are also clearly shown. Gun ports could not be cut in a clinker-built hull.

(PEPYS LIBRARY)

could also be when engaged in a battle when the wind was unfavourable, or when a final burst of speed was needed when coming along side an opponent in order to grapple with and board the enemy ship. Oared ships might also be highly suitable for some forms of fishing or the hunting of whales.[13] They would have had less room for cargo than round or sailing ships but were, even so, seldom exclusively used as warships. There were also undoubtedly many different local designs for small boats used on inland waterways, or as lighters and the like in harbours, which would have been rowed or poled. These are not our concern here, but larger seagoing ships which might find themselves conscripted for royal fleets. Generally speaking, these ships are often characterised as longships, deriving their form and function from the highly successful ships of the Vikings of Scandinavia. These were successful as warships and raiders as well as trading ships and, of course, were well capable of long-distance ocean voyages, as demonstrated by the colonisation of Greenland and the adventures of Erik the Red in North America.

The earliest representations of ships of this type in our period are those shown so graphically in the Bayeux Tapestry and which, of course, paradoxically, do not apparently have any oars in this representation. This may be because of the limitations of the medium (embroidery), or because the passage from Saint-Valéry was a swift one with a fair wind, with no need for oars. We have already noted that the term *esnecca* or 'snake' in some interpretations is used to describe the ship used in Channel crossings by later Norman kings. Was this something like a Viking ship with a snake or dragon head on the prow, and similar lines to those of the Gokstad ship? There is little evidence to support this idea, except the fancied etymology of the name; what can be said is that mentions elsewhere of ships of this type are rare, and are not found after the thirteenth century.

We have already mentioned the 'galleys' owned by English kings in the first half of the twelfth century. More detailed information comes from the series of accounts for building what are called 'galleys' (*galleia* in the Latin of the accounts) for the English Crown from 1295 into the fourteenth century. Again the name used in most of these accounts may cause some confusion. The clerks were using a standard Latin word; these vessels, however, were not designed or built on the same lines as the galleys of the Mediterranean maritime powers. They clearly differed from them in certain important respects: their sails were not lateen-rigged, for example, and their hulls were clinker-built. By the late fourteenth century, when Venetian and later Florentine trading galleys regularly visited Southampton and other English ports, the terms 'barge' and 'balinger' become those commonly used in English records for vessels of this type. To draw clear distinctions between English-built so-called galleys, barges and balingers is not easy. There is no reliable visual or material evidence for these vessels; looking at documentary sources will, however, allow some conclusions to be drawn.

*English galleys*
Looking first at the galleys of the late thirteenth and early fourteenth centuries, it is usually considered that Edward I issued the writ requiring twenty-six towns to build twenty galleys of 120 oars each in response to Philip IV's initiative in setting up the *Clos des*

*galées* at Rouen to build vessels for the French Crown, but in fact both monarchs took this decisive step towards increasing their naval power at very much the same time. The need for ships which could give a good account of themselves in a fight had been borne in upon both monarchs by the bloody encounter between Normans and Anglo-Gascons off Brittany the year before. Eight of these ships were in fact built, and the surviving accounts allow some deductions to be made about their design. The accounts are for the galleys built at Dunwich, Ipswich, London (two), Lyme, Newcastle on Tyne, Southampton and York.

The preamble to the account for the building of the Newcastle galley makes clear that it was intended 'for the defence of the realm and the safety of the sea'.[14] The total cost of the vessel was £205 2s 4¾d, rather less than those built at Dunwich, Southampton and York. Work began in mid December 1294, and the ship was ready to join a fleet by early September the following year. The materials used and the wages of the workmen are painstakingly recorded, but few measurements or other design elements are included. There is no doubt that the vessel was a shell-first clinker design, with overlapping planking forming her hull. These planks were secured by clench nails driven from the outside though the double thickness of the planking and then 'clenched' (bent over iron washers or roves) on the inside. Caulking made of a mixture of animal hair, coarse dry grass and tar was laid along each 'strake', or plank, before it was clenched to minimise leakage. The length of the keel can be deduced from the two great beams bought for the *fundum* or keel: one was 56ft long and the other 52ft. Allowing for the scarf, or join, between these, the galley would have been around 100–104ft long at the keel, making a length overall of *c*.120ft. Other timbers are named, making it probable that the vessel was double-ended much like a Viking longship.

The shape of the hull and the breadth amidships can only be speculative. The shallow U-shape of later galleys built in Venice is clearly shown in a group of Italian fifteenth-century manuscripts, illustrated with drawings dealing with shipbuilding, but there is no such information from this date nor in fact in English until Elizabeth's time.[15] The upper works of the Newcastle galley were gaily painted in bright colours: red, blue, yellow and green; this was taken seriously and took some time, with a special group of painters employed. The head (*brand*) of the galley was also covered in silver foil at a cost of 12d. She had one mast, of considerable size, erected by twelve sailors with the help of shear-legs, after she had been launched and was alongside the quay in Newcastle. She was steered by a sternpost rudder, although there is also mention of a free rudder, perhaps a lee board. The oars are recorded as forty-eight of 23ft, and twenty-four of 16ft in one batch, and eighteen of 23ft and fifteen of 17ft in another (105 in all).

The galley's superstructure included a fairly substantial castle, probably at the stern; the *castrum anterius* (forecastle) also mentioned seems to have been a much smaller affair. The *castrum capitale* mentioned in August at the end of the building period was probably a top castle, fastened to the mast, perhaps resembling a barrel since its panels were fastened with iron bands. There is no indication that any of these castles were temporary or could be easily dismantled. An attendant boat or barge with one mast was also built at the same time as the galley, and also equipped with twenty oars. When all the main works were finished, the galley was rigged. She was carefully waxed to minimise water damage, and also equipped with banners, awnings, bails, and brazen cauldrons and pots, and other implements, perhaps for the cook.

At the end of all this work, financed out of Newcastle's own funds with the promise of reimbursement by the Crown by a reduction in the fee farm, the money due annually to the Crown, the galley must have made a brave sight at the quayside in the town. She was not, however, a galley of 120 oars as the King had requested; 100 is a likely estimate with some necessary spares in reserve. There may also have been something of a question mark over the quality of the workmanship of her builders. She needed immediate repairs after a trial trip to Bamburgh. In the spring of 1296 after a voyage to Winchelsea to join a royal fleet she again needed quite extensive repairs. Finally, in 1301 she was sold back to the men of Newcastle for £40 because, 'the said galley barge and cock boat were almost rotten and their gear for the most part lost by storms at sea'.[16] This may have been the result of a lack of maintenance; well-built ships at this time often had much longer careers.

The other galleys built at this time varied in size; the Lyme galley was considerably smaller with fifty-four oars, implying a keel length of about 55ft, Southampton's had sixty, while the remainder had around one hundred. All, however, were clinker-built and had a stern rudder, with perhaps an auxiliary side rudder, and a single mast with a square sail. The Mediterranean galleys of this period had frame-first carvel-built hulls, twin side rudders and a lateen rig on two or more masts. The Lyme galley completed a voyage to Bayonne for the King, although she required repairs before she could undertake the return voyage. The financial aspects of her building were not finally settled until 1319–20, perhaps a reason why a small borough of the size of Lyme was not keen to undertake any other shipbuilding for the Crown.[17]

Accounts for the building of oared vessels from later periods are not plentiful, but give little indication that there was much change in the overall design of this kind of vessel.[18] There are detailed accounts for the repair of two galleys and a smaller vessel at Bayonne in 1320, but these have little information about the design of the vessels. The crews hired to bring the ships to England after the work was finished totalled forty-eight for the St George, thirty-three for the St Edward including the master, and eighteen for the galiot; this gives some idea of the size of these ships, but clearly the 360 oars made ready for this voyage included many spares.[19]

The need for an oared vessel in certain circumstances continued to be acknowledged into the sixteenth century. The vessels listed in the roll of Henry VIII's navy include one galley, the Galie Subtille, thirteen so-called rowbarges, small vessels of around 20 tuns, and fourteen galleasses in which the gun ports on the lower deck were replaced by rowing benches.[20]

## Balingers and barges

It is not at all clear how these vessel types were distinguished one from the other. Both were oared vessels, also with sails, which were popular both with merchants and as warships. It has been suggested that barges were larger than balingers but this is not always the case.[21] It may well be that contemporaries used the terms more or less interchangeably. Edward III encouraged port towns to construct barges for their own defence in 1355. In 1372 a more ambitious programme to build oared vessels was initiated by the King.[22] This has been described as 'reviving the barge-building programme … to produce balingers'.[23] This phrasing demonstrates the uncertainties about the design of these ships and the overlap between them.

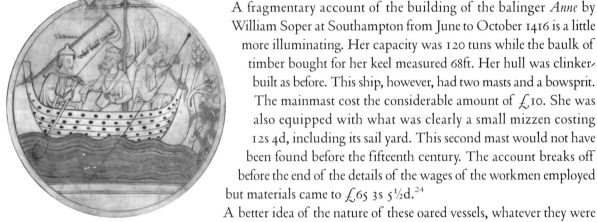

A fragmentary account of the building of the balinger *Anne* by William Soper at Southampton from June to October 1416 is a little more illuminating. Her capacity was 120 tuns while the baulk of timber bought for her keel measured 68ft. Her hull was clinker-built as before. This ship, however, had two masts and a bowsprit. The mainmast cost the considerable amount of £10. She was also equipped with what was clearly a small mizzen costing 12s 4d, including its sail yard. This second mast would not have been found before the fifteenth century. The account breaks off before the end of the details of the wages of the workmen employed but materials came to £65 3s 5½d.[24]

A better idea of the nature of these oared vessels, whatever they were called, may be gained by looking at how they were used and regarded by contemporaries, rather than the dry details of accounts. Balingers, perhaps because of their dual means of propulsion, both oars and sails, were seen as swift vessels – very useful for a quick Channel crossing. There is some evidence from the fifteenth century that most balingers were fairly small, normally of around 40–60 tuns. The *Anne* discussed above may have been unusually large, as was the *George* of the same size also built for the Crown at Small Hythe. In southwest France, balingers were seen as the vessel of choice of those who had more than legitimate trade in mind. They were to be found wherever some 'dark deed' was contemplated, preferred by pirates and corsairs from the Cornish ports to Spain. They also served as the lighters, or 'followers', of larger ships; they scouted for the enemy or took passengers from ships anchored off shore to the quayside. Their crews were on occasion augmented when it was clear that oarsmen might well be needed, so that the vessel could manoeuvre swiftly in adverse wind conditions. This happened particularly when balingers were included in royal squadrons patrolling the Channel in Henry V's reign.[25] There are graphic descriptions of their involvement in sea battles, including one in 1416 when six English balingers chased a Genoese carrack up the Channel but were unable to take her because of the way she towered above the balingers by 'more than a spear's length' and also because they had run out of missiles.[26] Their expertise as raiders did not prevent their also being used as trading ships (balingers can be found in the Customs accounts).

### Round ships, cogs and hulks

Round ships, the familiar vessels with a hull apparently shaped much like a half walnut shell, a single mast and a square sail are probably the most easily recognised of medieval ship types, appearing in many illustrations. Within this group, however, several different type names appear with the distinctions between them, as we have seen with the oared ships, lacking precision and clarity. The terms most often met with are 'cog', 'hulk' and *nef* or *não*. The last is the most problematic; it is merely the French or Portuguese translation of the Latin *navis*, meaning ship. There is little in the way it is often used in, for example, the ledgers of the Bordeaux Customs, to suggest that it is more than a general term with no more particular reference to a defined ship design than our word 'ship'. It is most frequently contrasted with the Latin *batella*, or boat. It seems to have been used for a vessel of perhaps more than 20 tuns or thereabouts, ranging up to the very largest of several hundred tuns capacity, but no clearly differentiated design features are associated with the term.

Ships were built at many locations along the shores and estuaries of the countries that faced the Channel, the North Sea and the adjacent coasts of the Atlantic. They would usually be designed to take into account the particular circumstances of their place of origin and local maritime trade and customs. Would the vessel trade mostly to harbours which dried at low tide? What cargoes were most likely? What conditions of wind and weather must the ship withstand? Any of these requirements might lead to small local adjustments to the design of the hull or the rig which would not be immediately obvious to royal clerks. As well as these local considerations, it is clear that there was a strongly developed maritime tradition which grew up along the coasts, and which encouraged well-tried traditions and customs of the sea to spread along the coasts of northern Europe. This is evidenced by the very widespread distribution of the Laws of Oléron controlling maritime trade and the duties of shipmasters, and the way the technical names of the equipment of ships can be found in very similar forms in many European languages.

In the same way, it is not surprising that evidence of sailing vessels with a beamy high-sided hull can be found all along the seaways of the same region. They had a good cargo-carrying capacity and a high freeboard, suitable for the choppy waters of this region. With a fair wind they could make good progress under sail. These ships were clinker-built; by the beginning of the fourteenth century, if not earlier, a sternpost rudder had become the norm. The rig of a single mast with a square sail was also more or less universal until, in the course of the fifteenth century, perhaps because of greater familiarity with ship types used in the Mediterranean, at first a mizzenmast, usually rigged with a lateen sail, was added, then a little later a foremast also made an appearance. The vessel shown taking soundings in the Hastings MS of the *Rutter of the Sea* dating from *c.*1480 shows a vessel rigged just like this, with three masts, including a lateen mizzen. By means of these developments, the ground was prepared for the more elaborate sail plans of sixteenth century ships.

At much the same time a highly significant change also took place in England in the design of a ship's hull. The well-tried clinker method was less and less used; shipwrights gradually adopted the frame-first carvel method of the Mediterranean. This allowed for

The seal of Winchelsea; this shows particularly clearly the fore and after castles which at this date (*c.*1290) may have been temporary additions to a ship's structure in preparation for war at sea.

(© NATIONAL MARITIME MUSEUM, GREENWICH, LONDON)

Bench-end carvings originally in St Nicholas Chapel, Lynn, dated *c*.1420: that on the left shows a two-masted vessel with a lateen mizzen, which may be based on a Genoese carrack.

(VICTORIA & ALBERT MUSEUM)

large vessels to be designed with more streamlined hull shapes. The method also used less timber than clinker building and overcame problems associated with the stiffness of large clinker-built hulls. The little Mataro model has a carvel-built hull. English shipwrights would have become familiar with this style of building as direct seaborne trade between northern and southern waters increased. Genoese carracks, large 'round' carvel-hulled sailing ships, had been making regular calls at English ports, principally Southampton, since the time of Richard II. This would have given local ships' carpenters some familiarity with this method of hull construction, something which would have been increased when no fewer than eight vessels of this type were taken by the English between 1416 and 1417, and absorbed into the group of King's ships also based at Southampton.

The gradual spread of carvel hulls in English shipbuilding practice is hard to trace in the absence of any relevant material evidence. Ship names beginning with 'carvel' are, however, increasingly found in the later years of the fifteenth century. John Howard, Duke of Norfolk, a notable shipowner at the time, agreed with Edward IV in 1468 to provide victuals for twenty-two ships. Among these are eight named carvels. These include 'john coles carvale, the carvale of Rye and the carvale Mary Shirborne', which was at Calais.[27] Howard also undertook the building of a carvel at Dunwich between 1463–66. This was a three-masted vessel with a top castle, but no measurements or tonnage are available.[28] An analysis of ship types listed in the particulars of the Customs Accounts for various dates showed that four ships identified as carvels were recorded in the Exeter and Dartmouth accounts in 1461, one in 1470, nine in 1480 and fourteen in 1508.[29] By the time the *Fragments of Shipwrightry* was written in 1586, carvel-framed hulls were clearly the norm for seagoing vessels. This MS makes clear how by this time the design of hulls involved mathematical calculations and the drawing of measured plans. If a vessel was called a *nef* or a *navis*, the meaning of this term changed over time from the stereotypical medieval ship already described, to something with better handling and sailing qualities, the forerunner of the Elizabethan galleons.

### Carracks

The development of sailing or round ships followed a rather different path in southern Mediterranean waters over the same period. While galleys were the dominant type of warship, something which was an inheritance from the navies of Greece and Rome, sailing ships had long been used for trade in bulk commodities. These vessels continued to have a quarter rudder until some time in the early fourteenth century. They also normally had frame-first (carvel) hulls. In northern European waters, the large trading ships of Genoa which were designed in this way became well-known, since they were frequent visitors coming up the Channel making their way to the international markets of Flanders, especially Bruges. In England, Southampton was the port most frequently visited. Carracks, two-masted at this date, captured from the French (who had employed the Genoese as mercenaries in their naval forces) became part of Henry V's navy. The large carvel-built sailing ships owned by English mariners in the later fifteenth century differed little in hull design from these ships, although most had a more seaworthy three-masted rig. The name 'carrack' was, however, associated with the Genoese and other Mediterranean traders and little used by the English.

*The King's great ships*
A little more can be said about this group of vessels built for Henry V from 1416. All were of quite exceptional size. The first to be built, the reconfigured *Trinity Royal*, was probably a two-masted clinker-built vessel of 540 tuns; the *Holy Ghost de la Tour*, 740–60 tuns, again two-masted and clinker-built; the *Jesus*, 1000 tuns of a similar config-

uration, and finally the *Gracedieu*, 1400 tuns clinker-built to a special design, three-masted. Although inventories of their equipment exist for all the vessels, which allow assumptions to be made about their rigging, as well as accounts which at least partially cover their building expenses, most is known about the *Gracedieu*.[30] She was probably the largest vessel with a clinker-built hull ever constructed. Excavation of her remains, which lie in the Hamble river above Bursledon, has made it clear that this hull was of an exceptional design. The problem was that for the hull to be stiff enough to prevent hogging in a very large vessel the thickness of the planking on the ship's sides had to be increased. It seems from the planking recovered from the wreck that this was done by an ingenious form

An illustration from a fair copy of the earliest known sailing directions in English (late fifteenth century). It shows typical vessels of the period with three to four masts rigged with a lateen mizzen, and square sails on the other masts, including a topmast in one case. On shore a beacon as a navigation aid is shown.

(PIERPONT MORGAN LIBRARY)

of modified 'triple thickness planking'. This is illustrated by the diagram below. The way this was designed relieved the pressure on the nails used to secure the planks, which otherwise would have been very considerable, and also increased watertightness. It did, however, require enormous quantities of ironwork for the nails and the roves, a great deal of high-quality timber, and a highly skilled workforce.[31] There is no reason to think that the design itself was flawed; the *Gracedieu* was seaworthy, although the use made of her was limited because of changes in the strategic situation in the Channel in 1420 when she was completed. It is not known whether her companion vessels had hulls of a similar design. This might be the case with the *Jesus* but the accounts of her building are fragmentary and there are no material remains.

Further details of the design of the *Gracedieu* come from the diary of Luca di Maso degli Albizzi, captain of the Florentine galleys in 1429–30, who visited the ship at anchor in the Hamble river with William Soper. He acclaimed the ship as the largest and most beautiful he had ever seen. He also gave some measurements; in his view the ship was about 177ft stem to stern, with a beam of 96ft; the height of the forestage above the waterline was about 46ft. The circumference of the mast measured at the level of the first deck was around 22ft while he estimated the height at 204ft. The hull measurements correspond well with those established during excavation.[32] Some concerns have been raised about the beam measurement, which seems too large, but there seems no doubt, looking at the proportions of length to beam of both the Mataro and the Ebersdorf models (2:1), that very beamy vessels were built. All this, however, adds up to an imposing ship, perhaps over-large for normal operations, but a potentially terrifying opponent in a battle at sea, the role for which she was specifically designed.

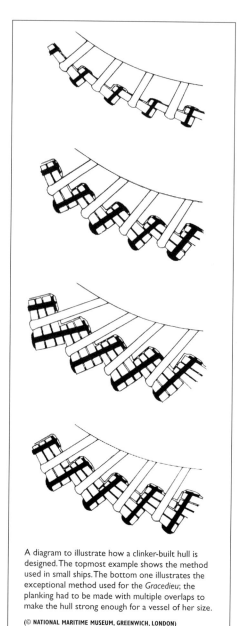

A diagram to illustrate how a clinker-built hull is designed. The topmost example shows the method used in small ships. The bottom one illustrates the exceptional method used for the *Gracedieu*; the planking had to be made with multiple overlaps to make the hull strong enough for a vessel of her size.

(© NATIONAL MARITIME MUSEUM, GREENWICH, LONDON)

## Cogs

There is much more certainty about the design of the cog than that of those ships called, rather enigmatically, *nef* or *navis*, or even the great ships. This is largely because of the amount of archaeological evidence which has fortuitously come to light. The most important find is that of the so-called Bremen ship discovered in the river Weser in 1962. This seems to have been swept downriver in a flood while under construction. Enough of the hull and a small proportion of the upper works remain for the design and method of construction of a cog to be understood, and in fact replicated in the modern version of the vessel which was built in 1988/9. There is no doubt about the

The Mataro ship model made in Catalonia in the early fifteenth century. Important details of ship construction are visible, including the scuppers. The detail of the bow shows the quality of the workmanship including the blocks on the rigging.

(WIKIMEDIA)

identification of the wreck as that of a cog; its lines, particularly the relatively short hull, straight stem- and sternposts and the centre-line rudder exactly mirror those of the vessel on the 1329 seal of Stralsund, a leading member of the Hanseatic League. This seal was also known to the townspeople at the end of the fifteenth century as 'the cog'.[33] The hull of this wreck was well enough preserved to enable the remains of other vessels, excavated earlier in the same region, also to be identified as cogs.

The ship had a flat bottom with the first planks adjoining the keel laid edge to edge, creating a pronounced U-shape; the planks rising towards the deck were clinker laid. It was also clear that the ends of the beams forming the frame protruded through the hull, a feature which the artists of seal and manuscript illustrations often attempted to portray. The vessel herself was 23.3m long, with a beam of 7.6m and a height above the keel of 4.2m. This would imply a capacity of around 80 tuns. The vessel can be dated by dendrochronology to c.1380, a period when the Hanseatic League was flourishing and its fleets perhaps at their peak.

This design would have made it easy for the vessel to take the ground in drying harbours or shallow estuaries. It was also very suitable for the bulk cargoes traded by the merchants of the Hanse, salted fish from Scania, salt from the bay of Bourgneuf, timber and corn. Although cogs have a long history in the Baltic and Frisia, it seems that ships of this type were not found in English waters before c.1200. Gradually after that date they formed a minority in the 'navy' of England. Very often in ship lists they are identified with 'cog' forming part of the vessel's name. Seven cogs were included in the fleet of seventy-five which took victuals to Berwick for Edward I's forces in 1299. All were based in the Cinque Ports, although the fleet as a whole was recruited much more widely.[34]

In 1303 nineteen cogs made up virtually all the ships recruited to transport horses to Scotland.[35] In Edward III's reign what might almost be called the flagship of his fleet, on which he sailed to command the fleet at the battle of Sluys in 1340, was the mighty vessel of perhaps as much as 280 tuns, the *Cog Thomas*. The royal ships also included the *Cog Edward* of c.240 tuns, bought for £450 in 1334, and several others of varying burthen.[36] Henry V briefly owned only two; the *Cog John* which was lost off the Breton coast in 1414, and a prize vessel renamed the *Redcogge*, sold to a Londoner in 1418 in poor repair.[37]

By the late fifteenth century, there is some evidence that cog ships had completely fallen out of favour among Baltic shipwrights, with carvel-hulled three-masted vessels replacing them. It is also the case that perhaps on short cross-Channel voyages they were still favoured by some conservative-minded shipmasters, or perhaps that the customs officials from whose records the figures come used the names of ship types very loosely. An analysis of the ships recorded in the Chichester Customs include, in 1499/1500, eighteen cogs belonging to aliens and thirty-nine owned by men from Calais, and in

The seal of Stralsund, a Hanseatic city on the Baltic, dated c.1250. The ship shown is a cog, the cargo-carrying vessel which dominated the seaways in this region. It shows the clinker-built hull and straight sternpost fitted with a rudder typical of this ship type.

(© NATIONAL MARITIME MUSEUM, GREENWICH, LONDON)

The wreck of the Bremen cog before it was removed from mud banks along the River Weser. The planking of the hull and its relative completeness are clearly visible.

(DEUTSCHES SCHIFFAHRTSMUSEUM)

1513/14, forty-eight alien cogs and ten from Calais.[38] Cogs were a highly important element in fleets in northern waters, especially suitable for the bulk cargo trades, but also a useful addition to fleets with more warlike purposes. Their distinctive hull design, however, seems to have fallen out of favour during the fifteenth century.

## Hulks

It cannot very often be said of a ship type that the evidence comes solely from iconography or images but that is the case with the medieval hulk. The crucial image is that on the seal of Shoreham in Sussex made in 1295. This shows a vessel with a banana-shaped hull, and planking running up to the castles at the bow and the stern not scarfed into a stem- or sternpost. Round the rim of the seal runs the inscription in Latin, *hoc hulci signo vocor os nomine digno*, or in translation, 'By this sign I am called Mouth which is a worthy name'. This somewhat obscure phrase becomes clear when it is realised that Shoreham was at one time known as Hulksmouth. Other medieval images have been found of banana-shaped vessels with a similar hull form. The earliest ones have side rudders, although the Shoreham seal shows a stern rudder, not an easy thing to attach to a curved hull form.[39] A kind of collar or rope binding also appears around the stem and stern in early representations. No remains have been excavated which show any of these characteristics. The word 'hulk' in various forms appears in documents, but rarely in English sources. None appear in lists of ships arrested by Edward I; Edward III owned one called *Le Michiel Hulke*. Fleets put together by Henry IV and Henry V included two, one of 200 tuns and the other of 160 tuns. The many hundreds of vessels recorded in the Bordeaux Customs and French notarial documents after the end of English rule as lading wine in that port include only one hulk, a ship from Middelburg in 1484. All this seems to contradict the view that hulks were cargo-carrying vessels of a particular design widely used before carvel building became the norm.[40]

It is, of course, possible that some new archaeological discoveries will confirm the existence of this ship type. It seems more likely, however, that the idea of clearly defined designs with significant characteristics differentiating one from another was not something that bothered the medieval shipwright. He worked from models he knew, modified by experience or the whims of a particular owner, or the conditions in his port and the surrounding region. Change came over time but slowly and gradually; occasionally stimulated by experimenting with a previously untried feature admired perhaps in a visiting foreign vessel. The names given to ship types sometimes reflected their purpose, a *passager*, or a *fisherboat*; or occasionally referred to a characteristic of their construction like *carvel*. Other than these obvious uses it is best to treat the various terms with some circumspection, rather than seeing them as definitive descriptions like the names given to naval vessels in the eighteenth century, or modern 'one design' racing yachts.

The seal of New Shoreham, one of the strongest pieces of evidence for the existence of the hulk as a defined ship type, since the inscription links the ship shown to the old name of the port Hulksmouth.

(© NATIONAL MARITIME MUSEUM, GREENWICH, LONDON)

CHAPTER 5

# Shipbuilding and Shore Facilities

THE ACCOUNTS RELATING to the building of the galley at Newcastle on Tyne in 1295 by order of Edward I begin with the money spent on making ready and securing the place where the galley would be built. The cost was 8s 3½d for preparing an area near the Pandon Burn, probably surrounded by some sort of hedge or fence. An additional 1d was spent on buying a lock for the gate of the garden where the timber was to be stored.[1] Clearly no very elaborate preparations were needed on land to set up a project like this, even though building the galley lasted more than nine months, with at times at least twenty men working on the ship. There was nothing very unusual about this arrangement in medieval terms. Ships were built in small ports and along rivers and estuaries in all parts of the country, with very little in the way of permanent facilities or advance preparations. The requirements seem to have been for a place near a watercourse where launching a vessel would be possible, where adequate supplies of timber were available at a reasonable distance, and where it was also possible to find or bring in skilled workmen. The usual method seems to have been to build the hull supported on props in a place where a 'dock' could be dug to help with the launching, or with the later rigging of the vessel. This was no more than a slipway cut out of the riverbank or the foreshore so the new hull could be eased into the water, probably on greased wooden rollers, and then floated out into the river or the harbour. This so-called dock was not, nor was it intended to be, a permanent facility.

**Shipbuilding for the Crown**

The arrangements made for the building of the group of galleys ordered in 1295 all mirror those set up in Newcastle. The site for the galley built at Southampton[2] consisted only of an enclosure protected with hurdles and *spinis*, that is, thorny brushwood.[3] In London an area was fenced off with old barrel staves and a hut was also built for stores.[4] This evidence sits oddly with the belief that King John in the early thirteenth century built something like 'a wet dock or basin with a lock' for his galley fleet at Portsmouth. The Latin word used, *exclusa*, certainly usually has the meaning of a dam or sluice. Here the term may mean no more than that an enclosure filled by the tide was built, where galleys could be safely moored and floated off as the water rose. Something very like this existed at Hartlepool at about the same time.[5] The sheriff of Hampshire was ordered to surround the dock with a wall to protect the ships and to build stores for equipment and tackle, but this was as protection against bad weather, not as a part of a permanent shipbuilding facility. Much more usual was the lack of special facilities we have already noted. This is also evident from the accounts of the building of a vessel at Conway in 1301, also for Edward I. There is no mention of any preparation of a shipyard, the main factors being the accessibility of timber in Lancashire and Cheshire, and the availability of forges capable of producing the ironwork needed at Beaumaris.

By the second half of the fourteenth century, a considerable amount of repair work and also the building of new vessels for the Crown took place on the Thames. The most important sites were at Ratcliff, near Limehouse, and on the other side of the river at Greenwich. The ships are often described as being on *les woses*, or the mudflats exposed at low tide, where their hulls would be supported by shores. There were some buildings at Ratcliff used as stores but it seems that the *delf*, or dock, needed for building a new ship or a major refit was dug out as required. This certainly happened in the case of the barge called the *Godesgrace* built in the 1380s. There is some evidence that by the end of the fourteenth century finding adequate supplies of suitable timber for shipbuilding in easy reach of Ratcliff or St Katherines's *flete*, near the Tower, a site also associated with the royal ships, was proving difficult. Timber for the *Godesgrace* came from Haringey Park to the north of London, and also from Horsley in Surrey. This had to be taken overland to Weybridge, and then brought up the river Wey and the Thames to Ratcliff. Some also came from Kent by way of Gravesend and down the river Lee from Waltham Abbey.[6]

A view of a waterway at Small Hythe in Sussex; this area was a thriving centre of shipbuilding for the Crown and other owners up to the reign of Henry VII. Many ship nails and other remains have been found along the former course of a branch of the river Rother.

**(AUTHOR'S COLLECTION)**

The reinvigoration of shipbuilding for the Crown which was so marked in the first years of the reign of Henry V, as preparations were pushed ahead for the reopening of the war with France, was also affected by the availability of timber. William Catton, the Clerk of the King's Ships in 1413, was charged with the complete rebuilding of Henry IV's *Trinity de la Tour*, originally built at New Hythe in Kent on the Medway. This took place at Greenwich, with timber coming from all over north Kent, including some from as far away as Yalding and Horsmonden. Other supplies came from Essex, including Colchester, and Hatfield forest. The reconstructed ship, now renamed the *Trinity Royal* of 540 tuns burthen, was the first of Henry's 'great ships'.[7] The others in this group, however, were all built on the borders of Sussex and Kent, and Hampshire, where it was easier to find timber of the type and quality needed, in the New Forest and the woods of the Weald.

Two great ships, the *Holy Ghost de la Tour* of 740 tuns and the *Gracedieu* of 1400 tuns, were built at Southampton between 1416 and 1420. At the same time a prize, the *Gabriel Harfleur*, formerly the *St Gabriel de Heybon*, was refitted, and a balinger, the *Falcon*, and a barge, the *Valentine*, intended to support the *Gracedieu*, were also under construction.[8] Another balinger, the *Ane*, was also built in the Southampton area while the *Jesus* of

1000 tuns was worked on at a slipway at Winchelsea. She also had a 'follower' or support vessel, the *Petit Jesus*, probably also originally built at Winchelsea.[9] Not far away up the valley of the Rother, now no more than a slow meandering weed-choked stream, at Small Hythe, another balinger the *George* of 120 tuns, described as being like a galley,[10] was also built during the same years. Small Hythe is now some distance from the sea and the only waterway near the village is a drain for the rich farmland of the isle of Oxney, the Reading Sewer. There is, however, strong documentary evidence for the fact that ships were built there, which has been confirmed by an archaeological investigation. Large quantities of roves and clench nails have been found in an area along the presumed medieval shoreline, together with fragments of ships' timbers. The way new and used ironwork was intermingled suggests that ship-breaking and the reuse of fittings in new or rebuilt vessels was common practice, with all the work taking place on the same site.[11]

One substantial refit did take place on the Thames at this date – this was that of the

A shipbuilding scene from a German chronicle: the carpenters in the foreground are working on the preparation of the planking. The figure on the right may be the master shipwright or designer.

*Thomas* of 180 tuns, which had been laid up on the mudflats at Wapping and was also repaired there, perhaps because she might not have survived the voyage to Southampton.[12] By any standards, the shipbuilding programme undertaken by the Crown from 1414–20 was a very considerable one, with the greater part of it being under the supervision of William Soper. Soper, who had been a successful merchant in Southampton before he became involved with the royal fleet, had property in the town including premises in the Water Gate which fronted onto the town quay. This was very well placed for his work as the collector of customs in the port and as a merchant, which he carried on at the same time as that for the King's ships. It was not, however, suitable for ship-building and there is no firm evidence for the location where this took place in Southampton. We do know that, as in earlier times, a temporary 'dock' was dug out in a suitable spot for each ship, and that this was fenced round with stakes to protect the stores from pilfering. After the *Gracedieu* had been completed the fencing, no longer needed, was sold to a local merchant. One suggestion is that the shipbuilding took place on the banks of the river Itchen; another tradition links this activity with Eling on the west side of Southampton Water but there is no firm evidence for either site.[13]

A shipbuilding scene from a manuscript of stories of Greek heroes. Workers on the shore are boiling pitch and other preservatives to treat the hull. Other workers are using a plane and other tools to prepare the timbers.

**(BODLEIAN LIBRARY)**

Soper, however, did construct in 1417 well-built and substantial facilities for the royal ships. These included a forge and a storehouse built out of Kentish ragstone and something called *holyngston*. The ships needed large numbers of iron nails, roves, and other fittings, most of which were made on site. A forge dedicated to this work was clearly desirable. The building was over 120ft long and has been tentatively identified with a building mentioned in the 1454 Terrier of Southampton called the Long House. This was adjacent to the town wall, next door to the Water Gate, conveniently placed, perhaps, for the storage of cordage and timber coming in by sea but maybe not for the forge if the shipyard itself was some distance away. The building was sold by Soper to the Master of Godshouse in Southampton in 1423.[14] The 1454 Terrier, however, records the owners of the Long House as the Mayor and Corporation of Southampton.[15]

After this tremendous burst of activity, as Henry V's fleet was dispersed following his death, shipbuilding dwindled to minor repairs to the great ships which went on till 1427. The only new work undertaken was not at Southampton but on the river Hamble above Bursledon, perhaps near the site now occupied by the Elephant boatyard. This was the rebuilding of the old *Petit Jesus* as a three-masted vessel in 1435.[16] No further shipbuilding was undertaken by the Crown until the 1480s. In 1487/8 the *Regent* and the *Sovereign* were built for Henry VII, followed by the *Sweepstake* and the *Mary Fortune* in 1497.

In the 1480s the royal ships were still principally based in Southampton, where the *Sovereign* (*c*.450 tuns) was built, or the anchorage in the river Hamble. The *Regent*, a vessel of about 600 tuns, was built at Reading on the Rother near Small Hythe. The building of a very substantial vessel was still possible in this location despite the continued silting up of the waterways.

There was also a rented storehouse at Greenwich. By 1495, when Robert Brygandyne was the Clerk of the King's Ships, a decision seems to have been taken to set up a new base for the ships at Portsmouth. A dock was built there, a rather more substantial construction than the mud berths of Henry V's reign, along with a forge and stores. Although dock gates are mentioned in the accounts, it seems that the dock was not a dry dock as usually understood, since the dockhead had to be dug out when a vessel needed to leave the dock when works were completed. Both the *Sovereign* and the *Regent* were refitted in the new dock, and the *Sweepstake* was built there.[17] Perhaps because of Brygandyne's connection with the village which was where he had been brought up, the *Mary Fortune* was also built at Small Hythe. This was possibly one of the last vessels to be constructed there, on land rented from his family on which a presumably temporary 'workehouse' was also constructed for 6s 8d.

*Shipbuilding supplies*

The large number of building accounts surviving from the period when Henry V was actively expanding the number of royal ships also allow a good picture to be built up of the nature and source of the supplies needed in large quantities. Timber was the first requirement. This was of many different types and qualities. It could be clove board, split from the original tree trunks, or sawn board, usually prepared by sawyers in the woods. The principal need was for oak used for the main structural timbers, easily available in the extensive woods of the New Forest, but harder to find near to London by the end of the fourteenth century. Soper was a verderer of the New Forest, among his many other jobs, which clearly gave him the authority and knowledge to seek out the best timber in these woods.[18] Knees (angled timbers supporting deck beams) were cut where a branch grew out from the main trunk, naturally creating the angled timber needed. Smaller branches and loppings had a use as shores or faggots for fuel. Locally-provided ash, beech and elm might also be used in shipbuilding. One calculation has suggested that 2735 oak trees, 14 ash trees, 1145 beech trees and 12 elm trees were used in the construction of the *Gracedieu* at Southampton.[19] Not all of this timber was bought. Some came from local landowners including monastic houses, ostensibly as gifts to the Crown. Timber was also imported sometimes over a considerable distance. The so-called Righolt boards (softwood) came from Riga, or at least were mainly imported by members of the Hanseatic League from the Baltic. What was sometimes called Prussian deal, also softwood, had a similar origin. What were called wainscot boards were widely used; this was oak of the best quality also imported from northern Europe, including Russia and Germany. Treenails (wooden fixing pins) were also needed and used on both hulls and upper works.

Building these ships likewise entailed the provision of large quantities of iron. This was for the nails, roves and other fixings needed in the construction, alongside the treenails, and other items, for example, the *flaill* for the windlass, grapnels and chains and the essential anchors. The nails used for the *Gracedieu* weighed, it is estimated, some 23,743 kg.[20] Some of this material was bought from local merchants in Southampton, which was a centre for the trade in iron bars with Bilbao. Six tons of iron for the work on the *Gracedieu* were provided by John Hawley of Dartmouth notionally as a gift but, given his involvement in actions at sea which were on the borders of legality, the gift may have been intended to placate an irate monarch.[21] It was only at the larger shipbuilding sites like Southampton that a forge was available to produce all the many kinds of specialised nails and other ironwork used in the ships. Normally these were bought 'ready-made', as it were, from local smiths. Apart from these materials, large amounts of pitch, rosin and tar were also needed to preserve woodwork and reduce leakage in the hull. The joins and gaps between strakes and deckboards were packed with caulking materials (often moss, oakum or animal hair woven into something called *sye*). The seams would be later coated with pitch and tar. When the Lyme galley was under construction a boy was paid to collect moss.[22] Those working on the Southampton

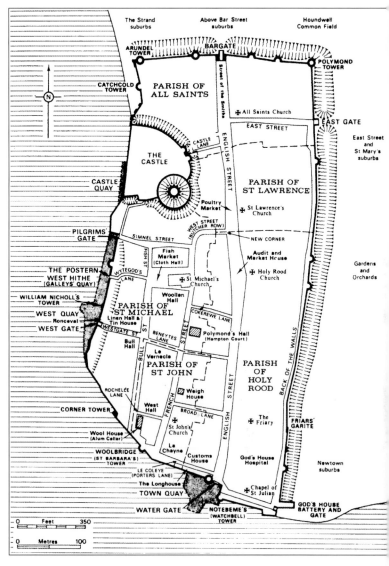

A map of Southampton in the mid fifteenth century based on the records of the Terrier or list of householders. The Long House which may have been a store for Henry V's ships is shown along with the Water Gate, the office of the Clerk of the King's Ships.

(FROM G HUTCHINSON, *MEDIEVAL SHIPS AND SHIPPING*)

A scene from the Bayeux Tapestry showing the felling of trees for shipbuilding; the small image below shows how the natural growth of branches springing from the trunks of oak trees was used to provide knees, the curved timbers supporting deck beams.

(AUTHOR'S COLLECTION)

The path along the ramparts at Sandwich known as the Ropewalk, which gives some idea of the size of the facility needed for the twisting of hemp fibres to make all kinds of cordage for medieval ships.

(AUTHOR'S COLLECTION)

galley used heather and pork fat,[23] tallow, oil and grease to treat the hull; sheepskin mops needed to apply these materials were usually provided for the final work on the hull.

Spars and masts, along with most of the cordage, were normally not fitted until after the hull of the vessel had been launched. The *mastspore* for the second London galley was brought from the park at Addington to Greenwich on a cart with six horses, so was clearly a heavy load.[24] There is also good evidence that the enormous mainmasts of the 'great ships' were composite; that of the *Gracedieu* was probably between 58–61m high, being around 2m in circumference at the level of the main deck, according to the measurements estimated by a Florentine galley captain.[25] No one tree could have provided a spar of such a size. This is confirmed by the explicit statement in the accounts that sixteen spars were bought 'for making the great mast' of the *Jesus*.[26] It is not clear where all the timber for large spars came from. It may have been imported like righolt or wainscot. One fragmentary account records how six large masts were brought by sea from London to Southampton, towed behind two crayers from Fowey.[27] The masts may have been bought from merchants from the Hanseatic

League based at the Steelyard on the Thames above London Bridge. At the end of the fifteenth century Robert Brygandyne gives few details about the provenance of timber and other supplies used in the building of the two rowbarges for Henry VII, but most seems to have come locally from suppliers in Hampshire or Sussex. Only the tar and pitch bought for the *Sweepstake* from a certain Clayece Dowcheman was probably imported, perhaps from the Baltic.[28]

The final rigging of the vessel was often carried out by the ship's crew or other mariners as the last process in readying the ship for use. Canvas for the sails came mostly from Normandy and Brittany, made of locally grown hemp, and was often called *olonnes*, after its supposed place of origin, Oléron. The main sources of supply of hempen cordage were Bridport, which had a thriving ropemaking industry, and Lynn for cordage imported from the Baltic or the Netherlands. It was described as 'white' or 'black', depending on whether it had or had not been treated with tar as a preservative. There is no mention of a rope walk at Southampton itself, although there is a long straight section of the town ramparts at Sandwich known by this name.

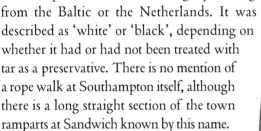

Medieval warships normally went to sea bedecked with banners and streamers. These bore the arms of the ruler (here the fleur de lys of France). Shields along the side known as pavises bore the arms of noblemen aboard. The oriflamme (the red streamer), the war banner of France received at the Abbey of St Denis at the beginning of a war, is also shown.

**(BRITISH LIBRARY)**

Most cordage was probably bought in bulk lots and then adapted for a particular use at the shipyards. It was accounted for by weight, and either 'cable' or 'hauser' laid, coming in qualities suitable for everything from anchor cables to the lines of sounding leads.

Both the accounts and the ships' inventories attached to them list other pieces of essential equipment: pumps and their component parts, pulleys and pulley shives, oars, tools like gimlets and hammers, lanterns, *watirscoupes* or bails, buoys, *bedews*, cooking pots. Also listed, usually for vessels which were in a reasonably seaworthy condition, were standards, gitons and streamers embroidered with royal badges; the *Holigost de la Tour* flew flags embroidered with emblems of the Royal Arms and the antelope, a personal badge of Henry V. Both the *Regent* and the *Sovereign* had old standards and streamers in the storehouse, with some of the *Regent*'s decorated with 'Red crosses and roses'.[29] Some of the later inventories also include basic navigation equipment like sounding leads and lines, bittacles which contained a compass and running glasses or *diols* to measure time, similar to a modern egg timer.

### The shipwrights

As well as allowing an overview of the materials used in shipbuilding at this period, the accounts also provide much information about the workmen who made the ships and the way their work was organised. The Newcastle galley was built under the supervision of a master carpenter called William de Waynflete, at the good wage of 2s per week. In the first week of the work he was helped by five carpenters earning 3d a day, others called clenchers at 2½d per day, and finally six porters or general labourers at 1½d per day. Later, ships' carpenters called holders were also employed at 2d per day. William de Wayneflete, the master shipwright, received his weekly wage irrespective of the number of days actually worked. All the others were on daily pay apparently meticulously accounted for.[30] Very similar rates were offered to those working on the galley being built at Lyme at the same time: 5d per day for the master shipwright, 3d for clenchers and 2d for holders.[31] The details of the Southampton account help fill out this picture. In this case, four master shipwrights were brought over from the Isle of Wight and from Shoreham, and offered wages of 6d per day. There may have been some initial problems with this arrangement, as a week later a further master shipwright, originally from Bayonne, was sent for from Portsmouth at the considerable cost of 8s, particularly to supervise the design of the galley. The ordinary shipwrights were divided into berders, clenchers and holders, much as before, but at the higher wages of 5d, 4d and 3d per day respectively.[32] The design role of the Bayonnese shipwright, together with the specific mention of a measuring device in connection with the building of the York galley,[33] implies that, while hands-on experience was essential for a shipwright, those at the highest level most probably were also literate and numerate, following some basic rules of proportion when building ships' hulls.

The smaller vessels built at much the same time in, for example, Conway and Great Yarmouth provide further evidence of the conditions of those working in a medieval shipyard. The most highly paid shipwright at Conway, one Richard Morteth, received 3s 6d for a six-day week. The pay of the other carpenters at this site was carefully graded but the most notable feature is that Welsh workers were consistently paid less (about half) than the amount offered to their colleagues from over the border from Chester and the Wirral. In Great Yarmouth, the highest pay was reserved for six carpenters at 2s a week each, followed by others at 4d a day, clenchers at 3d and rebators [sic] at 2d.[34]

By the first decades of the fifteenth century, Soper's considerable workforce at Southampton was organised in much the same way, with shipwrights known as berders, clenchers and holders making up the bulk of the workforce under a master carpenter. Other workers, particularly smiths and general labourers, were employed as necessary. One noticeable change, however, is in the wage rates. These had risen considerably, with the Exchequer clerk making up the accounts noting carefully that the provisions of the post-plague Statute of Labourers were not being enforced. Perhaps because of the complexity of organising work on several ships at once, an extra layer of management (to use modern phraseology) was imposed for the work on building the *Gracedieu*, the *Falcon*, and the *Valentine* from 1416. Robert Berd was employed at 12d per day. It is not clear what his qualifications for this job were. Was he a 'project manager'? Or an innovative 'naval architect'? There is no way of knowing, unfortunately, but it is clear that master shipwrights were also employed, including John Hoggekyn (8d per day), a very experienced man, assisted by three *quartermaysters shippewrights*, a description not occurring elsewhere. Joiners (6d per day) and master joiners (12d per day) who are also mentioned may have been employed on the 'fitting out' of the vessel, not on her basic construction. The rise in the pay rates of the familiar berders (6d), clenchers (6d), and holders (3d or 4d) compared with their predecessors in Edward I's time is clear.[35]

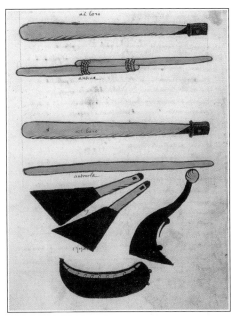

Suggested designs for rudders and whipstaffs (tillers) from the Book of Michael of Rhodes. The earliest known text on ship design, it originated in the Arsenale in Venice.

(BOOK OF MICHAEL OF RHODES)

In the 1490s, although the shipwrights working on the *Sweepstake* are paid at different rates varying from 6½ d to 4d per day, there is no mention of a master shipwright or of the old descriptive craft names. The men also received victuals as an expected part of their remuneration, not as an emergency measure in a difficult situation, as sometimes happened in earlier times. Each workman was entitled to 12½d per week in 'Bourde and Vitayle'. There are no details of the food apparently provided and it may well be, in fact, merely an extra cash payment. A payment for 'vitayle' was also made to the keeper of the vessel, which seems to support this supposition, since he is recorded as receiving 'xii d' for his wages 'by the weke' and 'for his vitayle xiiii d.'[36]

### Shipbuilding costs

This raises the issue of the costs of shipbuilding in our period. It has been pointed out that a ship, even one of modest size, represented one of the largest, if not the largest, capital outlays in the period.[37] It is not, however, easy to be precise about the cost of the building of the largest vessel of all, the *Gracedieu*; this is because the accounts for her building are rolled up into the costs of also building her followers, the *Falcon* and the *Valentine*. An attempted calculation of her cost, deducting the estimated costs incurred on the other two ships, produces the total of £3830.[38] This sum can be compared with some of the expenses listed in Lord Cromwell's estimates of the state of royal finances dating from 1433. At that date the costs of the seneschal of Aquitaine and his two hundred archers amounted to £2739 13s 4d; the total peacetime costs incurred in both the East and West Marches of Scotland came to £3816 13s 4d, all per annum.[39] These may not be entirely fair comparisons, but they do make the point that by building this ship, let alone the others constructed at the same time, Henry V was making a very considerable investment, and by implication a dramatic gesture in favour of the need for powerful royal ships.

The costs of building the 1295 galleys are easier to determine. These varied between £326 for the second galley built at London and £75 for the galley built at Lyme, which was just over half the size of that built at London. Most cost around £250. It is, perhaps, worthy of note that around two hundred years later the 'somme total of allmanner costes

The building of ships for the invasion of England in 1066 from the Bayeux Tapestry. The tools shown are little different from those used in the fifteenth century.

**(AUTHOR'S COLLECTION)**

charges and expenses concernyng the making with takelyng and apparelling the Kynges bark called the *Sweepstake* aforesaid', was £120 3s 2d, and that of the *Mary Fortune* even less, at a total of £110 17s. These ships had about fifty-two oars each, so were probably smaller than the earlier galleys (averaging 80–100 oars), but even so it is reasonable to suggest that building methods and thus productivity in shipyards had improved somewhat over this time span.[40]

## The stages of shipbuilding

There are, of course many areas of uncertainty when discussing the way in which ships were built for the Crown, and probably other owners as well in this period. As will have become clear from what has already been said, there is information about materials and about costs, but very little about the details of design. There is little alternative to reliance on accounts for evidence, with the dearth of archaeological evidence being something of a problem. When the accounts are set out with expenses being listed week by week with some indication of the work undertaken or the materials bought, it is possible to have an idea of the order in which work was carried out. The accounts for the Southampton galley of the 1295 group are particularly clear in this respect. After master builders had been found, timber was bought for the keel and the stems, and then quantities of boards in different lengths for the planking. The men employed are divided into berders (working on the hull), clenchers (nailing the timbers) and holders (attaching the roves on the interior of the hull over

A carving from St David's Cathedral showing two shipwrights. One is caulking the hull (forcing moss or other suitable material between the planks to prevent water seeping in). The other is enjoying his lunch with a flagon of ale provided. Victuals were often part of the shipyard workers' wages at this date, especially if the job was an urgent one.

(JULIAN MANNERING)

Repairs to ships taking place on the shore of a river; this was typical of the location of shipyards at this time.

(BRITISH LIBRARY)

which the nails were bent, an essential feature of clinker building). Iron worked up into nails was next bought in quantity as were the materials needed for the caulking laid along the edge of the planks. By the twelfth week it seems that the hull was largely complete and work moved on to the decks and the making of pavesades. The rudder was bought in the thirteenth week along with a windlass. Three weeks later attention was focused on greasing the galley, and the mast and sail were bought in Poole or the Isle of Wight. The final work in the seventeenth week was that on the 'castles' along with the purchase of a ship's boat, oars and anchors.[41]

Later enrolled accounts tend to follow a different pattern, with the provision of materials separated from wages, making it less easy to follow the progress of the work. It is, however, notable that, especially with regard to the works in Southampton and its neighbourhood in the years 1416–20, the building of ships for the Crown must have had a considerable impact on the town. The number of men employed on the *Gracedieu* project probably reached a maximum of over 120, with around forty more working as carters, bringing in supplies from the New Forest, and similar tasks. The strain that the need for a workforce of this size created in a town the size of Southampton is plain from the fact that extra experienced workmen were sought from Devon and Cornwall. Some who were conscripted for the work on Crown authority were imprisoned for failing to turn up for work in Southampton.[42] The much smaller workforce needed for the building of the *Sweepstake* at Portsmouth in 1495 varied from eleven to sixteen shipwrights working together. In addition, there were two sawyers employed preparing timber in the woods.

Comparing the accounts for shipbuilding for the Crown which survive for the period from the late thirteenth century to the end of the fifteenth century, a strong impression emerges of a craft tradition which was well organised and well understood. The order in which the work was carried out followed a traditional pattern. The organisation of the workforce with three 'grades' of shipwrights, berders, clenchers and holders probably emerged some time before Edward I commissioned galleys in 1295, and survived more or less unchanged as far as we can tell until carvel-built hulls became the norm.

*Salvaging materials*

It is also noticeable how both timber and ironwork was routinely salvaged from vessels which had been broken up and reused in major refits of other ships or even in new ones. Clerks of the King's Ships kept detailed records, which give the impression that almost every plank and nail was rigorously accounted for until it was finally of no possible further use. Once the sale of the majority of Henry V's ships had been completed, much of Soper's accounts for the years after 1427 consisted of inventories listing the dismal remains of the equipment of ships which were either no longer in royal hands or which were in no way seaworthy. Four small Breton wine ships appear in the 1422–27 accounts in this way and also, for example, four oars which had once been on board a vessel called the *Galley* which was acquired by the Crown in 1409, recorded as a wreck on the mudflats of the Thames in 1415, and the remains sold to a Londoner in 1417. The practice of the

Exchequer apparently demanded that they would not be removed from the inventory until no material trace of their existence remained.[43]

If equipment could be reused on another ship this was also meticulously recorded. The great ship the *Jesus*, for example, received cables, pulleys and oars from the *Katerine*, and other items from the *Rodcogge* and the *Nicholas c.*1422.[44] This was accepted practice. It is, however, hard to be sure to what extent these records, kept with such apparent care, reflected the reality in the shipyards. It may well be that clerks were better at creating the impression that not one piece of timber or cordage or ironwork ever went astray than in fact keeping track of all the supplies and materials and preventing pilfering. Because of the nature of the evidence, there are also many questions about the design of the ships of England's medieval navy which cannot be answered. Only the survival of the wreck of the *Gracedieu* in the Hamble river has allowed us to appreciate her unique three-skinned clinker planking. It may well be the case that some future archaeological investigation of a medieval wreck will allow some of these puzzles to be resolved. Nevertheless, the present state of our knowledge of medieval shipbuilding makes clear that it was a skilled and respected occupation, producing fine seaworthy vessels.

*Shipbuilding centres*

Over the whole period from the Norman Conquest to the accession of Henry VIII, it is also notable that while the majority of activity concerning ships in the ownership or the control of the Crown was concentrated on the south and east coasts of England, no one port could be described as the preferred base for these vessels. The ships requisitioned by the Crown came from any and every haven on the coasts of the kingdom which could provide a suitable vessel. Shipbuilding or repairs were confined to a smaller number of sites, but even so there were few purpose-built facilities for the royal ships. Some could be found mainly in the fourteenth century in the Thames below London Bridge near the Tower, further down river at Ratcliff, or across the water at Deptford and Greenwich. These areas were probably also favoured by those building ships for private owners.

The Cinque Ports' contributions to royal fleets varied widely but as far as dockyard operations are concerned the ports on the estuaries of the Rother and the Brede, Winchelsea and Rye, were most important, along with Sandwich. All were also, of course, important centres of maritime trade. The great increase in royal interest in ships in warfare notable in the reign of Henry V undoubtedly made Southampton and the Hamble river something of a naval centre, but this had largely faded away within ten years of Henry's death. Much has been made of the facilities for the repair of ships at Portsmouth constructed at the very end of the fifteenth century. There was, however, little reason to think that these would develop into a real naval base before Henry VIII turned his attention to naval matters and to the building of royal ships. It would seem that before the Tudor navy was created as a 'home fleet with its support centred upon Kent while Portsmouth and Plymouth became its forward operating bases',[45] ships were built for the Crown at any convenient location. Shipbuilders could be found in most ports and the Crown was happy to benefit from the widespread availability of the necessary skills.

## CHAPTER 6

# The World of the Medieval Mariner

IN SOME WAYS THE WORLD of the medieval mariner would be entirely familiar to his modern equivalent. The need to be aware of tides, wind direction, wind strength and currents remains an essential skill for all seafarers, as it was for those in medieval times. Medieval mariners, however, had few sources of information about matters like these, other than their own experience, and what they might have learned from personal contact with the proverbial old sea dogs. Written information of any kind was very rare until about the second half of the fifteenth century. The core of knowledge about weather patterns, navigation and seamanship, which was held in the collective memories of seamen, was extensive enough to allow quite lengthy voyages, for example, those to Iceland from Bristol or east coast ports, or from the south coast to Compostela, Lisbon and into the Mediterranean, to be successfully completed. There were, however, few if any manuals or almanacs to turn to if memory failed, or the voyage was in unfamiliar waters. Nor were sea charts or maps drawn for northern waters until the sixteenth century. The outline of the coast had to be committed to memory, a more complex task than might be imagined in some coastal regions of England.

## Changes in the coastline
It is easy to imagine that change has been almost imperceptible over the years in the configuration of the English coastline. Changes, however, were dramatic in our period on the south and east coast of England, and have continued at a slower rate in later periods. If we look at the gentle agricultural valley of the river Rother as it is today, it seems to be a most unlikely place for shipbuilding, yet, as we have already described, it flourished in this part of the world in medieval times. This change is one consequence of the many differences in the course of rivers, the coastline, and the nature of the landscape as a whole which particularly affected east Sussex and Kent in our period.

### Winchelsea and Rye
Between five and six thousand years ago coastal marshes developed between Fairlight and Hythe, protected by a massive shingle barrier offshore. Shingle or gravel banks are gently moved by the action of waves and tides, even in calm weather. The stones shift and grind one against another, with a bank being gradually built up or drifting away. In a violent storm a bank may collapse entirely or change its shape dramatically. Until

he final decades of the thirteenth century, the port town of Winchelsea stood on part of this bank, somewhere near the mouth of the Rother, facing the open sea. A series of storms in the thirteenth century began to affect the stability of the bank. The great storm of 1250 made the original breach in the barrier; Matthew Paris explained how 'the troubled sea crossed its usual boundaries flowing twice without ebbing and gave forth such a horrible roaring and crashing that it resounded in places remote from it'. In 1252 things became even worse: 'a raging east wind and an angry south-west wind occasioned much damage ... At the harbour of Winchelsea the waves of the sea as if indignant and furious at being driven back the day before covered places adjacent to the shore and drowned many men.'[1] The breach in the shingle bank made by these storms was gradually enlarged as tides ebbed and flowed, so that by 1258 the river Rother was tidal up as far as Appledore. Tides also ran up the Brede, a tributary of the Rother which flowed past the higher ground where the hamlet of Iham stood.[2]

In the 1260s and 1270s, the waters had advanced so far that the communities which had established themselves on the marshes to the east of the Rother acted together to build a 'great wall' to protect their farmland from the encroaching sea. This ran from a point southeast of Appledore to a point southwest of Lydd curving in a loop around the Wainway Channel.[3] As conditions worsened on the bank offshore, in 1280 the beleaguered townsfolk of Winchelsea, with the encouragement of Edward I, began to make preparations to move the town to a new site on high ground very near Iham. The decision to move came not a moment too soon. Three great storms in the space of fourteen

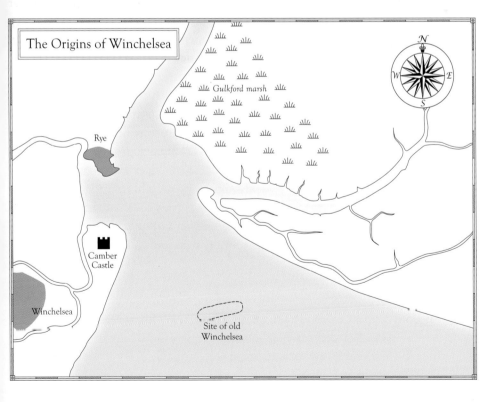

The Origins of Winchelsea

Gulkford marsh

Rye

Camber Castle

Winchelsea

Site of old Winchelsea

A map of the origins of Winchelsea based on a map drawn in the late sixteenth century.

(PETER WILKINSON)

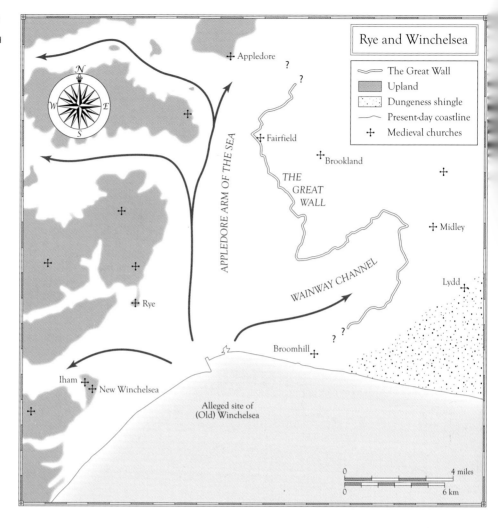

months in 1287/8 washed the old town away. The continuation of the *Chronicle of Gervase of Canterbury* records that in 4 February 1288, 'the sea flooded greatly ... in the marsh of *Romenal* and all adjacent places that all the walls were broken down and almost all lands covered from the great wall of Appledore towards the south and west as far as Winchelsea'.[4] The first rent roll of the new town was drawn up in 1292 and probably signifies the moment when the new community became a reality.[5]

The line of the coast, before the breach in the shingle banks occurred, is hard to determine and remains conjectural. What is clear is that 'old' Winchester, until disaster struck, was a prosperous port with a well-sheltered harbour in which a naval force could be assembled. After the breach Rye Bay opened up, creating a wide expanse of water extending from the land below the walls of the new town of Winchelsea to Guldeford Marsh on the east side of the bay. The quays of the new town were situated below the walls where the Brede entered the bay. Contact with Rye, also built on high ground, was easiest by water. This town had a good anchorage on the Rother but there was room for many ships to anchor in the area known as the Camber which lay between the two towns. Camber Castle, built to defend this anchorage in the early sixteenth century, lay on a spit of land at the edge of the bay. It is now, of course, a considerable distance from the sea or any navigable waterway and the anchorage it guarded is pasture land.

The gradual recession of the sea from this area was probably due more to the action of the tides in depositing silt and other material in the waterways than the action of the rivers. Another contributory factor was certainly the 'inning' and draining of marshland for agriculture. The strong eastward longshore drift and coastal current in the Channel also served to deposit shingle and silt along the shoreline near Romney and Hythe leading to the gradual decline of these ports and eventually the virtual destruction of their harbours.

## Sandwich

A similar process had a notable effect in reducing the viability of Sandwich as a major port. In the early medieval period, Sandwich Haven was sheltered from the rough weather in the Channel by a spit to the west of the town known at that time as Pepperness. The haven was also sheltered to the north by the Isle of Thanet (then truly an island) and another spit on which stood the village of Stonar. A channel, the Wantsum Channel, separated Thanet from the mainland, leading from Sandwich eastward to the Thames Estuary; this allowed vessels to reach London without making the difficult and sometimes dangerous passage round the North Foreland. The river Stour also flowed east and south into the Wantsum Channel, reaching the sea at Sandwich. The marshes around these waterways were drained for pasture over the years, often by monastic houses owning property in the area; other landlords built weirs to improve the fishing. Both activities reduced the flow of water in the Wantsum Channel and began to alter the course of the Stour. The river also deposited silt, slowing the flow of the water still further. At sea the longshore drift already mentioned built up sand and shingle on Pepperness or Deal Spit, its modern name, so that entry to Sandwich Haven was gradually obstructed. This process

Camber Castle, now some distance from a waterway: the fortification to protect the Camber was begun around 1512 and completed by Henry VIII in 1538–43.

**(AUTHOR'S COLLECTION)**

A picture from the late
nineteenth century when
the quays at Sandwich could
still be reached by sailing
barges. The large haven of
the middle ages, accessible
at all stages of the tide had
long ceased to exist.

(AUTHOR'S COLLECTION)

was well underway by the fifteenth century and would, of course, finally spell the end of Sandwich as a major port.[6] Although small trading vessels were still able to dock at Sandwich Quay in the early twentieth century,[7] the river Stour at Sandwich is now navigable only at high water after a lengthy passage up its meandering course. The river now reaches the sea at Pegwell Bay, well to the north of the town and its mouth in medieval times. The quays in the town have been reduced to moorings for pleasure boats.

### The east coast and North Sea coasts

The east coast of England has similarly suffered from the combined effects of coastal erosion and the silting up of waterways by the deposit of silt by rivers or tides. The best known change is probably the disappearance beneath the waves of most of the town of Dunwich, near Southwold. This was the result of a storm surge in the North Sea in 1286, with further disastrous floods in 1328 and 1327. Further north on Spurn Point in Holderness, the port of Ravenserodd which had supplied ships for the Scots wars in the early fourteenth century was similarly destroyed by storms in 1356/7 and 1362. In the Netherlands, on the other side of the North Sea, the configuration of the low-lying islands and coasts where the Scheldt and the Rhine reach the sea was altered a great deal by the effects of both efforts at land reclamation and drainage and natural processes, including severe storms and tidal surges in the North Sea. Both Damme and Sluys (now known as Sluis) were the sites of notable naval battles and outports for Bruges, but are now some distance from the open sea.

Navigation in the Channel and North Sea in general was undoubtedly made more perilous by shifting sand and shingle banks, especially off the Kent and Sussex coast. There were very few, if any, navigation marks or lights to guide mariners. Buildings on shore were sometimes used in this way; for example, to avoid a notorious sandbank in the Thames estuary the advice was to keep the steeple of the parish church (as seen from the deck of a ship) to the east of St Osyth's priory on the Essex coast.[8] Specially erected towers or carefully positioned buoys or stakes did not exist in English waters. Warnings of the advent of violent storms depended on an individual's experience of the signs of approaching weather systems, often encapsulated in well-known sayings and rhymes. Red skies in the morning are still taken as a sign of bad weather ahead. The presence of mare's tail clouds (cirrus) and mackerel scales clouds (altocumulus) accurately indicate that a storm is on the way so that the old rhyme, 'mare's tails and mackerel scales/make tall ships carry low sails', was good advice. In the 'Life of St Goderic', a shipmaster and merchant who found fame as a hermit, it is related how, 'by a prudence born of long experience ... he knew from the aspect of sea and stars how to foretell fair or foul weather'. It is no wonder then that 'though he fell into many perils of the sea, yet by God's mercy he was never wrecked.'[9]

## The responsibilities of shipmasters

In the uncertain world of the mariner it is perhaps not surprising that the relations between a shipmaster and his crew depended more on consultation and co-operation than the barking of orders. Our evidence for this comes from the Laws of Oléron. These were a collection more of the outcomes of legal cases which concerned ships and their cargoes, than of carefully drafted laws, which was widely disseminated in western Europe from the early thirteenth century. Versions exist in Flemish, German, Castilian and Anglo-Norman. Their common ancestor was similar compilations made in the Mediterranean, the *Lex Rhodia* and the *Consolate del mare*. In England the two earliest copies of the Laws are in the archives of the City of London, the natural place for a legal compilation which had great importance for merchants. A full transcript and translation of one version, that from the so-called *Liber Horn*, has been recently published.[10]

From the very first article the need for a shipmaster to consult the crew is apparent. The master can only pledge the ship's equipment to obtain a loan if the crew agree. Even more to the point, in the second article it states that a ship can only set sail if the crew agree. The shipmaster is described as saying to the crew, '"gentlemen you have this weather"... some will answer "the weather is not good" and others who will say "the weather is fair and good". The shipmaster has to agree on this with the majority of his companions.'[11] Since the majority of vessels which served the Crown were arrested merchant ships, this would have been the practice on board these ships at the outset of a voyage.

There is no evidence to suggest that the masters of royal ships behaved differently. When it suited the convenience of the Crown, royal ships were hired to merchants to carry out trading voyages. William Catton, in the first years of the reign of Henry V, raised a substantial sum by hiring royal ships to merchants for voyages to Bordeaux in connection with the wine trade, and also for a voyage to Danzig to obtain pitch, osmund (good quality iron) and timber.[12] On voyages like these the provisions of the Laws of Oléron would have undoubtedly been in force.

One of the rare insights into the behaviour of the crew on a royal ship also gives the impression that the sailors were tough and independent individuals who did not like being taken for granted. When the muster was being taken on board Henry V's *Gracedieu* in 1420, before a voyage to keep the seas, some of the crew swore at the royal officials checking the names of the crew, tore their clothes and refused to be mustered. The men then insisted on being put on shore at St Helen's in the Isle of Wight rather than continuing with the voyage. The report of the incident later mentions storms at sea so it is possible that the rebellious crewmen disagreed with the decision to put to sea and felt that their views had not been considered.[13] A master did, of course, have responsibility for discipline on board ship including matters like drunkenness and sleeping on watch. He also had a duty of care towards his crew if they were injured in the course of their service or fell ill and had to be put on shore. There is no information as to how these general customs of the sea applied to sailors wounded in battle. Since those serving on requisitioned ships or those owned by the Crown were paid wages, these may have been considered to have included an element to cover care after sickness or injury.

Many of a shipmaster's responsibilities related to the cargo and his relationship with the merchants who had entrusted their goods to his care. In desperate circumstances, when the vessel seemed to be in danger of foundering, the shipmaster was duty bound to consult the merchants on board before jettisoning any of the cargo or cutting the rigging. Their consent reduced the shipmaster's liability for the losses suffered. The merchants on the other hand, also had the right, if they eventually managed to reach land safely, to call the crew together and ask them to testify under oath whether the master had taken the correct decision.[14] The chaos on board ship in a situation like this was described by the poet of *Pearl:*

> And then the cry arises, they cut the ropes and throw everything out: many men jump about to bale and to throw‑scooping out the dangerous water when they would rather escape – for however heavy a man's load, life is always sweet. They were busy throwing bales overboard, their bags, and their feather beds and their best clothes, their cases and their chests and all their casks, and all to lighten the ship in the hope that calm should fall.[15]

### Food and drink

Victuals were provided for the crew both on ships owned by the Crown and those owned by private individuals. No standard ration scale for crews on English royal ships has survived from this period, although one does exist for those serving on the galleys in the service of the Venetian Republic. This provided 18oz of *biscotti* (ship's biscuit or hard tack, baked so hard that it was almost guaranteed to last for a considerable period in a more or less edible condition) or, where possible, 24oz of fresh bread per man per day. Wine, cheese and dried peas and beans to make soup were also supplied.[16]

English royal ships were provided with large quantities of both salt and fresh meat and salt fish. A flune called *Laurence*, with a crew of a master and thirty men, was loaded with flour, nine barrels of beer, one pipe of cider, nine beef carcases, eighteen mutton carcases, and half a quarter of fish, all supplied by Beaulieu Abbey for a voyage to Brittany in 1344.[17] The balinger *Petit Jesus* with a complement of thirty‑one sailors and the master was victualled with 'bread, ale, butter, beef, mutton, and salt and fresh fish and various other foodstuffs' at a cost of £21 11s 7d in 1426 for a voyage from

Southampton towards Spain 'to keep the seas'.[18] The bread might be in the form of biscuit or hard tack in some circumstances. The indication seems to be that an adequate, if plain, diet was provided, quite possibly more copious and more nutritious than that which was usual on land. It is clear that some kind of cooking facility was available since firewood was also provided. If elite passengers, or those of the blood royal might be on board, ships were provided with ovens. The *Cog Thomas*, which was the flagship of the fleet of Edward III at the Battle of Winchelsea in 1350 was adapted in this way in that year. The following year the *George Wesenham*, a very large vessel lent to the King by a leading merchant and royal servant, was similarly adapted.[19] This might have allowed for a wider range of dishes to be prepared than those given to the crew. Cabins were also specially built for noble passengers in the after castles of royal ships. When the future Henry IV travelled to Prussia to take part in the crusade of the Teutonic Knights, his ship was provided with what were described as a hall, chapel and chamber. These, however, were temporary structures of wood and canvas. A cabin for the cook is also mentioned, along with accommodation for other officers of the household.[20]

The Laws of Oléron have something to say about victualling in a general way. At least one cooked meal a day was expected. Wine should also be provided if the ship had docked in a wine-producing region. The crew clearly had the right to be provided with bread, since in an article dealing with the crew going on shore they are allowed to take with them 'only as much as they would have drawn on the ship; and such bread as there might be they should have according to that which they can eat'.[21]

The tower of the Church of St Nicholas (a favourite saint of seafarers) at New Romney was used as a navigational mark even when the harbour was silted up.

(WIKIMEDIA)

More details of a seaman's diet are provided by the accounts kept by the purser of the *Margaret Cely*, an English ship which made three voyages to Bordeaux for wine in the 1480s. This was based around bread, meat and fish (both probably salted). In 1487/8 en route to Bordeaux, the ship was provided with new 'flesh barrels' and 'steeping tubs' (to soak the meat), three oxen, three and a half 'beeves', and a large quantity of salt. She also had on board bread, fresh herring, salt herring, eight pipes of beer, and two barrels of 'new beer'. On the return voyage there was an opportunity at Plymouth to buy fresh food, again fresh fish, and beer. Very similar provisions were bought for a voyage the following year, but this time when the *Margaret* was stormbound in Fowey some vegetables were bought, as well as extra bread. When the ship reached Bordeaux, the diet improved considerably as fresh meat, eggs, more vegetables and wine were bought. On the return voyage the requirements of the Laws of Oléron regarding wine were fully obeyed, since over half a gallon per man was provided.[22]

## Life on board

Life on board for most mariners, however, was probably usually harsh and comfortless. The only form of sanitary arrangement was the ancestor of the modern yachtsman's 'bucket and chuck it' known as a *skettfatt*.[23] Bedding, probably just a rough blanket and perhaps a straw palliasse, was provided individually by the crew, and most clothing and other personal possessions would frequently have been perpetually damp at best. The work was physically hard and at times dangerous.

Little is known about the access which seafarers may have had to the comforts of religion. There was a widespread devotion to St Nicholas among seamen from most European nations. A church or chapel dedicated to this saint could be found in virtually all seaports. The church of San Niccoló on the Lido was both the first and the last sight of his city for Venetian sailors. The church of St Nicholas at New Romney has a tower which could serve as a navigation mark. In King's Lynn, the chapel of St Nicholas had bench ends carved to show the ships which frequented the port. The saint's popularity among seamen was rooted in his fabled ability to calm storms; this was depicted in stained glass and wall paintings in, for example, in the chapel at Haddon Hall in Derbyshire and in Beverley Minster. Other stories of ships in danger at sea occur frequently in accounts on pilgrimage voyages where the custom arose of pilgrims casting slips of paper into the sea bearing a saint's name and vowing to offer at the shrine of the saint if they reached land safely.[24] Fortunately, this manoeuvre was apparently usually successful.

## Experienced mariners

Analysis of the lists of ships requisitioned for service in royal fleets in the reign of Edward III has shown that there was a core group of professional shipmasters and seafarers in most ports. Often members of the same family served together. On a ship from King's Lynn in 1337 there were four members of a family called Halfknight, including the master, two from a family called Reppes, and a father and son called Hormynglowe.[25] By the time of Henry V there is evidence that an elite group of royal shipmasters had come into existence who had been granted annuities by the Crown and who were respected for their seamanship and leadership. These included men like William Payn who was master of several royal ships from 1416. His first command was the *Margaret*, a small vessel used mainly on trading voyages. He then took command of one of the carracks captured from the Genoese in 1416 and was granted an annuity of 10 marks (£6 13s 4d) by the Crown. He was finally master of the *Gracedieu*.[26] He also pursued a career as a merchant, trading largely with Ireland. Probably the most prominent of this group was John William from Dartmouth who was originally the master of a ship owned by John Hawley, the mayor of the town, who was both involved in privateering expeditions of doubtful legality and in 'keeping the seas' for the Crown. William then moved to Southampton and became master of the *Jesus*. His annuity was 20 marks secured on the revenues of Southampton. His later career was as a merchant and a prominent citizen of this town.[27]

## Navigation

One of the most valuable skills of a medieval shipmaster was the ability to set a course across the sea to bring a vessel to its desired destination. Hugging the coast, an option often suggested by those with little experience of the difficulties and perils which could await an unwary mariner, was often not a sensible or feasible procedure. More sophisticated methods were often needed.

### Navigation by experience

Discussion of the ways in which experienced and professional medieval shipmasters could set a course and be reasonably sure of their position has generated a certain amount of controversy. The ability of the Viking explorers to make voyages into the North Atlantic, returning safely to their starting point, to found colonies in Iceland and Greenland, and eventually to reach the shores of Vinland, has not only excited the admiration of mariners but raised queries about how these voyages were achieved. Did the Vikings have any access to navigational instruments of any kind, or were these voyages achieved solely by close and expert attention to natural phenomena – the patterns of waves, the flight of birds, the regularly changing position of heavenly bodies and the like?

As far as the possible existence of some sort of instrument is concerned, attention has focused on two possible items. One is a half-moon shaped disc excavated from the site of a Benedictine convent in Uunartoq Fjord in southern Greenland in 1948. This discovery at first was more or less overlooked, but recent research has accepted that it is at least plausible that it is the remains of a sun compass or bearing dial. The disc has a central hole into which a gnomon (a pin which cast a shadow allowing the time of day to be calculated like the similar 'pointer' on a sun dial) could have been fixed; the notches on the edge of the disc and the lines scratched on its surface could be interpreted to represent a course oriented to the shadow cast by the sun in the summer sailing season approximately along the parallel of latitude 60° N, on which lie the Hardanger Fjord, the Shetland Islands and Cape Farewell in Greenland. In the period before the magnetic compass was generally available in northern Europe, that is around the thirteenth century, this would have been a very useful tool.[28]

A piece of Icelandic spar, a form of quartz; this was probably the material used by Viking navigators as a 'sunstone'. It can polarise light and thus locate the position of the sun even if the sky is overcast.

(AUTHOR'S COLLECTION)

The other item which may possibly have been used for the purposes of navigation by the Vikings is an object mentioned in the sagas called a sun stone. The suggestion has been made that a mineral was known which could be used to determine the direction of the sun on a cloudy day by acting as a depolariser of light (like a prism); this would allow an experienced user to guess the direction of the sun even if the sun itself was not visible. Recent research has shown that this is possible by using common Icelandic spar (a form of quartz). It is, however, impossible to prove whether either of these instruments was used by mariners in English waters in our period. A piece of Iceland spar was found in the wreck of a ship sunk in 1592[29] off Alderney; by that date the calculation of latitude was a skill well understood by many shipmasters using a sea astrolabe or a quadrant.[30] The taking of 'altitudes', however, depended on 'shooting' the sun at noon; thus the sun stone would still have been of some value when sailing under cloudy skies, even at this date.

Despite the uncertainty which surrounds these navigational aids, it is clear that accumulated experience passed on from one shipmaster to another was sufficient to allow medieval mariners to complete successfully voyages in all the waters surrounding the British Isles. They did not creep from cape to cape as used to be suggested. Such a policy would have often resulted in disaster, since nothing is more dangerous to a sailing vessel than being driven onto a lee shore with no possibility of clawing the ship away from a rocky coast. Shipmasters relied a great deal on close observation of the patterns of the waves, known signs of the proximity of land, such as the behaviour of seabirds, and the formation of clouds. They were also skilled and knowledgeable in the observation of heavenly bodies, the sun, moon and stars, especially the Pole Star, when visible a sure indication of the north.

A good idea of what a skilled mariner should know at this time can be gained from the *Konnungs Skuggsjá*, a book of advice from a father to a son written in Norse around 1250. This makes clear that a successful merchant sea captain must understand the phases of the moon and the rotation of the stars. He must be aware of the relationship between the phases of the moon and the tides, and must be able to mark out the horizon into the eight wind directions commonly used. The father explains all this in poetical language, along with the varying pattern of the prevailing winds according to the seasons in northern waters. 'The chill north-east wind sits wrathful with snowy beard and blows hard against the hail-bearing clouds.' Tellingly, this work also has some well-observed things to say about the habits of walrus and seals, their presence often being a useful indication, for example, of the nearness of the edge of the sea ice in high latitudes.[31]

English seamen would have had need of the same skills, learnt by a close observation of their surroundings while at sea. A basic understanding of tides was particularly necessary in a period when many anchorages frequently used by trading vessels dried out at low tide. The direction and speed of the tidal flow in a particular place, which if misjudged could make it impossible for a ship to round a headland or access a harbour, could only be learned by experience. As mariners made longer voyages to more distant shores, the need for the accumulated experience of the maritime world to be shared more widely was something that would not have been hard for mariners to appreciate.

*Navigation using instruments and sailing directions*

Navigation using methods which had served generations of seafarers well on the sea lanes of familiar waters naturally became of less value on voyages into unknown waters. Indications of the near approach to land such as the presence of sea birds or the colour of the water still had their place, but much more emphasis was placed on the ability to plot accurately a ship's position in relation to its latitude, and where possible that of known landfalls. For this, navigational instruments and also almanacs of astronomical data were needed, together with the ability to perform the necessary calculations. These almanacs built on the shared experience of generations of mariners.

## Tidal information

It is perhaps for this reason that some of the earliest surviving navigational documents in northern waters contain detailed information about tides. The times of high tide at London Bridge in relation to the phases of the moon were recorded by monks in the thirteenth century. To suit their particular circumstances, mariners also devised a system of recording the times of high water at important ports in terms of the bearing of the moon, at what was called 'full and change' (the days of the full and new moon). This information was known as the 'establishment of the port'; this would be expressed as, for example, 'Dieppe is north-northwest and south-southeast'. A skilled mariner understood this to mean that high water at Dieppe occurred on days of full and new moon when the moon bears NNW and SSE, that is 10.30pm and 10.30am. At Dover, conveniently, the moon was 'south — full sea', that is, with high tides predicted at midnight and noon at these times.[32] The prevalence of this method of describing the establishment of a port from at least the beginning of the fifteenth century is well demonstrated by a section in the *Book of Michael of Rhodes*, dealing with 'the waters and tides of Flanders how the moon is when the tide is high or when it will be low for the ports and out of the channels ... that is in the parts of Flanders and in the gulfs and island of England.' This book was put together by a Venetian galleyman as a collection of maritime lore. It dates from around 1434 but also includes earlier materials.[33]

Calculation of the time of high tide on days other than 'full and change' involved working it out on the basis that the high tide would occur rather more than an hour later for each day that the moon had waxed or waned. A set of tables providing this information for major ports would clearly be a boon to a shipmaster. The printed tide tables which survive are mostly from the sixteenth century, but there is evidence that they existed in written form from at least the early fifteenth century.[34] Since these tables would have been constantly consulted at sea, often in unfavourable conditions, it is not remarkable that none have survived.

The seal of San Sebastian; boys are seated on each end of the sail yard, an image found in quite a number of the seals of port towns. This provides evidence of the method used to rig the sails and secure the sail yard.

(© NATIONAL MARITIME MUSEUM, GREENWICH, LONDON)

## The compass

This method of dealing with tides also shows how the invention of the magnetic compass was of great use to seafarers in a range of applications. The first mention by an English writer of the use at sea of a magnetised needle to indicate north comes from the treatise *De Natura Rerum*, written by Alexander Neckham around 1187. He describes how sailors rubbed a needle on 'the magnet stone' and twirled it around till it came to rest indicating the north. It seems that the original basic device involved the insertion of a magnetised needle in a straw which was floated in a bowl of water, something which would have had clear disadvantages on board ship. At first this may have been used more to check wind direction than to lay off a course to steer. The development of the compass into an essential instrument for the navigator took place in the Mediterranean.[35] The

This comes from an illuminated copy of the adventures of Marco Polo and shows a mariner consulting a compass on the foredeck of a ship, while another adjusts the sail; probably the first depiction of the use of a compass at sea.

(BIBLIOTHÈQUE NATIONALE, PARIS)

wind rose had developed from the eight points of classical times to a diagram with sixty-four points. The magnetised needle attached to the card and on a pivot was enclosed in a wooden box. The compass is in fact called a *bussola* or box in Spanish. In northern waters during the fourteenth century a thirty-two-point compass card was more usual. English mariners used the term binnacle or bittacle for the wooden container for the compass, which was made without any iron nails, and fixed where the steersman could easily see it. Bittacles like this were listed in the inventories of royal ships in England from the early fifteenth century.[36]

Some form of compass was, however, carried on royal ships from at least 1345, and probably somewhat earlier. In his accounts for 1345/6 Thomas de Snetesham, the first Clerk of the King's Ships, records buying in Sluys in Flanders, 'twelve stones called adamant called sailstones' for the royal ships. These were undoubtedly lodestones and would have served to find north even if not fixed to a compass fly or encased in a bittacle.[37] Another of his purchases at the same time was several sandglasses described as *horlog*; these would have been used to time manoeuvres, for example the time spent on a particular tack, which would have been of great help in the process of dead reckoning or estimating a ship's position. Merchant vessels were probably also provided with them for a voyage of any length. By the end of the century a compass was a normal part of the fittings of a vessel. In 1485 George Cely bought for the *Margaret*, 'a grett compass a lodston' and, from another supplier, 'a glasse [a running glass or timer], a compas'.[38]

In the Mediterranean, compasses were used in conjunction with portolan charts to set courses following the rhumb lines which led from the compass roses drawn on the charts. In northern waters, where charts were not used at this period, a compass was used, as we have said, in conjunction with tide tables, but was also necessary to follow the directions in the rutters (the word is a corruption of the French *routier*) or sailing directions which were put into written form in the fifteenth century. It is very probable that before this time the directions were memorised by shipmasters.

The earliest surviving rutter in English survives in two fair 'library' copies dating from the 1460s to 1470s, and may contain some material going back to the fourteenth century. The rutter gives directions for several voyages around the coasts of England and France, with the most distant going as far as Bordeaux and Spain.[39] There is much information about tides and compass courses, but also a great deal of detailed information about soundings, the practice of taking the depth of the water by lowering from a vessel a lead on a line knotted at one fathom intervals. The lead also had a cavity filled with grease so that a sample of the material on the sea bed might be retrieved. There was nothing new about this practice; nautical archaeologists have found lost leads dating from classical times in the Mediterranean,[40] but the way in which the technique was evidently used was perhaps particular to northern waters. In the rutter, mariners are advised, for example, that they can be sure of the course from the Gironde to English ports by the use of soundings. They are clear of the Gironde 'when there is mud and sand together and it is between 12 or 14 or 16 fms. deep.' Open of the Loire, 'there are striped stones and white shells'. Very important directions were given for a ship sailing from Brittany to ports on the west coast of England:

> And ye come oute of Spayne and be at cape fenestir [Finisterre] go yowre cours northe northe est and ye gesse yow ii partes ouyr the see [estimate you are two thirds of the way across] and be bounde in to seberne [the Severn] ye muste goo northe and be est til ye come in to soundynge and yf ye haue an c fadim deep or ellis iiii[xx] [80] and x than ye schal go northe until ye sownde ayen in lxxii fadim in fayre gray sonde and that is the rigge [shoal] thast lieth between clere and cille [Scilly].

This section continues with further directions on how to reach Bristol or a similar port. There is also an explanation of how to change course for ' the narrow see' [the Channel]. Once in soundings of a hundred fathoms the course should change from northeast and by north to northeast.[41]

The writer of the rutter clearly expected that any skilled shipmaster would have access to a compass and sounding leads; the master would also be well aware of tidal streams

Part of the cover of *The Mariner's Mirror*, derived from a sixteenth-century Dutch book of sailing directions. It shows a medley of navigational instruments: a quadrant, astrolabe and backstaff (all used for taking altitudes), a sailor using a sounding lead, dividers for measuring distance on a chart and a bittacle, or boxed compass.

til ye come in to iiij fadmu deep and yf it be stremy
grounde it is berwene Huschaut and Cisle in the entre
of the chanel of ffaundres and soo goo youre coure
til ye have svyi fadmu deep. than goo eft northe est
a longe the see. + c

A vessel taking soundings off a rocky shore; making sure of the depth of the water and the nature of the sea bed from samples stuck in the grease on the sounding lead were essential to navigation in this period.

(AUTHOR'S COLLECTION)

and the establishment of ports. With these instruments and techniques at their disposal shipmasters in our period could navigate with confidence all around the British Isles, into the Baltic and North Sea, in the Western Approaches and into the Mediterranean, and as far north as Iceland. For most, this was sufficient to meet their needs. They were unlikely to venture further afield, either on trading voyages or on the King's business. Compared with mariners in Iberia and the Mediterranean, however, their reliance on soundings, the absence of charts, and the lack of knowledge of mathematical and astronomical navigation might look somewhat old-fashioned.

## Mathematical navigation

Portolan charts had been used in southern waters since at least the twelfth century, in conjunction with compass bearings. The need for a more sophisticated system of navigation based on the calculation of latitude at sea became clear as voyages were made out into the Atlantic to the Canary Islands, Madeira and the Azores, and to the south following the coast of Africa. The Canary Islands were certainly visited by mariners from the Mediterranean in the early fourteenth century; settlers had occupied land on Madeira by 1420. The Azores appear on maps from around 1439. The series of Portuguese voyages southwards along the African coast began around 1420 and, of course, eventually culminated in the rounding of the Cape of Good Hope by Dias in 1487/8, and the voyage of da Gama to India in 1497.

On voyages like these, a method of establishing accurately the position of places on the coast, and, of course, of the ship itself, would clearly be invaluable. Surveying techniques which could determine the latitude of a place on land by means of an astrolabe were no novelty by the fourteenth century. The problem was to devise a practical way of measuring with reasonable accuracy the height of the sun above the horizon at noon or of the Pole Star, while at sea. To take an altitude on the heaving deck of a ship at sea was no mean task. To do this, tables of altitudes along with a reliable calendar were needed, along with an instrument which would operate in the conditions found at sea. The necessary written material was provided in Portuguese in the second half of the fifteenth century. The first printed edition of the *Regimento does Astrolabio e do Quadrante*, incorporating earlier material, dates from 1509. The instruments used were a very much simplified version of the astronomer's astrolabe and also the quadrant. A young man on one of the Portuguese voyages in 1456/7 described how he had 'a quadrant when I went to those parts. And I marked on the scale of the quadrant the altitude of the Arctic Pole. And I found it better than the chart.'[42] He may have had to go on shore to use his quadrant, but a sea astrolabe was designed, making the use of this method of determining a position practical on board ship. It rapidly became more common as more voyages were made and data was accumulated. By 1514 the nautical cross staff for taking observations was devised, overcoming some of the disadvantages of the earlier instruments.[43]

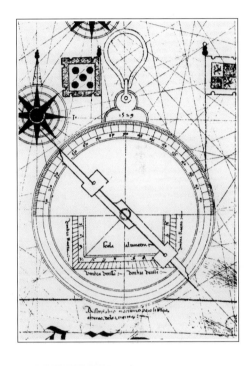

There is, however, no evidence that these methods were used by English seamen before the third or fourth decades of the sixteenth century. We may speculate that individuals who visited ports in Portugal and Spain may have become aware of them,

A mariner's astrolabe taken from the border of a chart; astrolabes were originally used by surveyors on land and were difficult to use at sea.

(© NATIONAL MARITIME MUSEUM, GREENWICH, LONDON)

Navigational instruments found in the master's cabin on the *Mary Rose*: sounding leads, dividers, a compass rose and a boxed compass, and rollers for charts.

(MARY ROSE TRUST)

but their interest has left no trace in the records. Fortunately, when it was obvious that these new methods were essential on 'blue water' voyages, English seamen rapidly acquired the new skills, greatly aided by publications like Richard Eden's *Arte of Navigation*, a translation of a Portuguese text which appeared in 1561. Even the ability to establish latitude with reasonable precision had not solved, of course, all the problems that faced a navigator in this period. There was no method of establishing longitude. Calculation of the speed of a ship and the distance it had travelled over the ground largely depended on the shipmaster's experience. The skill with which many were able to do this with reasonable accuracy and complete successful voyages can only be applauded.[44]

### Seamanship and ship-handling

There is little direct evidence of medieval standards of ship-handling. There are occasional vivid glimpses of a crew at work, such as that which appears in a poem about the pilgrims travelling by sea from England to the shrine of St James at Compostela. The poet describes the ship master ordering the crew to raise the sails:

> Anone the mastyr commaundeth fast
> To hys shyp-men in alle the hast
> To dresse hem sone about the mast
> Theyr takelyng for to make.
> With 'Howe! Hissa!' then they cry,
> 'What howe mate thow stondyst to ny
> Thy felow may nat hale the by'

When the passengers had got out of the way, the poet goes on to describe how the ship's boy was sent up the mast to lie along the sail yard, presumably to secure it as it was raised. This aspect of getting under way at this period is also depicted in, for example, the thirteenth-century town seal of San Sebastian, where the ship's boy is sitting on the end of the yardarm. The poet includes further snatches of the commands shouted to the crew as the voyage gets under way. They must haul in the bowline and veer the sheet and also obey his orders, ' Y howe! trussa! Hale in the brayles' and 'hale in the wartake'.[45] Many of the larger ships at this period had a windlass, but the basic power to raise sails or anchors came from the muscles of the crew, without the aid of the winches of a modern sailing vessel.

Rowing was a necessary skill for almost all seamen; most ships carried at least one small boat, often known as a *cokboat*, for contact with the shore when at anchor. Large vessels might draw too much water to moor at quays to unload cargoes or embark passengers. The Genoese carracks which frequented Southampton in the first half of the fifteenth century were loaded or unloaded by small boats, even when the cargo included bulky items like bales of cloth or raw wool, or alum and woad, needed for the dyeing of cloth. There is no clear information as to how the larger oared ships like balingers were rowed. Italian galleys used the system known as *al sensile* for most of our period. In this system each rowing bench was occupied by three men, each with his own oar; these were of differing lengths to avoid disastrous clashes between the blades. Later, in the sixteenth century, galleys had as many as five men per bench, all pulling on the same oar in the system known as *al scalocio*. There is little evidence that either system was adopted in England; the Antony Roll pictures of Henry VIII's rowbarges do not depict the oars in any systematic way.[46]

More is known about the way in which medieval sailing ships were able to reduce sail in stormy weather. There are many depictions from the twelfth century onwards of sails with reefing points. These were positioned so that the sail could be shortened either at its foot or at its head by the sail yard. This system, a variation of which is used in many modern sailing craft, seems to have fallen out of favour during the fourteenth century to be replaced by the use of *bonnets*; these were strips of extra canvas which could be laced to the foot of a sail in fair weather and removed if conditions worsened. It was possible to use at least two bonnets on a large and powerful main sail. The evidence for reef points comes from pictures; bonnets are shown in images but are also listed in the inventories of royal ships kept by the Clerks of the King's Ships.

Mariners taking bearings on buildings on the shore before entering port in order to identify the safe channel.

(AUTHOR'S COLLECTION)

## Crew sizes

Although it may seem to modern eyes that medieval ships were ludicrously over-manned, the lack of any auxiliary power source apart from the crew is one explanation. The rule of thumb, proposed by Nicholas Rodger, that ships at this time were manned in the ratio of one mariner for every 3–4 tuns of the ship's capacity is largely borne out by the manning levels of those ships of which we have both a tonnage figure and the total of the crew carried. There does not seem to have been much in the way of an 'officer class' on these ships. There was always a shipmaster, and often, especially on the larger vessels, a 'constable', both at 6d per day. It has been suggested that the constable was an apprentice master, which seems unlikely since he and the master were paid the same. Another possibility is that the constable had charge of the fighting men on a ship on a voyage with a warlike purpose. This may be so, but this officer is also found on vessels when no action was in prospect. The term 'constable' is only found on ships in the fourteenth century; the office held may have been more like that of a mate than that of a quasi-military officer.[47] Otherwise, wages for mariners on board a ship in the King's service were uniform throughout the fourteenth and fifteenth centuries at 3d per day, except for the one or two ship's boys who were paid half the adult daily rate.[48]

Two replicas of the Bremen cog under sail with the wind behind them. Both vessels have a low-aspect rig and each has a bonnet, an additional strip of sailcloth which could be laced to the bottom of the square-sail to increase its area.

**(WOLF-DIETER HOHEISEL)**

### Windward ability

Single-masted sailing vessels of the cog type could probably sail as close as 70° off the wind. This has been the experience of those who have constructed replicas of the Bremen cog. There are, of course, problems with this kind of 'experimental' archaeology. No rudder, mast or yard was found in the remains of the Bremen cog nor, of course, any of its rigging; the only clue was the position of the mast step. There was also the issue of ballast (none was found in the Bremen ship), but here there was some valuable information gained from another cog wreck, that found at Vejby in Denmark in 1976. This contained ballast and allowed a 'weight of ballast to length of keel' ratio to be calculated.[49] The rig itself was based on the information on the rigging of a 'round ship' in Giorgio Timbotta's notebook, which includes some data on shipbuilding and was written around 1444.[50] This replica, the *Wissemara*, was found to sail well, reaching 4 knots in a force 4 wind, but to roll and pitch so badly that the crew were almost incapacitated by seasickness. Other later replicas have altered some details of the vessel's construction, but the general conclusion is that medieval shipwrights had devised a 'quality vessel', without the technical aids available to modern shipbuilders.[51]

Despite some restrictions on going to sea in the winter imposed by members of the Hanseatic League, which, in 1403, forbade ships leaving port between St Martin's day (c.12 November) and the Feast of St Peter's Chair (22 February), probably because of the ice in the Baltic,[52] medieval seamen were quite prepared to go to sea in the winter months. The port books or local customs book of South-ampton, for example, show no fall-off of seaborne traffic into the port during this period. Often February and January were particularly busy because of wine ships bringing in the new vintage, and other craft unloading quantities of salt fish as Lent approached and the market boomed. The reluctance by monarchs to mount overseas expeditions in the winter was not caused by difficulties with seamen, but more general problems with logistics and supplies for an army.

*Manoeuvring*

Other aspects of seamanship are occasionally mentioned in chronicle

The adoption of additional masts and sails improved windward performance and aided vessels to tack through the eye of the wind.
In diagram **a** a vessel with a single mast and square-sail is quite far off the wind. As it tacks it points directly into the wind and as the sail backs the vessel begins to go astern. The rudder is reversed and the ship will fall off on the new tack. This manoeuvre requires skill and if not successfully completed the ship may fall off on the old tack or simply go a long way astern, losing valuable progress to windward.
In diagram **b** the vessel has a foremast with foresail and this can be backed to help the ship's head through on to the new tack.
Diagram **c** shows a vessel with a lateen mizzen and this helps the vessel point higher into the wind and also helps prevent the vessel falling off on the old tack.
Diagram **d** depicts a vessel with three masts and these both improve windward ability and help the vessel pay off on the new tack.

(© NATIONAL MARITIME MUSEUM, GREENWICH, LONDON)

accounts of encounters between ships at sea. It seems clear that with an experienced crew medieval ships could change course or tack with a fair degree of speed, even in the stressful conditions of a battle. In 1217 the English fleet, at the outset of the battle of Dover, had managed to convince the French they were making for Calais, before going about and coming up on the rear of the French.[53] In another encounter in 1406 somewhere off Calais, a squadron of galleys from Castile with a few French balingers, all under the command of Dom Pero Niño, a very experienced captain, came upon an English fleet composed of both great ships and balingers. The weather was calm so that the great ships of the English would have difficulty manoeuvring. The galleys, therefore, made ready for an attack. Just as a boarding action was under way, the wind got up giving the weather gauge to the English sailing ships. Dom Pero Niño himself seemed to be in real danger on his galley as it was soon surrounded by the English vessels, including two balingers. However, a French balinger managed to sail between the captain's galley and the attacking balingers and rammed one of them, shearing off her bowsprit and cutting a forestay so that she was disabled. This is described as a 'feat of seamanship' as the French balinger had backed her sail and hove to, luring the English balingers towards her before bearing up and going to the rescue of the captain.[54]

### Anchoring

Other aspects of good maritime practice, as it were, are touched on in the Laws of Oléron. Articles 15 and 16 deal with the problems that easily arise if several vessels are at anchor in a haven. Anchoring or mooring to a quay were usual at this period; ships might, of course, take the ground in a drying harbour at low tide, but only the smallest would normally have been drawn up on the beach. The Laws lay down that if a ship drags its anchor and causes damage to another the assumption is usually that costs of repair must be shared. In the situation where a harbour dries at low tide and ships are crowded together, the danger is that one anchor cable will drift over another; the Laws deal with the damage that may result, and also clearly expect anchors to be buoyed so that their position is visible to others. A rather later compilation than the Laws, *Les Bons usages et les Bonnes Costumes et les Bons Jugemenz de la Commune d'Oléron*, survives in one copy which, unusually, includes an article defining the responsibility of a shipmaster. It is his duty to see that the voyage is completed as required.[55] The overall impression created by the Laws is of a maritime community which extended to most European waters, and which had not only a clear understanding of good standards of seamanship, but also mechanisms to enforce them.

Given that the great majority of vessels in the service of the Crown at this time were requisitioned merchant ships, and that at times the King's own ships were rented to merchants for trading voyages, there is no reason to doubt that the same standards of seamanship and navigation could be expected from shipmasters in both ships in royal service and those acting as merchant vessels. Skilled mariners, like John William and Ralph Huskard in the reign of Henry V, were happy to be involved with voyages both for the Crown and for commercial purposes. Royal ships were involved in cases of robbery at sea or the breaking of truces almost as often as those in the ownership of individuals like the Hawley family of Dartmouth. This family happily served the Crown at the same time as organising the discreet dispersal of valuable cargoes seized at sea from furious merchants. In the later fifteenth century, as the Crown withdrew from the ownership and operation of ships, in favour of the contracting out of naval defence to private individuals, it was no more than the truth that there was indeed only one navy of England, the trading vessels carrying both goods and passengers in private ownership. In the next chapter we will turn to the role of ships of all kinds in the defence of the realm.

# CHAPTER 7

# War at Sea

ESPITE THE FACT that the most usual service provided to the crown of England by the navy of England was the transport of men and war materiel to the scene of conflict, occasions did, of course, arise when an engagement with the enemy at sea became unavoidable. How did these fleets largely composed of merchant ships with crews that, on the surface, had little experience of this kind of situation and no training acquit themselves in a war situation? What weapons were to hand? Was there any general understanding of the way in which a battle at sea should be fought? Was there any discussion of the nature of war at sea, or a code of conduct comparable to the chivalric code which had some influence on the conduct of armies and knights when fighting on land? The idea of a just war was well understood in this period and applied generally to all forms of conflict. In the opinion of Thomas Aquinas, war might only be undertaken by the authority of a ruler and in a just cause, that is, to right a wrong. It should also be fought out of a desire to bring about some good end, not in a spirit of revenge or for gain.[1] Widely-read works like Honoré Bonet's *Tree of Battles*, written around 1387, developed these ideas in some detail, setting out, for example, rules for the circumstances in which a knight might be paid (this was not permissible if he fought merely for vain glory), and decreeing the death penalty in all circumstances for those who broke truces without specific orders from a ruler to do so.[2]

## Writings on war at sea

The points about the need for a just cause and the avoidance of mercenary motives before going to war, and about the need to restrain pillage and truce-breaking, made with some force by writers like the author of the *Tree of Battles*, were

A battle at sea; the right-hand ship is flying the bear and ragged staff badge of the earldom of Warwick. The weapons shown include cannon, and also depict men in the top castles hurling missiles down onto the enemy decks.

(BRITISH LIBRARY)

problematic in the context of war at sea at this period. Monarchs undoubtedly saw themselves as fighting for a righteous cause, but there is room to doubt whether individual shipowners and masters saw things in quite the same light. The possibility of gain in the form of a prize cargo or a prize ship was often present. Events on the high seas, moreover, were often beyond the reach of any royal authority or royal court. Theorising of this nature, therefore, does not seem to have had much effect on war at sea. There were clearly great difficulties in enforcing even a modicum of laws about such matters as truce-breaking in a period when communications were slow and often interrupted, and the self-interest of a shipowner or master could take precedence over the letter of the law. The frequency and the vehemence of recorded complaints about robbery at sea by those who lost valuable property give some idea of the size of the problem. It is, however, very difficult to disentangle possibly legitimate actions authorised by the monarch from out-and-out lawbreaking. The violence of some attacks also makes it unlikely that any codes of chivalric conduct had an influence in the rough and lawless environment of many seamen.

The *Black Book of the Admiralty*, of which the oldest manuscripts date from the early fifteenth century but which contains even earlier material, includes among the articles relating to what the 'admiral is to doe in tyme of war at sea or land', the statement that 'noe man be soe bold as to robb or pillage the holy church nor to ravish any woman upon paine of death'.[3] The articles then go on to give directions about the division of prizes between the Crown, the admiral and individual ships' companies. This almost seems to be the main purpose of the articles. Their overall flavour emerges strongly from, for example, the entry which mandates that if any vessel tries to sneak away from the fleet with a prize without the admiral's consent, he will be fined twice the value of the vessel and its goods. The captor of the prize should, in fact, 'bring the same before the admiral there to take and receive what the law and custom of the sea requires.' This stated that the admiral would have two shares of the value of a prize vessel and its cargo, even if this had been taken by those not in the King's pay, or what the text calls *gaillioters*,[4] translated in the seventeenth century as 'privateers'. The aim of these articles seems more to ensure that the admiral received his due share of any prize than to maintain the rule of law at sea.

Discussion of the most effective way to wage war and organise military forces was also a feature of the later middle ages. Much of this discussion was based on Vegetius' *De Re Militari*, written at the very end of the fourth century. Book 4 of this work deals specifically with war at sea. It is not, however, obvious that Vegetius' views had much influence on how either war on land or war at sea was actually conducted in our period. It is true that the work was widely distributed and frequently copied, but it is much harder to find evidence of any military commander following his precepts in the field. The work was translated into both French and English in the late thirteenth century, was incorporated by other writers into their works, and even appeared in verse. One particularly notable adaptation was that by Christine de Pisan in her *Livre des Faits et Bonnes Meurs de Sage Charles V*, written in 1404. This included her suggestion that, in a sea battle, sailors who were good at swimming underwater should be provided with sharp instruments to make holes in the enemy ships, causing them to sink. This and similar works might imply that a wider audience for the book developed in the fifteenth century. It has, however, been pointed out that in the surviving copies the naval chapters have few if any marginal marks and look as if they were seldom read.[5] Vegetius' own recommendations were perhaps either obvious to a good commander, or too closely tied to the style of galley warfare usual in the Mediterranean of his day to be very useful to later commanders in northern waters. Using scouts to try and find out the preparedness of the enemy, as he recommends, or linking ships with grapnels in a boarding action seem very much like 'best practice' to use a modern phrase. Other recommendations like the hurling of containers of lime or soft soap onto an enemy's deck to make then slippery have left no trace in any medieval records, except in the chronicle accounts of one or two battles. There is a suspicion that this was what a chronicler felt should appear in an account of a naval battle rather than any actual event. As far as the disposition of a fleet is concerned, Vegetius was in favour of an attacking fleet being drawn up in a crescent shape so that the wings could envelop a fleeing enemy. Nothing like this seems to have happened in any encounter in northern waters before 1500.

A late-fifteenth-century view of a ship in port, clearly showing the rigging, four masts with lateen sails on the mizzens. There are also guns visible positioned to fire over the gunwale. The incident depicted shows Henry VI welcoming Richard Beauchamp, Earl of Warwick.

(BRITISH LIBRARY)

## Training for war at sea

Knights, of course, trained from their youth in the particular skills needed to fight on horseback and to use a sword when on foot. The tournaments and jousts which were a popular part of many medieval celebrations were a necessary part of this training. In the same way, archers, particularly longbow men, needed to train and practise for long periods to build up the skills and the physique needed to be successful with this weapon. The crossbows which could be found on some English ships, and to a much greater extent on those of the Castilians and Aragonese, also needed some expertise to use effectively. If, therefore, a ship had embarked fighting men, whether men-at-arms or archers, these men would very probably have had some training in the use of their weapons, but there is no trace of any specific training for fighting at sea even for this group. The same applies to the mariners with even greater force. They probably possessed some basic personal weapons, knives or daggers, and had some protective clothing. Helmets and some items of body armour appear in the inventories of royal ships but there are no records of any formal training of men for fighting at sea or for masters in the details of the tactics to use in a sea battle. It is not surprising that shipmasters and crews of vessels which had previously engaged in commerce raiding or 'piracy' also appear in squadrons of ships keeping the seas for the Crown. These men would have had useful experience in laying a vessel alongside another prior to boarding and in taking another ship. This could be deployed to the advantage of the Crown when needed.

The command structure in a war situation is also unclear. The master of the ship was in overall charge of the vessel and apparently senior to any military commander who might also be embarked. There is nothing recorded about how this system operated in practice

An image from the mid thirteenth century showing an attack on a town. Weapons here are longbows, crossbows and a flail.

(CORPUS CHRISTI, CAMBRIDGE)

in battle. Many ships from the late thirteenth century with crews of more than around twenty mariners also carried at least one constable, but there is no clear indication that this officer (he was paid the same as the master) had a special responsibility for fighting the ship. As we have seen, constables can be found on board ships when no fighting men other than the general run of mariners were carried, and when the voyage was not expected to include any naval action. The seventeenth-century translator of the *Black Book* inserts the word 'gunner' after that of constable but medieval documents do not suggest that constables at sea had special responsibilities for weapons of any kind, let alone guns.[6]

## The weapons used at sea

The nature of fighting at sea changed only gradually over the period from around 1000 AD to 1500 AD. At the beginning of the period, the weapons used would have been largely the same as those used by foot soldiers on land. Swords and daggers were normally personal possessions so do not appear in ships' inventories but illustrations,

A gun of the type found at sea in the late fifteenth century mounted on a replica carriage. This one was excavated from the wreck of the *Mary Rose*.

(MARY ROSE TRUST)

particularly one showing an engagement between two cog ships, indicate that longbows, clubs and swords were used. In another picture from a version of Matthew Paris's chronicle, crusaders attacking the city of Damietta from the sea are using a flail, longbows and slingshots, while the defenders have crossbows and are also hurling stones. Crossbows were the weapon favoured by the fighting men on galleys in the Mediterranean in the

This graphic image makes clear the ferocity of fighting at sea between vessels grappled together.
There was little prospect of the taking of prisoners for ransom as was common on land.

(BRITISH LIBRARY)

thirteenth century and later, with their expertise being renowned, especially that of those from the kingdom of Aragon. The galleys rebuilt for Edward II at Bayonne in 1320 were equipped for the voyage to England with 100 shields (normally these were arranged along the gunwales as protection for the crew), twenty dozen lances and thirty dozen 'darts'. The lances would have been hurled at the opposing crew to disable them before the two opposing vessels grappled with each other; the darts, made of iron with a pointed end, were thrown from the top castle on the mast onto the deck or among the rowing benches of the opponent to cause the maximum number of injuries among the crew. The galley *Philippe* built at Lynn for Edward III was equipped with pikes, basinets (light helmets), and mail jackets. She also carried 'engines', that is, mechanisms capable of projecting missiles by means of tension wound cords, probably springalds, rather like large crossbows mounted on some sort of plinth.[7]

## Guns

The basic armament of royal ships in the fifteenth century did not differ very much from this. Personal armour like *jakkes* (leather tunics sometimes reinforced with metal), hauberks (mail shirts), basinets, and *vambraces* (armour for forearms) was available, along with darts and *gadds* (pointed iron spikes) to hurl from the top castles, and bows and arrows. The new element was the presence of guns. The first recorded gunpowder weapon on an English ship was an 'engine', perhaps an adaptation of a springald, which fired quarrels (crossbow bolts) or lead pellets, listed as on board a vessel called the *All Hallows Cog* in 1337/8. It does not seem to have been a success, since there are no further mentions in royal records of similar weapons until the reign of Henry V. Along with difficulties with the design, it has been suggested that a further reason for the slowness with which gunpowder weapons were taken up may possibly have been the difficulty in obtaining supplies of saltpetre, necessary for making gunpowder.[8]

By the first decades of the fifteenth century, however, the squadron of royal ships was armed with a number of guns. These are listed in the ships' inventories recording what was on board at the date these were taken; more may have been carried if a vessel was setting out to meet the enemy. The guns listed were made of iron and were breech-loaders; that is, the charge of gunpowder was contained in a separate reusable chamber which fitted into the breech. Guns like the ones on these ships were often provided with more than one chamber to speed up the cumbrous process of loading. Henry V's *Graunt Marie* and *Thomas de la Tour* had three 'chambers' for each of the cannon carried.[9] The oldest gun recovered in English waters is that from the Studland Bay wreck which is dated to around 1520 and was probably made in Spain.[10] The gun barrel was formed of iron staves arranged as a cylinder, bound with iron hoops. The oldest surviving guns for use on land which were made in this way date from around 1450 and clearly show the same method of construction. Various alloys of copper were also used to make guns at this date, but no copper alloy guns are clearly identified among those on the King's ships until the reign of Henry VII.[11]

In the early fifteenth century four or five cannon seems to have been the greatest number carried on one ship. Even Henry V's great ship, the *Holigost* carried no more than seven, the highest number on any vessel at this date.[12] Two of the ships built by Sir John Howard in the 1470s, the *George* and the *Edward*, were more heavily armed than this. The *George* had sixteen 'bombards' with seventy-two 'chambers' and the *Edward* had fifteen with sixty-four chambers.[13] On these ships, and on the royal ships earlier in the century, the most effective weapons were probably not these guns but the gads, or iron darts, thrown from the tops, along with the arrows and quarrels fired from longbows and crossbows. The most effective tactic was the boarding action with ships grappled together and the crews fighting hand-to-hand on the deck and in the hold. From the fifteenth century, the guns were probably mounted like those depicted in *The Beauchamp Pageant*, where they are shown positioned in the waist of the ship with the guns firing over the gunwale. In that position, with at most six or seven cannon available, it would have been very hard for gunfire to do more than contribute to the noise and confusion of battle with billowing smoke to obscure the fighting men on the deck. The real damage would have been done by the bowmen, pikemen and men in the tops.[14] By the reign of Henry VII, perhaps more attention was being paid to the possibilities presented by the use of gunpowder weapons at sea. By 1497 the *Sovereign* of 600 tuns carried 141 guns of various types deployed on the fore and aft castles as well as in the waist and the *Regent* of 1000 tuns carried 181.[15] Even so, the deadly ship-killing broadside of the seventeenth century would not be possible until gun ports, cut in the hull, had become an established feature of the design of vessels equipped with cannon.

## Sea battles

A medieval land army normally set forth with the intention of meeting the enemy on the field of battle. Most accounts of campaigns describe how the opponents manoeuvred so as to encounter the enemy in favourable circumstances and thus win the day. Battles at sea were very seldom preceded by any kind of campaign in this period, often occurring almost fortuitously. Their very rarity also ensured that accounts of sea battles made for stirring tales in contemporary chronicles.

### The Third Crusade

While the rulers of England controlled both sides of the Channel, there was little prospect of conflict between national forces in these waters. The first chronicle accounts which purport to record how English ships were involved in a notable action at sea in fact relate to the Crusades, and more particularly to the expedition of Richard I to Outremer, the kingdom beyond the sea established as a result of the First Crusade in 1095. Richard's intention as a leader of the Third Crusade was to recover the territory lost to the Saracens, led by Saladin, after the disastrous defeat of the forces of the Kingdom of Jerusalem at the battle of the Horns of Hittin. He ordered the assembly of a fleet from all over his domains at Dartmouth, which was intended to sail south across the Bay of Biscay, down the coast of Iberia, and eventually into the Mediterranean to meet the King at Marseilles, to which he had travelled overland. For English seamen this was an extraordinary voyage

An attack on the port of Brest in Brittany. The transport fleet is shown in the background but the emphasis is on the fighting on land.

(BRITISH LIBRARY)

OPPOSITE PAGE:
A battle at sea between the English and the Flemings; the English ship is wearing the banner with three leopards and the Flemish the lion of Flanders. The fighting is at close quarters with high casualties.

(BRITISH LIBRARY)

quite outside their usual experience. It is not clear if the vessels concerned were sailing ships or oared vessels like galleys; in either case it has been suggested that once they had passed the Straits of Gibraltar they would have had great difficulty in retracing their steps against the strong eastward flowing current. The voyage is related in detail by Roger of Hoveden in his chronicle, including a storm in the Bay of Biscay, and involvement in actions against the Moors on behalf of the Christians in Portugal. Some 106 ships are said to have reached Marseilles at the end of August, after a voyage on which the chronicler details each stage, only to discover that Richard had already left with a fleet of ten hired busses and twenty galleys.

From this point, Richard's activities, including his involvement in the tangled affairs of Sicily and the conquest of Cyprus, are well recorded. How involved the fleet from England was in the doings of the King is not so clear. Some ships seem to have followed the King to Messina but no numbers are given. After the success of the campaign in Cyprus, the expedition set out for Acre where the crusading forces were laying siege to the town. On the way, the fleet encountered a large vessel from Beirut attempting to bring in supplies to relieve the town. A bitterly fought engagement followed between the crusading fleet and this ship. We do not know how many, if any, of the attackers were English, but to the chroniclers of the deeds of Richard I it was a famous victory with

the King a 'hero of a naval battle', the first time this had happened since the days of
Alfred. Roger of Hoveden describes the Saracen ship as 'of immense dimensions', greater
than any 'with the exception of Noah's ark'.[16] Later chroniclers then added more and
more detail to their accounts of what was undoubtedly a hard-fought encounter between
the English king's galleys and a large sailing ship. One version has a galleyman diving
into the sea and attaching ropes to the enemy ship's steering oar or rudder so the steersman
lost control. The galleys are described as ramming the ship and holing her, even though
no galleys at this date had rams like those used in classical times. There was even a
story that the ship was carrying two hundred serpents which were fortunately drowned.[17]
On a more sober note, the account of the engagement by a Moslem chronicler accepts
that the fighting was hard, but states that the ship was in fact scuttled by its commander
to deny the enemy possession of the stores and war machines which it carried.[18]

### The battle of Damme

Even if the action against the enormous Saracen ship off Acre rapidly acquired a
semi-legendary veneer in the hands of chroniclers, the battle of Damme was both better
recorded by contemporaries, and also has more to teach us about the nature of warfare
involving ships at this date. The whole episode is described by Roger of Wendover,
whose work was later incorporated into that of Matthew Paris, his successor as historian
monk at St Alban's Abbey.

In the struggle for dominance in northern France between John, King of England,
and Philip Augustus of France, the various rulers of the counties in the Low Countries
were inevitably drawn into the conflict in support of one or other of the major combatants.
In the last months of 1212 Philip began to pursue with some determination his desire
to invade England and set about raising a fleet to carry his forces across the Channel.
The fleet was largely made up of vessels and mariners from Poitou under the command
of Savary de Mauléon. Boulogne was settled on as the rendezvous for the ships. John,
however, made the invasion very problematic for Philip by submitting to the Pope in
April 1213; now any invasion of England would be a deadly sin, as the realm was under
the protection of the Church. Philip nevertheless moved his forces to Gravelines, but
then decided to attack Flanders because he felt he had been insulted by an envoy from
the count. In the meantime, John had also summoned a fleet which was divided into
three squadrons based at Dover, Faversham and Ipswich. According to Paris, he then
received a plea for assistance against the French from the Count of Flanders.

A fleet of five hundred ships with seven hundred knights on board, along with many
foot and mounted soldiers under the command of the Earl of Salisbury, put to sea. After
a good voyage the ships approached the estuary of the Zwyn and sent in scouts. They
discovered that a large number of French vessels were either beached on the mud or at
anchor in the estuary near Damme, laden with valuable stores. All the French except a
few sailors had left their ships to pillage and lay waste to the surrounding Flemish territory.
The English rapidly took the ships at anchor (said to number three hundred) and
dispatched them and their cargoes of 'corn, wine, flour, meat and arms and other things'

back to England. The beached ships, around a hundred in number, were burnt after the stores had also been taken as spoil. The English horsemen then set off to attack Philip's forces which were near Bruges. It is not clear if this group were themselves routed by the French, but they returned speedily to their ships and set sail for home. Philip, now deprived of his transports and most of his stores, had little option but to abandon his plan to invade England.[19]

It might be argued that this engagement hardly involved ships at all, and that to call it a naval battle is not really justified. Certainly, no great skill in ship-handling was required by the shipmasters, and what fighting there was took place on land. Yet without the English being able to put a fleet to sea they would not have been able to respond to the Flemish cry for help. The danger that England herself faced came from the threat of a seaborne invasion. The battle itself, in some ways, looked back to the age of Viking raids as more a successful amphibious operation than a true sea battle. It did not perhaps add much 'to the naval renown of England', but for the first time it had been made clear that England would always take very seriously the matter of who controlled the coast of Flanders. It could have a crucial impact on the security of the realm.

### The battle of Dover

This encounter, however, did not resolve the conflict between John and Philip Augustus, nor did it greatly affect events in England itself, where tensions between the King and the nobility grew more serious. Within two years the King and the barons were at war. In the autumn of 1215, after the meeting at Runnymede in June, the King was making strenuous efforts to put together a fleet based in the East Anglian ports, and was also

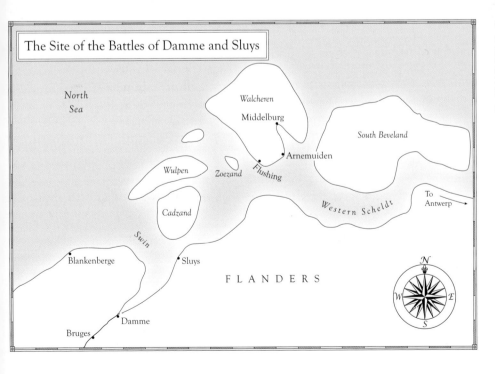

### The Site of the Battles of Damme and Sluys

This map shows a reconstruction of the possible coastline, islands and navigable waterways in the estuary of the River Zwyn and the River Scheldt in the middle ages.

(PETER WILKINSON)

English ships ready for battle, displaying the cross of St George and the royal arms of England quartered with the lilies of France. Men-at-arms in the illustrations in chronicles are always shown as crowded on the deck.

looking for aid from Flanders. His fears of French intervention were proved well-grounded when Louis, the Dauphin of France, managed to land with a small force in April 1216 at Sandwich. Louis managed to take control of the Cinque Ports and moved towards East Anglia. The barons' party seemed to be in the ascendancy when in October 1216 John died, leaving a child of nine, Henry III, as his successor.

William the Marshal, Earl of Pembroke, who had made his reputation as a young man as a knight of consummate skill, a hero of the tournament circuit, was one of thirteen named executors of John's will. He soon, however, became the dominant figure, well deserving of the title of '*rector regis et regni*' bestowed on him by chroniclers and of the verse biography commissioned shortly after his death by his oldest son. Because of the survival of this lengthy work (19,000 lines of rhyming couplets) we have an account largely by eyewitnesses of much of his career.[20] In October 1216 he was over seventy years old but still a formidable soldier and military leader; he had been close to Henry II and Richard I, and had also served John in the last years of his reign. His aim was to throw the Dauphin and his forces out of England and restore power to the rightful king, the young Henry III.

By the spring of 1217, the Marshal had gone a long way to achieving this. Indecisive fighting over the winter around Rye and Winchelsea had prevented the Dauphin receiving reinforcements from France. In May, the Marshal and his royalist forces won a victory over the remaining baronial rebels and Louis at Lincoln, with the old man himself rushing first into the melee. Over the summer Louis' wife managed to raise fresh troops and supplies in France; the success or failure of the French intervention in England

These two images are on facing folios in the original manuscript; storms at sea could devastate a battle fleet and lead to shipwrecks and death. The coast of Brittany near Ushant was particularly dangerous.

(BRITISH LIBRARY)

depended on the successful reinforcement of the Dauphin's army. By the end of August, the French supply fleet was ready to sail from Calais. It was led by one Eustace the Monk, whose colourful career as a soldier of fortune and a pirate has made him a figure of romance and legend in much the same way as Robin Hood.[21] His depredations on the shipping of the Cinque Ports had also made him cordially loathed by all local seamen.

The old Marshal had news that the French had put to sea, and marched to Sandwich declaring that he was ready to lead the English fleet himself until dissuaded by his companions. The poem recites how the English forces were at Canterbury but could get little sleep; at first light, on a clear summer's day, they set off for Sandwich where they could see the French fleet approaching, sailing for the North Foreland driven on by a southwest wind.

The description of the ensuing battle differs a little between that in the Marshal's biography and that in the chronicles, principally that of Matthew Paris. In the biography the English ships put to sea led by a 'fine well-armed ship' with Hubert de Burgh, the justiciar, on board along with Richard, a bastard son of King John. The French laughed at the advancing English ships, saying that they 'would soon take them with us to London or else they'll fish for flounders in the sea'. Sir Hubert sailed past without initially giving battle but then made for 'a great ship of Bayonne', carrying the leaders of the French expedition and the French king's 'treasure' (probably the funds for the mercenaries with the Dauphin). This ship was low in the water because it was also carrying siege engines, including a trebuchet, and many fine horses. Also on board was the hated Eustace the Monk. Sir Hubert's cog was high in the water and was able to send boarders to take the French vessel; the defender had been thrown off balance by '*granz poz pleins de chauz/Qy'il jeterent sor els de val*' (great pots of lime that they threw down into the ship). Soon all on board had been captured or killed, including Eustace, who was offered the choice of having his head cut off on the trebuchet or on the side of the ship. He said that he didn't fancy either, but was decapitated anyway. After this successful action the remainder of the English forces routed the French and took an enormous amount of valuable spoil. The poem describes mariners strolling through Sandwich clad in scarlet and silk and boasting to each other of the value of their attire: 'Bah! Mine is all cisemus[22] fur, cote and surcoat mantle and cape. There isn't a better between here and Aleppo'.[23]

According to Matthew Paris in his *Chronica majora*, which may be based on the recollections of Hubert de Burgh in old age, de Burgh set forth in company with the best Cinque Port ships, around sixteen altogether, with another twenty smaller vessels. When they came up on the French fleet they changed course as if to make for Calais; the wind then dropped and the English fleet changed course again as the wind strengthened, allowing them to take the weather gauge and come up on the rear of the French fleet. De Burgh's ship grappled with that of Eustace the Monk, and de Burgh's men were able to cut the stays of the mast of this ship. The sail came down and trapped the French crew like birds caught in a net. The nobles on board were captured and all other crew members were killed. Eustace himself was found hiding in the bilges, dragged out and decapitated. Hubert was greeted with great rejoicing when he reached shore after this famous victory.[24]

Of all the sea battles fought in our period, this had the clearest and the most important consequences. Louis had no alternative but to abandon his intervention in English affairs and return to France. In England the victory provided the breathing space necessary to restore royal government under the guardians of Henry III. An invasion which had had a degree of success and could have had far-reaching consequence had been decisively defeated. It was also, of course, fought not in an estuary but on the high seas somewhere off Sandwich or Dover. The English success depended on a change of course and the intelligent use of the prevailing wind conditions. It was a boarding action, and we may doubt the accuracy of some of the details, but victory depended on co-operation between mariners and fighting men.

## The battle of Sluys

The victory at Dover did not, of course, ensure any long continuance of peace on land or at sea. In many ways the sea was a world beyond the reach of laws and courts, so that low levels of violence were endemic, often in pursuit of feuds between towns or individuals, or as a means of personal gain or at times as a kind of unofficial warfare. We will look more closely at some aspects of this later in the next chapter, but at this point it is as well to remember that though the battle of Sluys occurred over a hundred years after the battle of Dover, this did not mean that the sea was a zone of tranquillity. The role of ships in transporting armies and their supplies was frequently needed by the Crown, most notably perhaps in the reign of Edward I for his campaigns across the Channel and in Wales and Scotland. Intermittent warfare also occurred between England and France as the French sought to extend the areas ruled directly by their king, while the English struggled to maintain their power in areas such as Aquitaine where the English king was dominant.

This conflict reached a new intensity as Edward III emerged from the tutelage of his mother and began to set his own seal on policy. One aspect of this was that he resuscitated his claim to the throne of France as the nearest living male relative of his late uncle, Charles IV of France. Charles had died in 1328 and had been succeeded by his cousin Philip of Valois. To renew the claim in 1337 probably reflected English anger over the French alliance with the anti-English party in Scotland, and continued French encroachments on the duchy of Aquitaine. The overall effect was to increase tension between the two realms, and especially increase the level of violence in the seas off the south and east coasts of England. One commentator on this period has stated that the English showed themselves as having no strategy for a war at sea. Their enemies, on the other hand, 'thought about the war at sea and put their thoughts into action.'[25]

The French had concluded treaties with the Genoese and the Grimaldis of Monaco to supply them with galleys fully manned and ready for war. The French *Clos des Galées*, founded in 1295 at Rouen, was also able to supply a number of galleys to the crown. With these forces the French were able to mount devastating raids on English ports, burning ships and stores, looting warehouses and killing and raping the men and women of these unfortunate towns. Early in 1338, Portsmouth was burnt. In September Guernsey

The battle of Sluys, the most renowned sea battle fought
before 1500. The opposing ships are identified by their
banners and the heavy casualties are indicated.
The inclusion of the shore in the picture
does reflect the site where the
battle took place in the
estuary of the Zwyn
near Sluys.

(BRITISH LIBRARY)

was taken by the Genoese and in October an attack which took the town completely by surprise was mounted on Southampton.[26] Froissart describes how the French fleet under Hugh Quieret sailed into Southampton harbour one Sunday morning when the townspeople were at mass and 'pillaged and looted it completely'.[27] The King himself lost wool and wine stored in the town. Later archaeological investigations have uncovered pits of burnt debris, of tiles and slates, while a new seal had to be cut to replace that carried off by the raiders along with all the town's muniments.[28] The King had also lost five large royal ships seized in Arnemuiden harbour while the crew were on shore and unable to offer any resistance. To attacks like this, the English had no effective response at sea. The following year threatened to be as bad with the French raiders at sea all summer and threatening Harwich, Hastings, Plymouth and the Cinque Ports. English shore defences had been strengthened, however, and in the autumn Philip was faced with the defection of his Genoese mercenaries. The majority mutinied over dissatisfaction with their pay and sailed for home, followed by the Grimaldi fleet.

In January 1340 fortune also seemed to favour the English. Around 13 January, according to the chronicler Adam Murimuth, the sailors of the Cinque Ports with many small, well-equipped ships crept across the Channel on a foggy day and burnt nineteen galleys, four big ships and twenty small ones in the harbour at Boulogne. They also set fire to a storehouse full of oars, sails, arms and crossbows – everything that was needed for the crews of the nineteen galleys.[29] This counter-raid weakened the French at sea and also strengthened the hand of Edward III, who was endeavouring to build alliances with the Flemish towns and others hostile to the King of France, including his brother-in-law, the Count of Hainault. If this was successful Edward would be able to use Flanders as a base for an attack on France itself in pursuit of his claim to the French throne.

By the summer of 1340, Edward had managed to raise funds from Parliament to pursue the war; he had also had some success for his policies in Flanders. By Whitsun the King was at Ipswich trying to raise a fleet for the expedition to Flanders, but had only collected a small squadron when news reached him that Philip VI had put together a large fleet of over 250 ships in the estuary of the Scheldt off Sluys, with the intention of invading England. Some chronicles then have a dramatic story of Edward declaring that he would set off immediately to confront the enemy to the horror of his chancellor, Archbishop Stratford, who warned the King that in that case he would lose both his life and his kingdom. When the King took no notice of this advice Stratford precipitately resigned. The King then summoned his Admiral Robert Morley and one John Crabbe, a very experienced Flemish sea captain, both of whom agreed with what Stratford had said. The King, in fury, accused them of acting in conjunction with the Archbishop, and of cowardice, saying those who were afraid with no reason should stay at home rather than crossing the sea with him. Both, not surprisingly, then changed their minds and agreed to go with the King into danger. In the heightened atmosphere of an imminent engagement with the enemy, within ten days a much larger fleet of from 120–147 ships was assembled with many men at arms and archers embarked. This set off from Orwell on 22 June.[30]

Sailing with a fair northwest wind, the fleet reached the Flemish coast near Blankenberghe the following day. Scouts were sent out on land to reconnoitre the position of the French fleet while tactics for the battle were finally settled. The following day the fleets engaged; the French forces were crushed with heavy losses, with some of the victors making the gruesome joke that if fish could speak they would talk French after nibbling at so many corpses.

The course of the battle is less certain. There are some differences in the chronicle accounts and some differences in interpretation. The story that one ship carried a party of English ladies off to visit Queen Philippa, who had stayed in Ghent for the birth of her son, John, seems unlikely; this was no pleasure outing. More seriously, there is some doubt about the initial attack by the English. The best source would seem to be the letter written by Edward in French shortly after the battle, while still on board his ship the *Cog Thomas*, to his eight-year-old son, Edward of Woodstock.[31] This states that the English entered the Swyn with the tide in their favour shortly after the '*houre de noune*'. This has been translated as Nones (the canonical hour, ie around 3pm) but since high tide on 24 June 1340 at this location was 11.23am, it seems that this must mean around noon. The chronicler Geoffrey le Baker, who describes Edward as setting off 'after nine o'clock when he had the wind and the sun at his back and the flow of the tide with him', was confused.[32]

The King's letter would imply that the English ships set off from Blankenberghe on the flood tide, sailing in an easterly direction, and reached the Zwyn when it was slack water. The wind was still in their favour from the northwest, allowing them to come up on the French fleet which Edward describes as being 'in a very strong formation'. This formation is described in many chronicles including that of Geoffrey le Baker and Robert of Avesbury; the French ships were chained together in three lines presenting an impenetrable barrier to the attackers. To any seaman this might have seemed like a very unwise thing to do; the seaway between the coast of Flanders and the island of Cadzand was not only narrow but obstructed with sandbanks. If the timing suggested above is accurate, the tide was on the ebb, increasing the likelihood of ships running aground. If chained together, the ships, whether galleys or round ships, would have been unable to manoeuvre speedily. It is significant that the Genoese commander of the few hired galleys still in the French forces advised strongly against this formation, and in fact left the fray in its early stages with his ships. The battle itself resolved into a series of very bitterly fought boarding actions in which the English had the advantage because of the presence of archers on their vessels and also many experienced men-at-arms. After fighting all day and much of the following night, the English took just under 160 enemy ships. Twenty-four managed to escape, but some of these were later taken at sea. The King estimated in his letter that French casualties numbered some thirty thousand who, he said, 'lie dead all along the coast of Flanders.' It was especially pleasing to him that his forces managed to retake 'the *Christopher* and the others which were lost at Middelburg [Arnemuiden]', and 'we have also captured from this fleet three or four others as big as the *Christopher*'.[33]

There is no doubt that this was a crushing victory; the French losses in manpower alone would have severely hindered their ability to put another large fleet to sea in the near future. English losses were put by le Baker at four thousand men including four knights, very low in comparison. It is not surprising that Edward III, who seems to have had a talent for projecting strong propaganda images, commissioned the well-known gold noble showing him on board the *Cog Thomas* on the obverse to celebrate this famous victory. In the context of the opening years of the Hundred Years war as a whole, it was of less significance; some raiding by the French on the south coast took place not long after the battle. The position on land was unaltered. The image of the King with sword in hand on his mighty ship, however, took hold of the English imagination and made Edward's claims to be Lord of the Sea seem to have some substance.

*Les Espagnols sur Mer (the battle of Winchelsea)*
This engagement which took place on 29 August 1350 illustrates very well the pleasures and also the potential pitfalls of evidence from chronicles. It took place on the high seas in the vicinity of Winchelsea between a squadron composed of English royal ships and a large group of Spanish ships, hence its contemporary name; the designation the battle of Winchelsea is a fairly recent one. It took place at a time when the Hundred Years war was in a relatively quiet phase. The disaster for the French at Crécy in 1346 had been followed by the fall of Calais to the English in 1347. All thoughts of war had then receded into the background as the full horror of the advent of the Black Death in 1348 had become apparent. Somewhat to the surprise of many, a truce for a year between the major combatants was agreed in June 1350. This did not, however, prevent Edward feeling the need to retaliate against the Castilian allies of the French. A Castilian fleet en route to Flanders had attacked and spoiled at least ten English wine ships on the way to England from Bordeaux laden with wine. His aim was to pay them back in the same coin and to that end collected a fleet at Sandwich when news reached him that a large group of Castilian ships laden with valuable cargo would soon leave the Flemish ports for their home waters.

Robert of Avesbury then relates how the English ships were ready for a fight, with many nobles on board and also many archers and men-at-arms. They encountered the Spaniards, who were also fully prepared to fight, off Winchelsea. A fierce battle ensued and twenty-four large vessels laden with choice goods including Flemish cloth were taken by the English.[34]

This story, however, in the hands of Froissart becomes one of high chivalry and romance. He describes how the King gathered a fleet and had with him not only most of his most battle-hardened nobles but also his two sons, the Prince of Wales and the ten-year-old John of Gaunt. They waited for the sighting of the Spanish ships, which had been equipped with a formidable array of weapons, and which carried large numbers of mercenaries, so the English were outnumbered ten to one. As the Spanish came in sight Edward and his companions were enjoying themselves on deck singing and dancing, with the King cutting a brave figure clad in black velvet. The Spanish, meanwhile, with the wind in their favour could have held their course and avoided a fight but, in the best traditions of chivalry, they accepted the challenge posed by the English fleet and battle was joined. It soon became a series of single combats much in the manner of a joust. Froissart supplies many colourful details. The King's ship was driven straight at a large Spanish vessel with the two colliding like a clap of thunder and the top castle of the Spanish ship being thrown into the sea. Other desperate boarding actions are described; the ship of the Prince of Wales was in danger of either sinking or being taken by the Spanish when the Earl of Derby came to his rescue. A ship carrying the King's household was being carried off by the enemy, firmly grappled to the side of a Spanish ship, when one Hanekin leapt on board the enemy and severed all the standing rigging, bringing down both the mast and the sail. All this is stirring stuff but it is impossible to say how nearly it reflects the reality of a hard-fought and bloody encounter. The end of Froissart's story is even closer to the conventions of chivalric tales. When all were on shore, 'the night was passed in great rejoicings and in conversations on arms and love'. The King 'thanked them for their brave conduct and loyal service. Then they took their leave of him and returned each to his own home'.[35]

A better idea of the battle perhaps comes from Geoffrey le Baker who wrote of the way the bodies of dead and injured Spaniards were thrown into the sea from captured ships and described the wounds suffered including those made by crossbow bolts and swords, torn out teeth, split noses and lips, and plucked out eyes.[36] The hand-to-hand fury of an action of this kind was far from the niceties of a romance.

For the naval historian, however, this engagement, though of little strategic significance, reveals the way in which war at sea was becoming more dependent on the skills of seamen and the design of the vessels they sailed. The relative size and height above the water of a ship was of importance in actions like these, as well as the ability of the master to lay one vessel alongside another and then to draw off if necessary. The success of showers of missiles in disabling the opposing crew before boarding took place was also clearly a factor in winning an action and taking a ship.

### The battle of La Rochelle

The development of battle tactics are also clearly illustrated in the course of this encounter, which took place in June 1372 at a time when England's military prowess was on the wane. Edward III was now old and had lost his wife, Philippa, probably to a recurrence of the plague in 1369. Both 1370 and 1371 had seen invasion scares, with the south-coast towns on alert for raiders, and stories circulating widely of large French fleets being gathered for a descent on the English coast. John of Gaunt was actively pursuing his ambitions in Spain and attempting to put together an expedition and a fleet for that purpose. In France itself, English forces in the southwest were under pressure. In these rather unpromising circumstances the young Earl of Pembroke was commissioned in April as royal lieutenant in Aquitaine. He finally left to take up his position in June, leading a small force of probably under twenty ships, mostly small transports, but with three large vessels as escorts. He had with him 224 knights, fifty-five esquires and eighty archers. He also received a large sum of money in gold and silver, about £12,000, so that he could recruit and pay an army of about three thousand men when he reached his destination.[37]

The various chronicle accounts then differ markedly as to what then ensued. Froissart as usual has a stirring tale to tell, which also changed between the different versions of his work. The foremost English chronicles hardly mention the incident. The *Anonimalle Chronicle* merely states that 'the young count set out towards Gascony with too few men to the great damage of England'. He encountered enemy ships and was captured along with some of his companions and others were killed.[38] A French chronicle, the *Chronique des Quatre Premiers Valois*, explains that on 22 June the English squadron arrived off La Rochelle and found a force of Castilian galleys already barring their way. The English thought little of the Spanish and were not unduly disturbed. An action ensued with the crossbowmen on the galleys opposing the archers on the English sailing ships. At nightfall this was still inconclusive so the two fleets parted. The chronicle also implies at this point that low tide was around dusk, perhaps around 9pm. This chronicle is then adamant that at dawn the next day after the first attack the English were aground because of the falling tide. The galleys, drawing much less water, were still able to manoeuvre freely and attacked, this time using flaming arrows and pots of grease and oil to set the English ships on fire. Soon most of the English ships were alight, with terrified horses in the holds adding to the confusion and uproar. The earl's vessel was grappled by no fewer than four galleys and despite fierce fighting on the deck those who remained alive were forced to surrender and were captured. The treasure intended to pay the army in Gascony also fell into enemy hands.[39]

This account of the battle has generally been accepted, although there is some

The entrance to the port of La Rochelle guarded by two towers. The battle in 1370 probably took place just outside the port, when low water in the early morning affected the ability of the English to manoeuvre.

**(WIKIMEDIA)**

disagreement over whether the English ships went aground. The timing of the crucial tide changes must remain uncertain without precise information but it seems likely that the tide was ebbing from around 2–3am on the morning of 23 June so that at dawn when the Castilian attack went in this would soon be a problem for the English ships if they had anchored not far from the shore. More controversial is the effect of this battle. One historian has called it 'the greatest defeat ever sustained by the English navy'. Another has claimed that the effect was, 'to stimulate naval activity'.[40] The most recent writer's view is that 'the loss of prestige incurred by this first major English defeat was incalculable.'[41] For most contemporary English chroniclers the most important matter was the capture of the Earl of Pembroke by the Spanish.

Despite the loss of ships in this disaster and the need to compensate the owners of three of the largest with grants of royal ships, a large fleet was raised later that same summer for an expedition to France, which came to nothing because of a long spell of adverse winds. There is also evidence that the fact that a galley fleet had destroyed one made up of sailing vessels lay behind the decision to set in train the building of more balingers and barges for the Crown. Feelers were also put out to both Genoa and Portugal in the hope that they might be able to provide galleys or oarsmen to power the new balingers. More generally, English military power was receding as Charles V of France reinvigorated his forces both on land and at sea; the era of English success and stunning victories seemed to have ended, as the enormous expense of the wars became more and more apparent to a people who had lost much of their enthusiasm for the whole endeavour.

*The battle of Harfleur and warfare in the Channel in the reign of Henry V*
For much of the remainder of the fourteenth century there was little reason for this enthusiasm to be rekindled. The initiative was with the French forces on land, while at sea threats of raids and invasions, coupled with commerce-raiding, continued unabated, with both sides trying to profit from the general climate of insecurity and uncertainty. One notable example of the expeditions undertaken in this period is that led by the Earl of Arundel in 1387. This was originally intended to mount a raid on Flanders to stir up opposition to the rule of the duke. The commanders, however, received news that a French fleet convoying wine ships from La Rochelle was in the Channel not far from Sandwich. The English intercepted them off Margate and harassed the convoy as far as the island of Cadzand on the estuary of the Scheldt near Sluys. An enormous amount of cargo was looted from the convoy and also some valuable ships were taken. Although the expedition was very expensive to mount and none of its strategic aims were achieved, individual participants, even the ordinary mariners, did well out of the division of the spoils. The Crown benefited too, selling off the captured ships and paying some of its major debtors, including Richard Whittington, in wine to the tune of 200 tuns.[42]

The reign of Henry V saw the rekindling of the desire of the English Crown to assert its rights in France. As we have already shown, this particularly impinged on naval policy and the attitude to the royal ships. The number of royal ships, their size and their ability to give a good account of themselves in a sea fight all improved markedly. The fleet which carried Henry and his army to Harfleur in August 1415, at the start of the campaign which ended in the victory at Agincourt, was led by the King on board the *Trinity Royal*. The major part of the remainder of the fleet was made up of requisitioned vessels, as in the invasion fleets of his great-grandfather Edward III. Seven other royal ships were certainly included. In the following summer his brother, John, Duke of Bedford, led the fleet which would attempt to aid the English garrison now besieged in Harfleur. The French, under the command of Bernard d'Armagnac, had blockaded the town very effectively both from the sea and on the landward side. By April the garrison were in desperate straits, almost facing starvation. Relief by sea was made very difficult by the ships hired by the French from Genoa, Gioanni de' Grimaldi and Castile patrolling in the Seine estuary which was obstructed by sandbanks. The Genoese contingent in this fleet included large carracks, the mighty sailing vessels which tended to dominate any boarding action because of their height above the waterline, and the large number of armed men who could be embarked. Grimaldi and the Castilians had provided galleys. The French and their allies also had a secure base just across the estuary, the town of Honfleur.[43] Henry himself was prevented from leading the relief fleet since the newly elected Emperor Sigismund was conducting diplomatic negotiations in England, which in fact came to a successful conclusion just as the English fleet engaged with the enemy.

The chronicle, *Gesta Henrici Quinti*, written by a cleric, probably a royal chaplain, explains how the two squadrons of the relief fleet had difficulty in joining one another because of adverse winds. The section from Southampton finally met that from the Camber off Beachy Head. By 14 August the whole fleet was off the Seine estuary with a fair wind, probably northwesterly. The next day at dawn they engaged with the enemy.[44] The English numbered around three hundred ships, according to a well-informed Italian source. The French may have been outnumbered, as shortly before the arrival of the English the Grimaldi contingent had withdrawn because their commander had been killed in a skirmish with a wine convoy. From the French point of view everything depended on the Genoese carracks and their ability to dominate the action.

After what the *Gesta* calls a 'long drawn out and most bitter fight of five or six hours' with iron gads from the tops, stones, and other 'weapons of offence' causing high casualties, the English had prevailed, taking three Genoese carracks, and had watched as another 'the greatest of the carracks' called 'the mother of them all was, in fear of her pursuers, driven violently upon a sandbank and wrecked.' The remaining French ships fled to Honfleur where, with the port protected by sandbanks and unknown channels, the English could not follow them. In the usual somewhat ghoulish manner of chronicles, the writer then describes the corpses of the slain 'being carried backward and forwards on the tide as if seeking other interment than the fishes could provide.'[45]

The victory was obviously important in allowing the lifting of the siege of Harfleur, but it also paved the way for Henry's campaign in 1417 which culminated in the conquest of Normandy. Moreover, the addition to English naval strength provided by the captured Genoese carracks was soon put to good use. The prize vessels were incorporated into the squadron of royal ships as the *George*, the *Marie Hampton*, and the *Marie Sandwich*. Their numbers were added to the following summer when on 29 June the Earl of Huntingdon 'fought with ix carrykkes off jene [Genoa], the grettest that euer was seyne in thes costs; and scomfyted hem and tooke iiii off hem with her patrones'. He also captured the French admiral and the 'Tresour' to pay their wages for three months. His fleet of royal ships welcomed the captured carracks as the *Andrew*, *Christopher*, *Paul* and *Peter*.[46]

These victories were not the result of chance or good fortune, or even the greater determination of men fighting for their king and country rather than as mercenaries. Henry and his naval advisers, probably the Earl of Devon and the Earl of Huntingdon, had been well aware of the threat posed by the Genoese carracks in the pay of the French, a threat more deadly than that of the Castilian galleys of the late fourteenth century. Why else had the King at the very beginning of his reign and then with increasing enthusiasm from 1416, set about building large ships whose clear strategic purpose was to oppose the carracks? The *Trinity Royal* and the *Holygost* played a key role in both the battle of Harfleur and the Earl of Huntingdon's action. The *Jesus* was ready to carry the King and his suite when he set out on 30 July for Touques at the beginning of the campaign to conquer Normandy. The earl had successfully cleared the Channel to allow this crossing to take place unmolested.

The difficulties which could face smaller ships attempting to engage with the carracks of Genoa are made clear by an incident which occurred in 1416 after the battle of Harfleur. A carrack sailing fast before the wind under full sail was spotted in the Strait of Dover. The Captain of Calais, the Earl of Warwick, Richard Beauchamp, set out in hot pursuit with a force of six balingers on Thursday, 24 September. On the following Saturday one returned to Calais. She had lost the rest of the squadron in the dark and had failed to catch the carrack. The next day another balinger limped into harbour; she reported how at dawn on Friday the balingers had caught up with the carrack which loomed over their vessels with a much lower freeboard. Nevertheless, they had grappled with this huge ship and had fought all day until nightfall and had finally run out of weapons and missiles. The casualties on both sides were high but just when victory seemed in sight they had been forced to break off the engagement and the carrack escaped, sailing towards Sluys. The balingers had then made for Orwell but a storm had driven them back towards the French coast and Calais. This ship had lost her consorts in the storm and had, in fact, been unable to enter the harbour with the tide against her, and had been forced to beach the ship with the crew wading ashore. Another balinger of this group made it back to Calais a day later, followed by the remaining three on 30 September. All had left harbour in the excitement of the chase without supplies and were suffering badly from hunger and thirst. Finally, the story of the death of one English knight was also revealed. He had been killed by a stone being hauled up to the top castle for use as a missile falling from its sling and crushing him.[47]

In many ways, this account gives a better idea of the reality of war at sea at this period than the often brief and bland accounts of more notable encounters. The relative height above the waterline of the hulls of opposing ships was an important factor in these boarding actions, but one which could be overcome by force of numbers and adequate supplies of munitions, that is, iron gads, stones, arrows and darts. There is no mention of gunpowder weapons at this date, though they may have been available. In the fourteenth century Froissart had deplored the ferocity of fighting at sea and there is plenty of evidence that this was no more than the truth. The dead and injured were usually hurled into the sea and few if any prisoners taken. The aim was not 'ship killing' but the 'taking' of the enemy's vessels, which represented a huge capital investment, and incorporating them into the fleet of the victorious nation. It is also clear that by this date the almost static battles between fleets in which the vessels could plausibly be described as chained together in an estuary or near the shore were giving way to encounters where the skill of the shipmaster in manoeuvring his vessel was as relevant as the bravery and attacking spirit of those leading the boarding parties.

## Patrols in the Channel

There is also evidence that a much more coherent and considered plan for the use of the King's ships and the protection of English coasts was in existence in the period from 1412–20. The number of ships in royal ownership had been greatly increased, with emphasis placed on the building or acquisition of large sailing ships on the lines of the carracks of Genoa. Oared vessels still had a place in an English fleet, but the preferred balingers were also fast and manoeuvrable under sail. The galleys which dominated warfare in the Mediterranean had perhaps proved to be less useful in northern waters. What was virtually a corps of royal shipmasters had been created, paid by annual grants from the Exchequer. Most importantly, a regular system of patrols was implemented in the summer months to counter any attempts by the French and their allies in Castile and Genoa to interrupt the supply and transport of royal forces to northern France and to disrupt seaborne commerce. The Earl of Huntingdon's successful cruise which had resulted in the capture of four carracks was one of three patrols at sea in the summer of 1417. The other two patrols led by Thomas Carrew and Pons, Lord Castelhon, captured another five smaller ships, at least three of Spanish origin. In 1418 and 1419 strong patrols also went to sea but no more prizes were taken, perhaps because the enemy was now much less able to put an opposing fleet to sea, as most of the Channel coast of France was in the hands of the English or their Burgundian allies.[48] The last recorded patrol in the summer of 1420 is notable for the near mutiny on board the *Gracedieu*, rather than any action against the French.[49]

At this point Henry's naval policy must have seemed to be resoundingly successful. The Channel was once more a waterway dividing the domains of the English Crown or under the control of their allies, and no longer a hostile frontier. On the sudden death of the King, the dismantling of his navy and the abandonment of his policies must have seemed only prudent with all attention turned to the continuing war on land in France. By the middle of the next decade the fortunes of the English had begun the decline which ended with the defeat at Castillon and the loss of all territories in France, except Calais and the Pale in 1453. There was little expectation of set-piece battles at sea involving the navy of England, however defined, for the remainder of the fifteenth century.

## CHAPTER 8

# Corsairs and Commanders

A LTHOUGH SET-PIECE NAVAL BATTLES were rare in our period, low-level violence at sea was commonplace, and much of it has often been treated by later historians as piracy. This word has connotations of flamboyantly illegal and brutal activity and has been much influenced by representations of pirates in a somewhat later period in films and popular fiction. In our period, the same word was used but without the same cultural baggage attached. Particularly from around the fourteenth century, it has been argued that rulers of maritime states bordering the Channel and the Atlantic, France, England, Spain and Portugal and the Low Countries were gradually establishing a distinction between 'pirates' and 'corsairs or privateers'; that is to say between those who acted solely for their own gain without any sanction from a ruler or other authority and those who had some justification for their actions which therefore made them at least arguably legitimate.[1] We have already mentioned this problem in chapter 2 but will deal with it in more detail here. It is hard to determine whether a trend in this direction is discernible in the way activities of this kind were viewed in England in our period. The precise impact of robbery at sea or commerce-raiding on trade or inter-state relations at this time is also hard to determine.

## Prizes and the law of the sea

It is true that the enforcement of law on the high seas posed particular difficulties for medieval rulers, as ideas like territorial waters were not recognised. It is not true, however, that it was widely accepted that attacks on shipping and the looting of cargoes need incur no penalties at all and no attempts could be made to control activities of this nature. The problem for seafarers, merchants and legal authorities was that in a wide range of cases the capture of a ship with its cargo could be plausibly justified. It was accepted, for example, that if an individual had suffered loss in a way in which legal redress had not been available, he had the right to recompense himself as best he could. The principles underlying the concept of reprisals were relatively clearly defined; in medieval times it was well understood that, if undertaken according to the correct procedures, reprisals were not acts of war but a legitimate way of getting justice when all other means had failed. A shipowner or merchant who had lost goods had to be able to show in court that the loss had occurred as a result of violence, and that all previous attempts to get redress via the law or personal appeals to the authorities and the like had failed. The amount claimed must also not exceed the amount originally lost. Many of those involved in legal cases or incidents referred to in the Patent Rolls and similar sources in our period would not have considered themselves as thieves or robbers but as injured parties seeking just recompense.

It was also the case that, in some circumstances, rulers encouraged shipowners and shipmasters to go to sea with the intention of attacking enemy shipping by allowing them to keep all, or more often a proportion, of the value of any prizes taken. An idea of 'general' reprisal for the costs of war might be involved; also the masters of such vessels might be given authority by letters of marque to prey on enemy shipping. Such letters usually specified that attacks should be confined to the 'King's enemies', something which might be very hard to define when truces could come into operation at short notice, or when safe-conducts were issued to named individuals, or when the goods of 'friends' were carried on 'enemy' ships. In many of the cases for which records survive, the issue was not whether the ship and its cargo had fallen victim to attackers but whether the attackers had reasonable justification for their actions.[2]

Marsden suggests that as the political importance of piracy or robbery at sea became more important during the wars of the fourteenth and fifteenth centuries so its criminal aspect 'seems to have been lost sight of'. The English Crown certainly negotiated numerous agreements with other states to try and bring an element of control or greater certainty into the area of the legitimate taking of prizes at sea. A treaty with Spain in 1351 set out that French goods in Spanish ships would not be treated as prizes, since the French had agreed that English goods in Spanish ships would be similarly exempt. Another treaty with Portugal in 1353 stated that both English and Portuguese goods captured in enemy ships would be restored, provided no help was offered by either state to these enemies. The particular difficulties which affected traffic in the Narrow Seas between England and Flanders were subject to intense negotiations between the Crown in England and the Count and the Four Members of Flanders, Bruges, the Franc of Bruges, Ghent and Ypres, in the first decades of the fifteenth century. All parties had a strong economic interest on the free flow of trade in wool and other goods between both sides of the Channel. Merchant truces and arrangements for safe conducts were signed at frequent intervals in these years although enforcement was patchy at best.[3]

The English Crown finally made an attempt to deal with clear breaches of truces by vessels of all kinds in 1414 when an act was passed to appoint officials called conservators of truces in ports, who would be under the direction of the admiral and his court. The breaking of truces would be considered treason, subject to all the awful penalties of that crime. There is little record of the activity of these conservators and the act was suspended in 1436 and 1442 and then re-enacted in 1450 without the provisions about treason which had perhaps made it unenforceable.[4] To a medieval seafarer the sea, particularly in time of war, could be a dangerous and unfriendly place, with the possibility of losing both ship and cargo to robbery at sea always possible.

At least some of those involved in this so-called piracy, however, would have felt they were acting legitimately. Despite the number of complaints made to the King and his council and which later reached the courts, particularly Chancery, in our period, it is very hard to ascertain whether the overall level of violence seriously affected the level of seaborne traffic of all kinds. Looking at the figures for the export of raw wool from English ports in the second half of the fourteenth century and the whole fifteenth century it is very hard to find any correlation between variations in these and what is known about the incidence of robbery at sea. The reign of Henry IV (1399–1410) has been characterised as a period when piracy was a particular problem, but there is no sudden or obvious deterioration visible in the figures from the Customs accounts. Looking at the similar figures for cloth exports, these fluctuate from 1399–1410 but begin a steady rise around the mid 1430s when there were also many complaints of robbers in the Channel.[5] It was essential for petitioners in cases taken to court dealing with the loss of goods at sea to prove that their property had been taken from them by violence. This might well have been an incentive to emphasise this aspect of the case in the petition. It is also the case, however, that at certain periods the Commons in Parliament complained bitterly about the lack of security on the high seas for merchants and their goods. Even so, trade continued and merchants managed to prosper throughout our period.

## Corsairs

What is more to the point when writing about the navy of England is that some of those who have been labelled pirates were also consummate seamen. The skills needed to board a merchant ship in order to take over the vessel and the cargo were, of course, hardly different from those needed to board an enemy ship in an engagement. The general navigational skills honed by frequently cruising in the Channel and off the coast of Brittany were equally valuable to a corsair or to a shipmaster in the service of the Crown. It is also probable that shipmasters who had proved themselves successful as 'pirates' or 'corsairs' would have had the support of crews made up of experienced seamen probably adept at boarding hostile ships on the high seas, exactly the kind of men needed to man royal ships. The careers of some of the best known 'piratical' shipmasters in our period make clear that rulers were not averse to using their skills in time of need.

### Eustace the Monk

Eustace the Monk was probably the first to make a reputation as both a 'pirate' and as a commander of a royal fleet. His career in this case became a matter of folklore enlivened with stories of his abilities as a wizard who could make his ship invisible, and who had something of the same appeal as Robin Hood. On a more sober level it was still extraordinary. He was born around 1170 in the Boulonnais and for a brief period entered the Benedictine Order at the monastery of St Samer near Calais. He left the order around 1200, perhaps to avenge the murder of his father, and became an outlaw and fugitive in northern France, at some point acquiring skills as a shipmaster. By 1205 he was intermittently in the pay of King John and had set up a base on the Channel Islands from which he conducted attacks on shipping. John used his services as a way of exerting pressure on Philip II Augustus of France. Eustace, however, fell out with John around 1212 and transferred his allegiance to France not only to the King, Philip II, but also to his son Louis the Dauphin. The ships and merchants of the Cinque Ports seem to have suffered particularly from the depredations of their former ally.

When Louis invaded England in 1216 in support of the baronial rebellion against John, landing at Stonor, across the harbour from Sandwich, Eustace was in command of his fleets and instrumental in ensuring the arrival of the French forces and their supplies. The French in fact rapidly took Sandwich and used it as their supply base. In August 1217 it was again Eustace who commanded the French fleet, once more attempting to resupply the French, and whose death was greeted with so much joy by the triumphant mariners of the Cinque Ports, not surprisingly particularly Sandwich, after the English victory in the battle of Dover. This career pattern could easily be interpreted as that of a man of violence whose main concern was his own interests, a typical pirate in modern eyes. He was, however, an effective corsair in the pay of the English Crown and a fleet commander for the French Crown in his last years. Much if not all of his commerce-raiding could have been included under the heading of legitimate reprisals. His competence as a seaman, however, was never questioned. The author of the *Romance of Eustace the Monk* was convinced that he only finally met his death because the English adopted unorthodox tactics:

> Eustace's men defended themselves so strenuously that their opponents could not get on board. Then they [the English] began to hurl well-ground lime in large pots which they smashed to pieces on the ship's rails. The powder rose in great clouds and it was this that caused the most damage ... their eyes [the French] were full of powder. Those who were tormenting them were up wind ... All the barons were captured and Eustace was killed.[6]

The execution of Eustace the Monk; the beheading of Eustace on board his own ship at the end of the battle of Dover, probably by men of the Cinque Ports, was seen as just recompense for the destruction he had wrought as a corsair and in the pay of the French Crown.

(CORPUS CHRISTI, CAMBRIDGE)

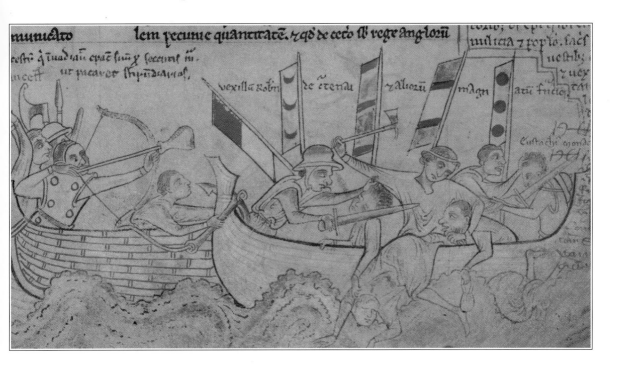

## John Crabbe

That this kind of swift changing of allegiance was not all that uncommon at this period is also shown by the somewhat similar history of John Crabbe. His activities were first recorded in 1305. He was of Flemish origin from the maritime community of Muiden on the Scheldt estuary. He was caught up in the political rivalries in this part of the world, where the Count of Holland and Zeeland was a bitter rival of the Count of Flanders. This was further complicated by the opposition of the leading Flemish commercial cities, including Ghent and Bruges, to the Count of Flanders and his overlord the King of France. Some at least of the attacks on shipping between 1305 and around 1317 in the Channel and North Sea for which Crabbe and his men were responsible can be related to the intertwined relations of England, Scotland and France with each other and with Flanders. To many, including the writer of a poem, he was just an evildoer:

> He wrought great damage on the seas showing mercy to no one. Now he appeared here. Now he served one person next he turned against him and sought the favour of another. Such is the evil company of robbers. [7]

A section of the walls of Berwick, the frontier town, the possession of which was long disputed between the English and the Scots. Its good harbour made it a vital part of an English supply route to an army in Scotland.

(JULIAN MANNERING)

He had a particularly valuable association with Berwick and Robert the Bruce from 1318, being responsible for the defence of the town against the English. In 1333/4, however, English fortunes in Scotland were in the ascendant and Crabbe fell into the hands of Edward III. Despite the demands in Parliament for his crimes against English shipping and mariners to be punished, Crabbe was taken into the King's service and soon proved his worth. He organised shipping for the Crown, advised once more on the defences of Berwick, now in English hands, and helped patrol the seas against raiders in the opening years of the Hundred Years War. He was present at the battle of Sluys and commanded the English vessels, a squadron of around forty ships, ordered to give chase to those French ships which were attempting to flee the battle and the slaughter. He was still in the service of the English Crown around 1346 and died at Somerton Castle in Lincolnshire in 1352, probably well into his seventies and a respected member of the gentry. It is hard to judge all of his career; some of his exploits were on the very borders of legitimacy, but others often involved the goods or shipping of enemies of the ruler to whom he owed loyalty, whether Flanders, Scotland or England. To some extent at least this made them fair game in his mind. It is also the case that, as with Eustace the Monk, his skills as a seaman and as a commander of a fleet were evident to his contemporaries. They were sufficiently obvious in fact for Edward III to gloss over speedily Crabbe's service to the Scottish Crown and to make use of his skills for the benefit of the navy of England.[8]

*Harry Pay*

The lack of a clear division between robbery at sea for personal gain, legally sanctioned reprisals against the King's enemies, and official 'seakeeping' patrols and voyages is also particularly evident in the first years of the fifteenth century. Much attention has focused on a group of seafarers and shipowners from the west of England. The best known are Harry Pay of Poole, also known as 'arripay' by the Castilians, and the Hawleys of Dartmouth, a father and son both called John. Harry Pay probably acted more in his own interest than some of his contemporaries. He achieved notoriety in Castile by sacking Finisterre, including the shrine of the Virgin in the town.[9] He was, however, evidently a skilled navigator with experience of routes as far south as northern Spain as well as in the Channel. In 1405 and 1406 he took part in seakeeping expeditions on behalf of the Crown.[10]

John Hawley from his memorial brass in St Saviour's Church, Dartmouth. He was a local worthy, as well as a famous ship owner and promoter of privateers.

**(REBECCA WRIGHT)**

*The Hawley family*

John Hawley the elder was a man of considerable local importance, who had begun life as no more than the younger son of a tenant farmer from Allaleigh. He had come to Dartmouth to make his fortune and had risen to be the town's mayor on several occasions and an MP. He was wealthy enough at his death to be commemorated by a brass in St Saviour's church, of which he was a benefactor. The brass shows him as a knight in full armour; in fifteenth-century terms he had made the leap from the common people to the urban elite and the fringes of the gentry.[11]

There is no doubt that the rise of the family was due in large part to their activities as shipowners and ships' masters as well as merchants. Both father and son were a vital part of the maritime community of their town and would have had a great deal of experience in the best way to deploy their own vessels and those of their colleagues and collaborators. To recent historians, however, the Hawleys are pirates, corsairs or privateers (the terms are used interchangeably), robbing other seafarers without shame, and a problem for Henry IV which he was unable to deal with. The exploits of John Hawley the older, however, as described in legal documents, involved considerable organisation and nautical skill. One major enterprise was the capture of seven Spanish ships in the Channel, in conjunction with Thomas Norton of Bristol, with mixed cargoes including iron, wheat, cloth, oil and white soap. Some of these goods belonged to Flemish, Italian and Navarrese merchants and some to Castilians. All the prizes were taken into Plymouth in October 1403, setting off prolonged litigation by those robbed for the restitution of their property. There was at least an arguable case that the seizure of some of these goods could be justified as legitimate reprisals.[12]

Another case concerning the younger John Hawley in 1412 gives an even more vivid picture of the world in which these men operated. Hawley was at sea with Lord Carrew and others from Dartmouth, cruising to 'destroy the enemies of the king and the realm'. Off Brittany they took a crayer (a small merchant ship) loaded with wine which was the property of Frenchmen, the King's enemies. Hawley put a prize crew of six men on board to bring the ship and cargo into Dartmouth. The Breton crew got free and killed four of the English mariners. Another English balinger, the *George of Paignton*, then re-took the Breton ship and sailed it into Torbay. Hawley then caused two of his own balingers 'to be arrayed in unlawfully hostile manner with a hundred men or more arrayed

Dartmouth Castle and the entrance to the harbour. Dartmouth was one of the most important West Country ports in this period.

**(WIKIMEDIA)**

for war' to sail to Torbay. There the crew of the *George* were so frightened when they saw Hawley's ships approaching that they fled ashore leaving the vessel and the wine to Hawley's men, who took it into Dartmouth. The Chancery case was brought by the Paignton men who petitioned for £250 damages. There is no record of whether they were successful.[13]

Cases like these, however, do provide an insight into the commerce-raiding which was undoubtedly rife in these waters at this period. There was not, as we have said, an entirely lawless free-for-all. The ownership of a vessel or the goods carried was important; were the King's enemies involved? Was a truce in operation or some other form of treaty? The law, as it was understood, and the courts, had a role in these matters as the surviving documentation demonstrates. On the other hand, the men involved were used to a harsh and violent environment and acted at least partly in self-interest; they would have little compunction in taking what they could get. It has also been suggested that another strand to be considered in the matter of piracy in the Channel at this date is the attitude of Henry IV. Was he pursuing the policy of conducting a form of semi-official economic warfare at sea against the French and their allies, in which men like Hawley and Pay were his tools? It is often forgotten that English merchants and shipowners suffered from the seizure of ships and the loss of cargo to much the same extent as their French and Flemish counterparts.[14]

Developments in the reign of Henry V, when there was no question that England was at war with France and that this war had an important maritime element, demonstrate how useful to the Crown, perhaps more precisely how essential to English actions in the Channel and adjacent waters, was the experience and seamanship of men like John Hawley the younger and his associates. The older Hawley had a record of service to his community as mayor and a Member of Parliament, as we have seen. He held office in the customs administration and as an escheator for Devon. His son followed much the same career path as mayor and MP, and was also escheator and from 1422–31 a JP. This made both men part of the machinery of royal government, an essential element in ensuring the continuity and stability of national life.

Their sea service was much more exceptional and not always at odds with their official roles on shore. At this time the clear division between the royal navy and privateers as properly understood in the eighteenth century did not exist. It is clear that the Hawleys were able to put together a squadron of ships which was well able to give a good account of itself in a fight. We have already seen the younger Hawley at sea with Lord Carrew in 1412. In 1419 and 1420 he was involved with patrols in the Channel with Sir Hugh Courtenay. Before this in 1416 he had donated his balinger *Craccher*, a 56-tun single-masted ship to the Crown. On the death of Henry V this was sold to a group of Devon men, including John William of Kingswear. This man was one of the most distinguished of Henry V's group of royal shipmasters, being master first of the *Jesus* and then of the *Gracedieu*, the largest of the King's great ships. He had begun his career in Dartmouth with the Hawleys, was promoted in the service of the King, and ended his days as a respected citizen and merchant of Southampton.

The fifteenth-century tower at Polruan which protected the harbour at Fowey, the leading Cornish port and base for many 'sea rovers'.

(AUTHOR'S COLLECTION)

### The Mixtow family

Similarly, the Mixtow family, from a village near Fowey, moved easily between actions seen as piratical by their accusers in the courts and service to the Crown at sea. In 1402 Mark Mixtow led a group of ships from Fowey acting against a fleet sailing under the Scottish flag, led by the Earl of Crawford, but in fact largely made up of French ships.[15] George Mixtow was the first master of Henry V's new barge, the *Falcon*, and was one of the group of royal shipmasters paid by annual Exchequer grant. In the 1430s, John Mixtow, together with a group of West Country sailors from St Austell, Polruan and Taunton, captured a Genoese carrack with a valuable cargo, some of which was the property of John Chirche, a leading London merchant. It was alleged in the petition in Chancery that the attack had taken place as far south as Cape St Vincent, and that the wretched crew of the caravel had been put ashore destitute in Portugal, accused of being 'saracens'. This Cornish family were clearly excellent seamen, even if sometimes operating on the borders of legality.[16]

All these men and their colleagues had the skills in ship-handling, navigation and in engaging with the enemy, which were badly needed for the King's ships. It is neither surprising nor an indication of royal weakness that many were recruited for service to the Crown. There was no other source of the experience needed to handle and command ships in warfare at sea. Fleets setting forth in the King's name might have the monarch himself on board and ostensibly in command. Otherwise a noble, often one distinguished in land warfare, might hold the highest rank; all, however, needed the help and support of men like John Hawley. As long ago as 1924 a historian called piracy emanating from West Country ports at this period, 'the school of English seamen'; this judgment perhaps still stands.[17] The distinction between men like these and groups like the *Vitalienbrüder*, a group of renegade seamen not controlled by any ruler, who preyed without mercy on shipping in the Baltic and the North Sea, *c*.1390–*c*.1402, was not lost on contemporaries. A chronicle written in Lubeck records how a fleet from the Hanseatic towns defeated them and captured seventy of the pirates: 'all were beheaded; their heads were set up in a meadow beside the Elbe as a sign they had committed robbery at sea.'[18] These men did not end their lives as members of the gentry like at least some of the West Country seamen.

## Commanders

The leaders of royal fleets in this period did not achieve the same fame as the leaders of land armies, and perhaps had less prominence in popular report than the best-known corsairs. The office of admiral was not usually associated with valour, but with more mundane matters of fleet organisation and supply.

### Admirals

The office of admiral first appeared in the reign of Edward I with the appointment of Sir William Leyburn by the King in 1295. The title was originally given to individuals appointed on an 'ad hoc' basis for a particular year or campaign with responsibility for a geographical area. Normally this would be for the North, in fact the east coast from the Thames northwards or for the South, from the Thames estuary and the Kent coast to the West Country. Those appointed were often distinguished soldiers and commanders on land, but often had little or no experience of the sea. This was not a matter of great importance in many cases, since their duties were largely concerned with the assembling of a fleet, its manning and the maintenance of discipline, largely before their embarkation, among the large body of men assembled as both mariners and soldiers. Since, as we have seen, the great majority of royal fleets were engaged in the logistical support of a land campaign, the skills needed of an admiral were mainly very similar to those needed on land by the leader of an army. The lack of continuity may have caused difficulties; between 1295 and 1407 over one hundred separate appointments were made to this office according to one list which has been compiled. Another, looking in more detail at the reign of Edward III reveals that certain individuals were frequently reappointed. None, however, were similar to the admirals of later centuries. They were not trained as seamen and probably seldom went to sea themselves, with the exception of one or two individuals whose careers will be discussed below.[19]

Admirals' responsibilities relating to the command or organisation of royal fleets were defined probably in the late fourteenth or early fifteenth centuries. A copy in Norman French in the *Black Book of the Admiralty* of rules for the office is entitled 'Old rules for

the Lord Admiral'. This sets out regulations for a fleet, including the need to keep together and the use of lanterns at the masthead at night, for example, but also lays stress on the admiral's jurisdiction and the conduct of his courts. The incidence of violence at sea, and the equivocal position of those apparently committing robbery at sea already discussed, naturally encouraged the growth of admirals' courts dealing particularly with this problem. The courts, however, reflecting the lack of differentiation between royal and merchant service at sea also dealt with 'commercial' cases. The text in the *Black Book of the Admiralty* claims that 'any contract made between merchant and merchant or merchant and mariner beyond the sea or within the flood mark shall be tried before the admiral and nowhere else.'[20] These courts certainly functioned in this way from the first half of the fourteenth century but never had exclusive jurisdiction in either commercial cases or those involving violence at sea. The legal powers of the admirals were restricted by legislation in the fifteenth century, leaving the courts largely concerned with technical cases dealing with matters such as collisions, jettison and errors by pilots.[21] The operation of the courts, however, remained among the admiral's responsibilities.

The regulations for the fleet lay out wage scales and the like. They make clear that supreme command rests with the King if he is present and that the royal ship must be identified by three 'great lanterns' with one hung above the other two. The admiral's ship and that of his lieutenants must also be identified so the fleet can keep together at night. The document lays down the signal needed to call shipmasters together for a council and sets out the way in which the value of prizes should be allocated. It has, however, nothing to say about warfare or tactics or conduct in the face of the enemy, except that the ship which first sees 'any enemies vessel upon the sea then he shall putt a flag aloft', so that the admiral may then 'contrive the best they can to meet therewith'.[22]

*Gervase Alard*

One commander from the early thirteenth century, who has some claim to the title of admiral, but whose activities were also comparable to those of the Hawley family around a century later, was Gervase Alard. By popular report, he is commemorated in a magnificent tomb in St Thomas's Church in Winchelsea. On this he is described as the first Admiral of the Fleet in English history. The chantry, however, which included the tomb was founded in 1312 by another member of the family, Stephen Alard; the very similar adjacent tomb dates from between 1319 and 1323, and was associated with a chantry founded by one Robert Alard, the son of John Alard. There is no doubt that the family was very prominent in the town and the Cinque Ports as a whole, even if the identification of the figure on the tomb has little documentary support.[23]

Gervase was a master mariner and described as the Admiral of the Fleet from the Cinque Ports in Exchequer accounts and the Wardrobe Books from this period.[24] This fleet was operating off Scotland in support of the forces of Edward I in 1300, 1303 and 1306. He was also, like the Hawleys, involved in at least one case of robbery at sea. As Admiral of the Fleet in Scotland, although there are no records of any involvement of him or the ships in his charge in naval action, his pay was 2s per day, four times that of a shipmaster. In old age he petitioned the King for the seisin (legal possession) of some land at Pevensey called the Island, since he had received little for all his efforts for the crown in Gascony, Flanders, Normandy and Scotland, except a horse worth 4 marks and a sum of money handed over to him at Ross in Galloway.[25] He was, however, granted the town of New Winchelsea for life in November 1306, in succession to the late keeper, Thomas Alard, who may have been his father.[26]

*Noble commanders in the fourteenth century*

During the reign of Edward III those appointed admirals were usually of noble status with a reputation as leaders in land warfare. Clearly, little weight was placed on any nautical experience they might have but some were, even so, frequently reappointed. This was possible because the specifically maritime responsibilities of the office were carried by their lieutenants, some of whom are known to have been seamen, although it is hard to find many details of their careers. Examples of the appointment of leading soldiers and colleagues of the King to the position of admiral are Walter Manny (Admiral of the North in 1337 and 1338), the first and second Earls of Suffolk, and Richard Fitzalan, Earl of Arundel. Walter Manny was Admiral of the North in both 1337 and 1338 in conjunction with Robert Ufford, later Earl of Suffolk, and Thomas Drayton. Manny has been described as 'the model soldier of his age ... gallant and courageous', even though it has also been claimed that he had 'little strategic grasp'. He was also something of a hero to Froissart, who gave his exploits prominence in his writings. In warfare at sea, more or less nothing is known of his personal actions, although he was said to be present at Sluys and very probably also at Winchelsea.[27] His most important achievement as far as the navy of England was concerned was probably his capture of John Crabbe at the siege of Berwick and his sale of Crabbe, because of his value as a captive, to Edward III for

1000 marks.[28] Richard and William Ufford, successively Earls of Suffolk, and Richard Fitzalan, Earl of Arundel, had very similar careers to Manny, all being successful soldiers and supporters of the King fighting in campaigns in Scotland and France. Their appointments as admiral, whether of the North or the South, seem to have been more a token of the regard in which they were held by the monarch, than any indication of their interest in or prowess at the art of command in war at sea. The lieutenants, who in all likelihood supplied the expertise in naval matters, included Thomas Drayton, who had had some involvement in 'piratical' attacks on enemy shipping in the Channel,[29] and Philip Whitton, of whom little is known. Philip Courtenay, another lieutenant, came from the well-known Devon seafaring family of which the most prominent member was Hugh Courtenay, Earl of Devon in the reign of Henry V. The family seat was at Powderham Castle, looking out over the River Exe, facing the port of Topsham.

### Robert Morley, 2nd Lord Morley

The most prominent of these noble commanders of royal fleets in the middle years of the fourteenth century was Robert Morley, who was in command at Sluys in 1340, and perhaps also at the engagement in the Channel off Winchelsea in 1350. He was born around 1295 on the estates of his father, the first Lord Morley, in Norfolk, and is likely to have had the usual upbringing of a young man of the nobility, training in knightly pursuits, and the art of fighting on horseback. There is some evidence that he may also have gained some early experience at sea as a shipmaster and as a shipowner.[30] He began his career fighting in Scotland for Edward II and was also at the battle of Halidon Hill in 1333. The first indication of an aptitude for maritime affairs came when he was appointed keeper of the maritime land in Norfolk, although this post was concerned with the defence of coastal communities on land, not seakeeping or the like.[31] In February 1339, however, he was made Admiral of the North, in charge of the east coast ports north of the Thames estuary. The summer of this year was notable for a series of determined French raids on the Cinque Ports. Morley's fleet cruised in the Channel and successfully drove the raiders away from Rye. In the course of protecting a convoy of wool ships bound for Flanders, Morley came up with a French fleet escorted by Genoese galleys. Morley's fleet chased the enemy into Sluys and caused a lot of damage. This had some unfortunate legal consequences, since one of the most valuable ships attacked was in fact a neutral Spanish vessel, but it gave Morley and his colleagues up-to-date recent knowledge of the port of Sluys and the waters around it.[32] The affray may also have awakened Morley's interest in war at sea.

This experience was certainly of great value to Edward III's forces in the summer of the following year. We have already seen how in the days before the battle of Sluys, the King sent for Robert Morley and John Crabbe to ask their advice.[33] At least one chronicler commented that Crabbe, the former 'pirate' now in Edward's service, was involved because of his skills as a seaman and knowledge of the Flemish coast.[34] A sizeable fleet was collected within ten days and set sail for Sluys. At the battle Morley, the leader of the northern contingent with many vessels from Yarmouth and Lynn, is recorded as being in the van, together with the Earls of Gloucester, North-ampton, and Huntingdon. There is little reliable information about the precise tactics used in the battle, but Morley with his lieutenant, Crabbe, seems to have played an important role in the crushing English victory.

After this episode, although still Admiral of the North, Morley was more involved in fighting on land than at sea. He died in 1360 a few days after the successful French raid on Winchelsea, leaving the Admiralty of the North in a state of some confusion, with many shipowners refusing to serve the Crown. It is hard to be certain of Morley's own prowess as the commander of a fleet, but at least he had enough awareness of the skills necessary to use the services of John Crabbe, whose reputation as an excellent commander of ships was well-founded. He also benefited from the help of the experienced Thomas Drayton, employed in the role of lieutenant from 1337–55. John Wesenham, a well-known mer-chant, shipowner and royal financier from East Anglia, was something of a disaster as Morley's final lieutenant in 1359 and 1360. He was probably more adept at building up his own fortune than organising a fleet and was not trusted by other shipowners, leading to the confusion on Morley's death.[35]

## Commanders in the fifteenth century

Since naval actions had so much greater prominence in the reign of Henry V, it might be thought that greater prestige would attach to those who filled the role of commander at sea in this period. There was, however, little consistency over the course of the whole century in attitudes to commanders; some, especially in the period when the Crown had ceased to own ships of its own, acted as much in their own interests as those of the realm

A picture of John, Duke of Bedford, in a Book of Hours commissioned by himself and his wife.

(BRITISH LIBRARY)

### The Duke of Bedford

The Duke was the first to benefit from a major change in the way the office was designated and in the responsibilities attached to it. A sole Admiral of England was appointed, who could expect to hold the office for life unless dismissed. All holders of the office of admiral in the fifteenth century were, moreover, members of the highest rank in the nobility, with many being closely related to the monarch himself. There were by this time perquisites attached to the office which made it a profitable appointment. The most notable among the admirals of the first half of the century was John, Duke of Bedford, Henry V's brother, appointed in 1426. Some ten years earlier he had in fact been credited with a notable naval victory when he successfully relieved Harfleur and captured four Genoese carracks.[36] After 1426, however, despite holding this office, his notable service to the Crown was in northern France where he was in charge of the governance of those areas which were ruled by the English.

### John Holand, Earl of Huntingdon and Duke of Exeter

Bedford was succeeded as Admiral in 1435 by John Holand, Earl of Huntingdon and Duke of Exeter from 1444. He had had some experience at sea as a young man, leading a successful Channel patrol in 1417, but by the time he was appointed the squadron of royal ships had been dispersed, and his interest in the office was probably purely financial. By this time, of course, the Crown owned no ships of its own, the last being the balinger, *Petit Jesus*, handed over to its last master, Richard Rowe, some time after being rebuilt in 1435.

Later holders of the post in the fifteenth century continued this trend of regarding the post as an honour bestowed by the Crown with useful perquisites, but necessitating little personal involvement in naval affairs or fighting at sea. Richard, Duke of Gloucester, the later Richard III, was Admiral from 1462–83. A brief interregnum in his hold on the office in 1471 and his replacement by Richard Neville, Earl of Warwick, was related to the turmoil in English affairs linked to the readeption of Henry VI. John Howard, 1st Duke of Norfolk, held the position from 1483–85 when John de Vere, 13th Earl of Oxford, took over. Responsibility for the defence of the realm by sea was in the hands of leaders serving under individual indentures rather than the Admiral of England.

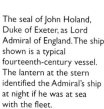

The seal of John Holand, Duke of Exeter, as Lord Admiral of England. The ship shown is a typical fourteenth-century vessel. The lantern at the stern identified the Admiral's ship at night if he was at sea with the fleet.

(© NATIONAL MARITIME MUSEUM, GREENWICH, LONDON)

## Defence by indentured forces

The lack of 'seakeeping' in the Channel became a constant plaint of merchants and others in Parliament, with a scheme being put forward by a Commons petition in 1442 for a force to be 'upon the sea continually' from Candlemas to Martinmas, consisting of 'eight ships with forestages', each attended by a barge and a balinger, with four pinnaces presumably for scouting purposes. This force was estimated to cost in wages and victualling for six months over £4500. The great ships would be provided by major

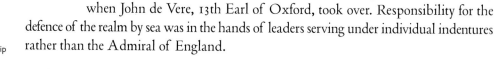

ports including Bristol, London, Hull and Newcastle, while the barges and balingers would come from ports like Saltash, Fowey, Sandwich and Winchelsea. Particularly prominent among those providing ships was Sir Philip Courtenay of Powderham Castle, who clearly owned a number of ships based at Dartmouth. Despite the Crown apparently accepting the petition there is no evidence that the scheme in the form set out in the petition was ever implemented.[37]

The Crown should have had adequate resources to finance a scheme of this kind since the duties on imports known as tonnage and poundage had been imposed on a regular basis since the accession of Henry IV and were specifically intended for the keeping of the seas. Royal finances, however, were under so much stress by the 1430s that money for naval expeditions was hard to find now that Henry V's squadron of royal ships had been dispersed. The situation in the Channel had also begun to change decisively in favour of the French. The alliance between the Burgundians and the English had broken down, with the Duke of Burgundy reasserting his loyalty to the French crown. Boulogne was part of his territories, while Calais and the Pale, besieged by the Burgundians in 1436, were now surrounded by hostile territory. Control of the ports on the Norman coast was crucial to English efforts to hold on to their conquests in northern France, and to protect English shipping from French corsairs. Dieppe, with a good harbour and an aggressive and skilled population of seamen, was under French rule from 1435. Harfleur, the starting point for English successes in France, was also in French hands from 1435–40. Crotoy, on the estuary of the Somme, was also under extreme pressure from French forces in the early 1440s, but remained in English hands until 1448. Other major ports on this coastline all came under French control in the final campaign of 1449/50. By the end of this year, Rouen, Harfleur and Cherbourg were all restored to the rule of Charles VII of France.

In the immediate crisis of 1435/6 the English Crown has issued licences to individual captains to take to the seas against the King's enemies. In 1440 an English force had been organised under an indenture to help in the retaking of Harfleur.[38] In 1442, perhaps as a partial response to the Commons petition, Sir Stephen Popham undertook in June to take a force to sea to deal with the King's enemies under the terms of an indenture, but little was achieved. The force itself was not mustered till September and then nothing more is recorded of it.[39] It is not surprising that the rebels led by John Cade in 1450, who came predominantly from Kent, should have included in their list of complaints to the King the claim that 'the sea is lost'.[40] The consequences for the towns on the south coast of England of the loss of control of the Norman coastline were finally made brutally clear by the French raid on Sandwich in 1457. The newly-built fortifications were no match for the French forces who killed the mayor and thoroughly pillaged the town.

With the Crown having withdrawn from shipowning, defence against raids on coastal towns or against attacks on merchant shipping could only be provided by ships owned by private individuals. These would be liable for requisition, as in earlier periods, or could form part of forces serving under indentures at royal expense, but there was little sense of continuity in service of this kind. Since, as we have pointed out, many of the most successful commanders of vessels in sea warfare of any kind had gained what experience they had as corsairs or pirates, however these terms are defined, this situation tended to blur even more the distinction between lawful defence and unlawful robbery at sea. Shipowners and shipmasters could slip only too easily from one category to the other. It is also the case that since there are very few records of ships in private ownership which give details of their construction or armament, or the way they were operated, it is hard to have a clear idea of the maritime resources of England in this period. It has been stated that at least some shipowners were of noble or gentle status. Lord Say owned a carvel, while one of the Rivers family owned the vessel known as the *Star Rivers*. Most is known about the ships of John Howard, Duke of Norfolk from 1476, because of the survival of his Household Books which include some of the expenses incurred by his ships. These include the accounts of the building of his carvel, the *Edward* of Dunwich. He was also involved with some indentured service to the Crown at sea, employing at least three of his own ships.[41]

### Richard Neville, Earl of Warwick

Against this depressing background of the apparent lack of any coherent plan by the Crown to protect English shipping and trade or even, it must have seemed, coastal settlements, together with the increasing divisions among the nobility which eventually led to civil war, it is something of a relief to turn to the maritime aspects of the career of Richard Neville, the Earl of Warwick. Warwick is perhaps not often thought of in this context; his soubriquet of Kingmaker rightly reflects the view that he was a highly skilled political operator who used the divisions between the rival royal clans of the Lancastrians and the Yorkists to advance his own interests and those of his family. As far as can be ascertained, he did not himself have any experience or nautical skills, whether as a tactician commanding ships at sea or as a navigator. He did, however, have a clear and sophisticated grasp of the possibilities and advantages of the strategic use of sea-power and how this might be used to advance his aims.

His first commission with a maritime element undertaken in 1451, to suppress piracy in the Channel Islands, was perhaps of a conventional nature. From around 1455, however, he became gradually more involved in maritime matters in a way in which allowed him to exercise considerable power and influence over events in England. He was appointed Captain of Calais in 1455, and once installed in the English enclave in the following year he was frequently resident in the town, making good use of its potential to control traffic in the Channel as a base for sea patrols. At the same time, he also cultivated good relations with the mariners of the Cinque Ports, particularly Sandwich, the port

Richard Neville, Earl of Warwick, with his wife Anne, from a family tree.

(BRITISH LIBRARY)

from which Calais was usually supplied. In 1457 after the disastrous raid on the town by the French, it was not surprising that he was commissioned to go to sea against the King's enemies for a term of three years with the costs covered from the proceeds of tonnage and poundage.[42]

This period of seakeeping is also associated with the accusation that Warwick in fact used Calais as a base for piratical attacks on any shipping in nearby waters with the aim of increasing his personal fortune. One commentator has claimed that the Crown had so little control over Warwick that 'at Calais and on the high seas' he 'was a free agent'.[43] This is certainly a possible interpretation of two sea battles fought by his vessels in 1458. The first took place in May and was reported in a letter to Margaret Paston by John Jernyngan. 'Five schippis of forecastell and iii carvels and iiii pinnaces' sailed from Calais to engage with twenty-eight Spanish ships, 'wherof there was xvi grete shippis of forecastell'. This was perhaps more foolhardy than dashing and certainly the casualties were high, with some eighty of Warwick's men slain and another two hundred briefly captured. Six Spanish ships were sunk, however, and six taken. Tellingly, Jernyngan reported that once the squadron was back at Calais with the news of this encounter, the Earl's reaction was to send 'for more shippis and lyke to fyghte togedr agayne in haste.'[44] Later in the same summer Warwick's men attacked the Hanseatic fleet, returning from the bay of Bourgneuf with salt, taking as many as seventeen ships as prizes. Both this and another attack on Genoese carracks and Spanish ships in the summer of 1459 have been called flagrant but expedient piracy. Certainly these actions filled Warwick's own coffers, allowing him to pay his seamen and the soldiers of the Calais garrison. They also went down very well with many Englishmen in the southern coastal counties who could rejoice that the 'erle of Warrewyk, having a strong and myghte naveye kepte the strayte see', in a way the King could not. And moreover, 'all the cominalte of this lond hadde him in greet laude and chierte.'[45]

In the following year, exploits which can be compared with those of the West Country corsairs of the earlier part of the century were no longer Warwick's main concern. Matters in England, with the Crown in dispute between the supporters of the Lancastrian Henry VI and the Duke of York and his followers, including Warwick, were sliding rapidly towards civil war. It is at this point, rather than in his activities as a buccaneer, that Warwick showed his understanding of the uses of sea-power. Warwick and York had attempted to bring things to a conclusion in the summer of 1459, but had suffered a disastrous defeat in the Midlands, with York fleeing to Ireland, but Warwick and other Yorkists managing to slip back to Calais. The possession of this base and a fleet of ships were crucial in what followed. Warwick could not be dislodged from Calais by Henry's supporters, and was still being supplied from Sandwich. The Lancastrians formed the plan of seizing his ships in the harbour there to isolate the Earl; as a chronicle recorded, the plan was that 'the seyde Lord Ryvers [a leading Lancastrian] shulde kepe certyene grete forstage shyppys that were the Erles of Warrewyk the whyche lay at anker there in the hauene.' News of this plan reached Calais. A small squadron of vessels slipped across the Channel at dawn, 'the whyche took the sayde Lorde Ryvers and Antony his sone in thyre beddes and lad theym ouer to Caleys and took with theym alle the grete shyppes.'[46]

Warwick then sailed for Ireland to join with the Duke of York and, in fact, to plan a Yorkist invasion of England. Henry VI's government, well aware of the threat this posed managed to put together a fleet of their own under the Lord Admiral, the Duke of Exeter. The two forces came up with each other, probably off Dartmouth. The scene seemed to be set for a set-piece naval battle. Waurin, a French chronicler, imagines the news of the presence of Exeter's fleet being brought back to Warwick by a scouting carvel. In his account, the Earl then held a council of war with his shipmasters and prepared for battle, sailing towards the enemy.[47] In one English chronicle, however, it is recorded that Exeter 'durst not sette oppon the erle' or, as another English chronicle explained, 'they fought not for the people being wt the Duke of Excetir ought more favour to therle then to hym'.[48] In either case Exeter withdrew to Dartmouth, while Warwick continued unmolested to Calais. The invasion which led to the crowning of Edward IV and the deposition of Henry VI was launched from this base at the end of June 1460.

It is not easy to be sure of the number and nature of the ships which Warwick himself owned at various times. A vessel named the *Gracedieu* is associated with him in the 1460s and the name can be found in the records as late as 1486, but this was a fairly common ship name at the time, and there is no certainty that the references are all to the same ship.[49] The types mentioned, great ships of forestage, balingers and pinnaces, are those familiar from the earlier part of the century, but by at least the 1460s would have included carvels and ships with three or even four masts. A list of ships used in various seakeeping expeditions by Warwick from 1462–64 includes ten names with tonnages varying from 500 tuns, the *Mary Warwick*, to 80 tuns, the little *Mary Richardson.* Most were around 250 tuns. It must be emphasised that although available to 'keep the seas', none of the ships was in royal ownership.[50]

Warwick's maritime activities were of great benefit to the Yorkists and Edward IV while he continued to support them. The earl, however, turned his forces against them in 1470, when he attempted to seize Calais to use as a base for an attack on England, this time in support of the Lancastrians in the way he had done ten years earlier for the Yorkists. He was frustrated in this, but still managed to exert pressure on shipping in the Channel by attacks by his fleet from a base in the Seine estuary where he had taken refuge. With the aid of the French King Louis XI, he finally crossed to England to restore Henry VI to the throne in September. Edward fled to Flanders while Warwick was able to add the title of Lord Admiral to those he already possessed. His triumph, however, came to nothing in the spring of 1471, when Edward won back his crown with a crushing victory at Barnet at which Warwick was slain.

It may seem strange to praise as a naval commander a man who died the ignoble death of a rebel cut down and stripped of his armour in a wood in Hertfordshire at the age of forty-two. He has often been described as no more than a ruthless pirate,[51] but as his biographer concludes: 'if no future magnate was to deploy sea-power or to commit the Calais garrison in domestic power politics it was because Warwick's example was remembered, feared and guarded against'.[52] In his case, moreover, even as his cause collapsed, his shipmen remained loyal to him and were prepared to fight in his support.

*John Howard, 1st Duke of Norfolk*

It is notable that the strongest statement of the need for a navy in the ownership and control of the crown was made by Sir John Fortescue, probably in 1471 in the immediate aftermath of the events of the previous year and the death of Warwick. His plea that the King 'always keeps some great and mighty vessels for the defeat of an army when any shall be made against him upon the sea. For then it shall be too late to have such vessels made', would have not only resonated with the newly restored Edward IV in relation to foreign states, but also in relation to an 'over-mighty subject' like Warwick. This was, in fact, a topic which Fortescue dealt with very shortly after that of the need for royal ships.[53]

Fortescue's views may have also influenced the organisation of the naval aspects of Edward IV's campaign in Scotland in 1481. John Howard, now Duke of Norfolk, who has already been mentioned as a major shipowner in this period, was put in charge of these arrangements. Many details of the expedition can be found in the second of his surviving sets of household accounts, not in the royal archives. Since his return in 1471, Edward had acquired some ships of his own including the *Antony* bought in 1472, the Spanish ship the *Falcon* bought in 1475, and the *Carvel of Portugal* bought in 1481. The *Carvel of Portugal* and the 'grete Antony' sailed north with Howard, together with his own *Mary Howard* and *Parker Howard*, and at least eight other ships. Another group of seven ships was deployed at the same time to 'kepe the narowe see'.[54] All the ships carried soldiers as well as their crews, and were victualled from the royal purse at the rate of 12½d per man per week. The expedition left Sandwich in May and reached the Firth of Forth a month later. Once there, however, successful raids were carried out along the southern shore of the Firth, while Kinghorn and Pittenween were also attacked. The major aim of the fleet to prevent the French reinforcing the Scots was achieved, and the value of at least a minimum number of royal ships was perhaps demonstrated.[55]

Looking at the way in which fleets in the service of the Crown were commanded from the beginning of the thirteenth to the end of the fifteenth centuries, the impression is created that each separate campaign or expedition was treated in isolation. Early admirals were appointed for a relatively brief period of time to serve a particular purpose. Very often a nobleman, perhaps with considerable military and administrative experience on land, would be appointed, but must have had to rely on the experience and skills of his lieutenants, of a much lower social status, when at sea. It was also the case that many of these 'lieutenants' would have gained their experience of fighting at sea from encounters of at least dubious legality in modern eyes. The Crown was also, it seems, reluctant to undertake the high expenditure necessary to keep a fleet of royal ships ready for action at sea. The realisation that this might be not only desirable but in fact unavoidable, if the realm was to be adequately defended, was only being slowly accepted by the late fifteenth century.

## CHAPTER 9

# The Navies of
# Other European States

THE IDEA THAT ALL SHIPS in the possession of Englishmen and able to go to sea made up the navy of England was deeply rooted in the minds of English monarchs and accepted by English seafarers. However reluctant they might be at times to obey a royal summons to serve the King and defend the realm with their vessels at sea, the existence of this principle was not questioned. English kings from at least the tenth century had at times also owned ships themselves and had used these in a variety of roles. The twists and turns of external circumstances and royal policy ensured that there was little continuity in the royal ownership of ships, or in the way they were financed or maintained. We have seen that some English kings devoted considerable time and energy to the well-being and the proper use of their ships, while others neglected them, or in fact disposed of them entirely. How did the rulers of other states approach the same problem of defending the dwellers on their coasts, their ports and their trade? How did they also attempt to supply the need for ships that could give a good account of themselves in war at sea?

## France

Facing the North Sea and the Atlantic, the kingdom of France possessed, in theory, around 2500 kilometres of coastline, stretching from the estuary of the Zwyn in Flanders to Hendaye on the frontier with Castile. At the beginning of the thirteenth century, however, only the counties of Ponthieu and Artois on the north coast were ruled directly by the French king; other territories including Flanders, Normandy, Brittany, Poitou and Gascony were fiefs of the French Crown, but were ruled directly by dukes or counts who often followed their own policies. This was particularly the case with the territories which were ruled by the Kings of England as dukes, first of Normandy from the Conquest till c.1204 and from c.1417 to c.1450, and second of Gascony (also known as Aquitaine) from 1152, when the future Henry II of England married Eleanor of Aquitaine, till 1453. Brittany, under its own duke, also pursued independent policies until the last years of the fifteenth century, when the French king took over the direct rule of the duchy by marrying Anne, the heiress of the last duke in 1491. As a consequence of this situation, kings of France had taken little interest in maritime matters, until the collapse of English rule in northern France in the reign of King John extended their power over most of the Channel coast. The kings of France, initially Philip II Augustus, now had control over a coastline in the north of their kingdom with excellent ports, where maritime trade was on the rise, and where skilled and adventurous seamen could be found in large numbers. They also had the power to demand feudal service at sea from these mariners and their ships in much the same way as the English Crown could rely on its power to conscript ships and crews for royal fleets. As Michel Mollat put it, 'Philip [II] did not have a fleet but he had ships'.[1] It was a fleet raised in this manner which met with the English at the battle of Dover in 1217.

### Sources for French naval forces

There are not, however, many surviving French equivalents of the letters patent, commissions and accounts which allow historians to examine in detail the fleets largely made up of conscripted merchant ships raised by English kings from the thirteenth century onwards. It is easier to find evidence of the measures taken by French kings to defend their coastline by fortifying ports and building castles, for example at Montreuil-

A fleet at sea; this gives an impression of the imposing spectacle of a royal fleet putting to sea; the majority of the vessels were probably requisitioned and not in royal ownership.

(BRITISH LIBRARY)

Fortifications built along the north coast of France to defend towns and harbours from English raids. *Top left:* Montreuil sur Mer; *bottom left:* Boulogne Castle; Boulogne was raided by the English in 1339–40 just before the battle of Sluys. *Right:* the Tour St Nicolas at La Rochelle; this town changed hands between the French and the English several times in this period.

(WIKIMEDIA)

sur-Mer and Boulogne. After their control also extended by the mid thirteenth century to the coast of Poitou and Saintonge, the fortifications of the major port of La Rochelle were also strengthened, although it was not until 1345–47 that the twin towers which guard the harbour entrance were built. These still exist and the Tour St Nicholas, in particular, is a very imposing structure; the watch tower is more than 35m above sea level. A chain was stretched across the entrance to the harbour between the two towers on which cannon were also mounted. Harfleur had similar towers, while at Honfleur across the estuary of the Seine one tower was built by the French in the mid fourteenth century, and another built *c.*1430 when the town was ruled by the English.[2]

### Le Clos des galées

The idea of special facilities for French royal maritime forces first took shape in 1240 on the Mediterranean coast of France. In that year Louis IX founded the port of Aigues Mortes in the marshes of the Camargue, on the small section of the southern coast of France between Marseille and Montpellier, under direct French royal rule. From this vantage point the French monarchy acquired direct experience of the sophisticated form of galley warfare which dominated these southern waters in the second half of the thirteenth century. The war between Charles II of Anjou, Louis IX's nephew, and ruler of Provence, and successive kings of Aragon, usually known as the war of the Sicilian Vespers, had a major naval component with galley battles fought in the waters off Sicily and Catalonia.[3] Both the Aragonese kings and Charles built galley fleets and, from *c*.1270, began the development of large galley-building shipyards at Barcelona or Marseille.[4] It is very probable that awareness of these events and the effectiveness of galleys as warships was one of the motivations for Philip IV of France to establish a galley-building yard of his own, in the north of his kingdom on the river Seine at Rouen. Shipbuilding had gone on at Rouen since at least 1226, and the tidal regime in the river ensured the town's success as a port, despite its distance from the sea. It was also, of course, well placed if the primary opponent of vessels to be built in the yard was England.

The yard was established around 1293–95, with the initial task of setting up the enterprise in the hands of Genoese shipwrights, some of the most successful and experienced workers in this field in the Mediterranean. It was initially quite a modest enclosure, defended only by ditches and a palisade, but eventually became a galley yard on the model of those in Genoa or Barcelona, with substantial buildings including housing for the officers and workers and covered galley sheds. It was designed round a basin leading off the river itself, with the entry and exit of vessels controlled by lock gates.[5] It was certainly a much more impressive establishment than the temporary buildings and hedged enclosures used by the English Crown at Ratcliff on the Thames in the mid fourteenth century.

It is hard, however, to be sure how effective the *Clos* was as a shipbuilding yard since there are considerable gaps in the surviving documentation. In some ways it was more use as providing winter shelter for galleys according to the usual practice in the

The walls of Aigues Mortes, the town built on the Mediterranean coast in the marshes of the Camargue by Louis IX to serve as a base for Crusader fleets.

(WIKIMEDIA)

Mediterranean. At Rouen they could be taken out of the water and placed in covered galley sheds in the yard.[6] It is also the case that, under the supervision of the director of the *Clos*, ships were also built for the French Crown in other ports. Jean Ribaut was responsible for building three new barges at Rouen in 1369–70 and others in Dieppe and Caudebec. After 1376 more vessels were ordered by the Crown from the *Clos des galées*, but it is not clear that the work on all of these was finished.

It was certainly also used as a storage facility and victualling yard; the French fleet that fought at Sluys was assembled there, and in 1355 a fleet was provided with victuals for one month comprising biscuit, beef, salt pork, herring, dried peas and beans, salt, and onions.[7] The administration of the yard was reorganised in the 1370s in the reign of Charles V and given greater responsibility for the provisioning of expeditions and the provision of artillery, in addition to that for the building and repair of royal ships. The surviving accounts for Jean Champenois, master of the *Clos des galées* for 1382–84, however, make depressing reading. The inventory section of the accounts makes clear that despite the expenditure of a certain amount of money in wages and supplies, there were no vessels in the *Clos* ready to go to sea. The galleys *St Agnes*, *St Cross*, and *St Victor* required repairs and lacked some equipment. The *Madeleine* was rotten and beyond repair, while three old horse transports had been on the stocks for at least twenty-seven years. The only other vessels were four half-built barges.[8] In 1385, probably as part of the preparations for an abortive French attempt to invade England, biscuit for fifty-three vessels was provided by the yard; around thirty of these ships were, however, hired from Spain and most of the remainder came from Harfleur.[9] This flurry of activity was followed by a long slow decline into inertia under corrupt officials. By the time the *Clos* was overrun by the English and burnt down in 1417, the yard was no longer engaged in building or repairing ships. The final expenditure recorded was nothing to do with these matters but with the repair of the stained glass windows with armorial borders in the hall and the chapel of the '*ostel du clos des gallees lez Rouen*'.[10]

As the editor of the greater part of the surviving accounts has pointed out, the establishment of the *Clos* by Philip IV does not represent the fulfilment of a wish to have a permanent navy. In her view the only thing permanent about the *Clos* was the officials and their salaries. The number of ships built or based in the *Clos* was too small for any kind of permanent navy and, moreover, they were not kept in a 'sea-ready' condition but allowed to deteriorate in times of truce. There were no permanent crews for the vessels, with most of the galleymen coming from the Mediterranean when an expedition was in preparation, a process which could take some time and lead to delays in the fleet putting to sea. Finally, Philip IV and the kings who succeeded him had other means of raising a fleet. It has been estimated that a French king could raise a fleet of from one to four hundred ships in French ports using his powers of conscription, and also had the ability to hire at least forty of the best Mediterranean galleys, usually from Genoa or Castile, whenever he chose. Galleys were not suitable for commercial use or for fishing in northern waters, and therefore could not be put to other uses in time of truce. Even so, in the view of the editor of the surviving documents, the little 'nutshells', most with a capacity of less than one hundred tuns, built in the yard made 'England tremble for more than a century'.[11]

## The policy of Philip IV

Even if the galleys built in the *Clos des galées* did not have quite such a dramatic effect on English mariners as this remark implies,[12] there is little doubt that Philip IV was unusual among French kings in spending much care and attention on a maritime policy intended to deal with not only the English, but also the Flemings, especially those in the merchant towns on the coast who were in rebellion against the French Crown. As well as acquiring a squadron of his own ships, he also created the office of Admiral of France; the first was Otton de Toucy, followed by the Genoese Enrico Marchese, and the Castilian Benedetto Zaccaria. The King was able to defray the considerable cost of these innovations by imposing a duty on ships which had to be registered for royal service when needed.[13]

The highpoint for the *Clos*, and in some ways for the medieval French navy, was the preparations for a possible invasion of England in the first half of the fourteenth century. These began in 1338, some two years before the battle of Sluys. Ordinances for the French fleet were drawn up in the same year, which in many ways are very similar to some of those we have looked at for the English fleet, produced at much the same time. The French fleet was to be ordered in 'battles' or ranks with the mariners from the Seine and Flanders in the van, followed by those from Dieppe and Picardy. The systems of signalling by flag for councils of war, or for the first sighting of an enemy ship, was the same as those for the English fleet.[14] The administration of the admiralty was also clarified at this time; a vice admiral would be appointed with assistants in Leure, Dieppe, Abbeville and Boulogne. Payments for these officials and the *Clos* would come from the *Chambre des Comptes* via the *Clerc des arbaletriers* with funds provided from a special *aide* voted by the estates of Normandy.

Well might Philip VI consider that he now possessed a truly *Grande Armée de la Mer*, the phrase used in surviving orders and accounts.[15] To oppose the English in the early months of 1340 there were 200 ships mustered at Rouen from ports all along the northern coast of France. Among these were three galleys, twenty-two vessels which were either barges or the smaller *bargots* and seven *nefs* that are all described as being in royal ownership. In addition three Genoese galleys, commanded by one Barbavera, had been hired by the French.[16] In total, victuals and other provisions had to be provided for over twenty thousand men before they set off for the estuary of the Zwyn. As we have seen, the battle was a disaster for the French with very high casualties. Many of the men lost would have been skilled and experienced mariners; their loss was a serious matter for France and may have led to a curtailment of maritime endeavours for some time.

## Philip VI

In 1346/7, at the time of the invasion of France by the English which ended with the siege of Calais, it is notable that Philip VI's initial response to the threat posed by English preparations was to turn to galleys hired from the Mediterranean, not to rely on the resources of the *Clos* or French shipowners. In the first months of 1346 he concluded an agreement with Carlo Grimaldi to hire from him thirty-two galleys and one galiot crewed by around seven thousand men. Unfortunately for Philip, the force did not arrive in French waters until 19 July 1346, by which time Edward III's army had already disembarked at Saint-Vaast-la-Hogue.[17] During the long English siege of Calais over the winter and spring of 1346/7, the Grimaldi galleys did little to bring relief to the town. An early success in breaking through the English blockade was not followed up; at the end of October the galleys were taken out of the water and disarmed according to the custom in the Mediterranean.

The flotillas which did have some success in bringing in supplies to the starving town were made up of ships from all the ports along the French coast, acting, according to Bourel de la Roncière, the historian of the French navy, entirely out of patriotic fervour. He included in his account of the siege some stirring stories including the tale of hundreds of women in Dieppe who dragged an overloaded victualler free of the mud in the harbour by hauling on ropes. This vessel formed part of a relieving force which got through the English defences in late March.[18] No others were successful. The fact that Calais was in English hands from 1347 did to some extent limit the freedom of movement of French ships in this part of the Channel. As a consequence of these defeats, the French Crown had also to a degree lost its appetite for new maritime initiatives; better to rely on galleys hired from its southern allies than to use France's own resources.

### Charles V

The fortunes of the *Clos des galées* and the French navy, however, revived in the reign of Charles V, along with those of France in general. English fortunes were at a nadir, especially following the defeat at La Rochelle, which to one commentator signified the loss of English control of the Golfe de Gascogne.[19] Ordinances issued in 1373 and 1377 reorganised the *Clos* and the Admiralty under the leadership of Jean de Vienne, who proved himself as competent and imaginative a leader in warfare at sea as he had done on land. The letters appointing the new *Mâitre et garde* of the galley yard in 1374 make plain how bad things had apparently become before this date. Victuals and other equipment were rotten and spoilt, while the galleys themselves were in such a condition that they could not put to sea in any emergency. The new master Estenne de Brandiz came from the south where he had been in charge of '*pors et passages*' in Carcassonne and Beziers, and had proved himself by organising the return of the pope from Avignon to Rome.[20] The success of Vienne's strategy of destructive raids on English coastal towns is neatly summarised in the report on the doings of the *Armée de mer* drawn up at the end of 1380. The purpose of the report was to finalise the sums owed by Charles V to the King of Castile for the hire of twenty galleys which had been involved in many of these raids. The purpose of the squadron had always been to do as much damage as possible to the Isle of Wight, Jersey and Guernsey, and other places. The report declared that they had burnt 'Vincenezel' (Winchelsea) and Rye, had raided up the Thames in August, and had finally left for Spain at the end of September. Their base was Harfleur, more convenient for this sort of activity than the yard up the river at Rouen.[21]

*The fifteenth century*

It is also reasonable to suppose that Charles V had a deliberate policy of increasing the French monarchy's direct control over the maritime regions and coasts of France, both to extend his own powers and because of the economic benefit this would bring France. Most of this unravelled in the reign of his son Charles VI. The failure of the enormous efforts put into the projected invasion of England in 1386 perhaps created a climate in which no one in a position of power or authority wished to be associated with endeavours like this. Rather than grandiose projects including an invasion by a large French fleet, security in the Channel could be better provided by gaining the political support of the Burgundians and the Dukes of Brittany.

In the early years of the fifteenth century, as we have already seen, the French monarchy turned once again to the well-tried medium of hired vessels, at this period largely from Genoa, to defend themselves from the forces of Henry V. The issue of royal ships or even a royal navy did not come to the fore again until the 1450s when the defeat of the English had returned the northern coasts of France, with the sole exception of Calais, to French control.

The whole issue of the attitude of the French monarchy to maritime affairs at this time was debated with vigour in a pamphlet supposedly recording a debate between the heralds of France and England.[22] Written sometime after the battle of Castillon in 1453, which ensured the loss by the English of all their French territories except Calais and the Pale, the Herald of France pours particular scorn on the English claim to be '*roys de la mer*' and then mounts several arguments in favour of France exerting her own power at sea. Apart from better natural resources in harbours and shipbuilding materials than England, the Herald claimed that the King of France, without leaving his palace, could destroy all the great ships of England by shutting them out of the immensely profitable trades in wine and bay salt. He recalled the reign of Charles V and the way in which he had successfully deployed forces of galleys against the port towns on the English coast and had even sent a fleet up the Thames which had attacked the city with cannon fire. In his view, these raids could be easily repeated any time the French king wanted. The French could also easily wage war against the English at sea if they wished. It was true that the French nobility was not enthusiastic about going to sea – seasickness is mentioned as a particular problem – but this was not a matter of importance. The French could get as many ships as they needed from their Spanish allies and, moreover, since the French had authority over Genoa more ships, both carracks and galleys, could come from there. Finally, the writer makes a plea to the French crown:

> Item, et pour ce je prie Dieu qu'il doint au roy de France cuer et courage de vous faire guerre a la mer, car ce sont les verges de quoy il vous peut chastier et refroider vostre hault couraige et a tous vos voysins quant il luy plaira l'entreprendre.[23]

Unfortunately the precise date of the composition of this pamphlet is not known, otherwise the recommendation to restart raids on the English coast might be thought to have inspired that on Sandwich in 1457.

One individual who would have thoroughly agreed with the Herald's conclusions would have been Pierre de Brézé, the grand seneschal of Normandy from 1451–61. He had been in the service of Charles VII of France since 1437 and was much involved in the reconquests of Normandy by the French and the defeat of the English. A fragmentary account for the years 1452–58 preserved in the archives of the Musée Condé has cast light on his activities as an active promoter of the *guerre de course* against the English in the Channel. He held shares in at least two ships, the carvel *Marquise* and another ship called the *Poulle*. These were based at Honfleur and put to sea with the clear aim of taking English ships and profiting from their cargoes and the ransoms of their crews. A tenth of any profits after some expenses, including the victualling of the ships, had been taken into account went to the Admiral of France. Like the raid on Sandwich in 1457, of which de Brézé was one of the leaders, these were at least semi-official voyages. De Brézé's main aim was political and military, to wrest mastery of the Narrow Seas from the English. Any personal profits were a secondary matter.[24] The accounts reveal a degree of success; in 1456 his ships took the *Ghost* of London, the *George* of Hull and another smaller ship. The final profit after expenses and the tenth due to the admiral, made up of the value of the cargoes of wool and lead on the ships taken, the ransoms of the prisoners, and the sale of the *Ghost*, came to just over 76lt 6s.[25]

The Herald's impassioned plea for a coherent naval policy by French kings was also largely ignored by Charles VII's successor Louis XI. He was concerned to encourage French maritime commerce, but concentrated his efforts on political manoeuvres aimed at securing power in Burgundian territories and in Brittany. One of the principal ways in which he attempted to achieve this was by continuing the policy of encouraging the activities of the corsairs who swarmed in French ports, letting them attack Flemish and Breton shipping almost with impunity. Mollat summed up Louis' attitude to any form of navy by remarking that it was hardly possible to speak of the '*marine royale*' at this time. Since many of his political intrigues were successful, Louis XI would have cared little for this verdict. Once the long-running and destructive war with England was over, France had other preoccupations, most of which had little impact on maritime or naval matters. Her rulers' eyes turned southwards towards Italy, away from the Channel and the Atlantic, and made little effort to acquire their own naval forces.

## Aragon

The two Spanish kingdoms of Aragon/Catalonia and Castile looked on maritime matters in a rather different way. Both before and after the union of their crowns, Aragon and Catalonia were deeply involved in the maritime world of the Mediterranean, with its long history dating back to classical times of seaborne trade and galley warfare. The Moorish conquerors of the Iberian peninsula with whom both kingdoms were at war during the period of the *Reconquista* were equally inheritors of this tradition. War at sea was no new thing in this arena.

## Roger of Lauria

When the attention of the kings of Aragon turned to the possible conquest of Sicily, they were confronted by an enemy, the Angevins, well prepared to fight a naval war and familiar with an established system of naval administration derived from Byzantine models. The Aragonese themselves had, from the early thirteenth century, appointed ad hoc commanders of fleets as circumstances required. They later developed a system based on these early appointments which also used the Byzantine/ Sicilian model. Under this system, Roger of Lauria[26] was appointed to the office of Admiral of the Kingdom of Catalonia, Valencia and Sicily in April 1283. He had very wide powers: authority over all the arsenals, the power to control corsairs, rights to the possession of equipment and arms captured on all prize vessels, rights to ransoms, to shipwrecks, and to administer law throughout the fleet.[27] A number of officials were also appointed by the King, Peter III, who had duties regarding ports and trade and who were at least nominally under Roger's authority. After 1286 the admiral also had direct power over the finances of the fleet, including the right to collect a special tax known as the *marinaria*. A relatively complex administration developed with officials to control the arsenals, raise crews and pay them, and organise the baking of *biscotti*, the essential 'fuel' for the galleymen. When the situation in Sicily had largely been resolved and there was less need for a large fleet, this organisation was simplified but it was still possible for Aragon to send an effective force to sea within a relatively short space of time. Arsenals existed in several ports but that at Barcelona was a considerable establishment; some of the galley sheds, which still survive there, could house a good number of galleys. Here galleys could also be built and repaired; sails were made and arms and foodstuffs stored. The number of workmen was considerable, making the presence of an arsenal economically valuable to the towns where they were based.[28]

Peter IV of Aragon, who ruled between 1336 and 1387, issued *Ordinaciones* for the fleet, which set out regulations for the royal fleet. These emphasise the role of vice admirals, who commanded squadrons in the fleet, and how they should relate to the *comiti*, or masters of individual galleys. There would also be a helmsman or pilot on board who should have a good knowledge of the waters in which the vessel was about to sail.[29] The oarsmen, conscripts in the Aragonese fleet but legally free men, were divided into different groups with different duties, but all were paid at the same rate. All crew members were armed, even if only with some sort of sword or dagger, and had at least a minimum of armour, a helmet of some kind and a cuirass. The *Ordinaciones* also prescribed their rations, the main element being biscuit at the rate of 800g per man per day.[30]

The galleys normally carried a force of highly skilled crossbowmen, known as *almugavars*, who had a fearsome reputation among their likely opponents in the Mediterranean. If the galleys were needed for an amphibious operation, something which occurred quite frequently, more fighting men would be carried. The Aragonese fleet also included horse transports; these seem to have been built with doors in the stern so that the animals could be unloaded by riding directly from the ship up the beach. These are described in the surviving accounts as *galeae apertae in puppa*,[31] and a surviving illustration shows horses emerging from a large hinged hatch in the stern of a ship. None of them appear to be any the worse for their sea voyage as they are shown leaping eagerly into the waves.[32]

The system developed during the war with Sicily came under considerable pressure by the end of the thirteenth century. There were difficulties in raising money for the fleet since the tax-raising powers of the monarchy were restrained by the union of Aragon with Valencia (where the consent of the Estates was required before a tax could be imposed). Even so, the Catalan fleet based at the arsenal in Barcelona remained effective and capable of fighting when needed.[33]

The interior of one of the surviving galley sheds of the Arsenal of Barcelona, the base of the highly successful navy of Aragon. The ship shown is a later seventeenth-century galley.

(WIKIMEDIA)

## Castile

Aragon, despite its early development of a state-owned and organised navy, had little direct maritime contact with the states of northern Europe. Links between Castile and the realms of the north, however, were strong and frequent. Relations with England had been put on a secure footing in 1254 when a treaty had been signed between Henry III of England and Alfonso X of Castile.[34] This resolved the issue of Castilian claims to Gascony in England's favour, and provided a boost to trade between the two kingdoms. The north coast of Spain, especially Bilbao, was an important source of iron, while all manner of goods, including olive oil, oranges and other fruits, came from further

The conquerors of the Canaries; an illustration from a chronicle of the Castilian conquest of these islands at the end of the fourteenth century.

(BRITISH LIBRARY)

south once Seville had fallen to Castilian forces in 1248. The victory of Ferdinand III of Castile and Leon over the Moslem defenders of the city was greatly aided by a fleet raised along the northern coasts of Castile and sent south under the command of Ramon Bonifaz. This fleet defeated a Moorish fleet from Tangiers and Ceuta coming to the aid of Seville, at the mouth of the Guadalquivir. It was also two of the best armed vessels of this northern Spanish fleet which managed to break through the bridge of boats across the river which was the key to the Moslem defence of the city. The benefits of the ability to deploy naval resources in time of war were clearly evident to the King of Castile. Bonifaz, in his turn, was lauded in the chronicles describing these events as a great hero of this triumph of the *Reconquista*.[35]

### The conquest of Seville

The Moorish rulers of Andalucia had understood the need for some sort of centralised naval organisation on the coasts of Iberia as early as the second half of the ninth century, following the devastating Viking raids in 844. Lisbon, Medina Sidonia, Seville and Algeciras had all been sacked. Arsenals were set up in several ports including Algeciras and Seville in the tenth century, while an admiral in charge of the whole region was based in Almeria. This system seems to have been in operation during the period of the Almohad emirs in Seville, but it is not known to what extent Ferdinand III built on this structure when setting out his own plans.[36] After the taking of Seville, the Moslem population had been expelled; the King's first priority was to re-people the city and ensure its incorporation into Christian Castile. This entailed large numbers of land grants and the creation of privileges to reward those who had been involved in the campaign to take the city and who had undertaken to live in this magnificent conquest. The most important grant in 1251 was that of the *fuero*, or charter of the city, based on that already given to Toledo. One section related particularly to the maritime community which had established itself along the river front. This was largely peopled by the former crews of Bonifaz's galleys. The king saw their future as shipbuilders, merchants and fighting men. The *fuero* laid down that they would spend three months a year at sea in the service of the Crown in their ships; in return they would receive trading privileges and their own court as well as payment for their time at sea.[37]

Almost exactly a year later Ferdinand died; his successor Alfonso X then proceeded to implement a much more considered maritime policy centred on Seville. He intended to create a naval force capable of supporting a Castilian expedition against the homelands of the Moors across the Strait of Gibraltar. The arsenal of Seville was established as a shipbuilding and repair centre on land between the river and the walls of the city. Although little of it now remains, there were originally around seventeen galley sheds with a considerable workforce of shipwrights employed. The leading employees were granted lands of their own which ensured their permanent employment and the right to pass their positions and lands to their heirs. The wood to build the galleys came from royal forests in the sierras, with the felled timber floated down the river to the arsenal.

The King then moved on to consider the way the fleet to be built in the arsenal should be manned and armed. The Castilian fleet would be made up of galleys, the type of vessel familiar throughout the Mediterranean and well-designed for the type of warfare at sea usual in that area. The arms provided included personal armour for the crews, a variety of personal weapons including swords and daggers, crossbows, grapnels and chains, and also soft soap and some kind of inflammable pitch.[38] The crews composed of oarsmen, steersmen and men-at-arms would be under the authority of the *cómitres*, or captains. These men had individual grants from the Crown of good agricultural land producing olives and figs, and also a house in the city and a money grant to fit out their galley. It was then their duty to keep this vessel in repair, ready to go to sea, with a complete refit every nine years. The office could also be passed on to their heirs. There were also provisions regarding the division of prizes and other booty with the Crown. The first group of galley captains included men from Catalonia, Genoa and France.

In 1254 Alfonso completed his scheme for a royal navy by setting up the office of the Admiral of Castile. This had a judicial function as in most other states and was based in Seville. The responsibilities of the office were set out between 1256–65 in the *Siete Partidas.* These make clear that the Admiralty controlled and licensed corsairs, the business of the arsenals and also ordinary commercial waterborne traffic, even down to the activities of fishermen. The collection of taxes on shipping entering the Guadalquivir at San Lucar was also one of the functions of this office.[39] The fortunes of the galley yard at Seville varied according to circumstances over our period, but the basic organisation remained intact and operational.

Our detailed knowledge of the career of Don Pero Niño, from the biography written by his standard bearer, reveals how the system of the licensing of corsairs worked at the end of the fourteenth and beginning of the fifteenth centuries. Niño's first voyage in 1404 is presented as an expedition against those preying on Castilian merchants. The King ordered him to man galleys with the best possible crews, including crossbowmen. All were paid in advance and also supplied with arms and supplies. A sailing ship was also included in the squadron. Unfortunately, little if any booty was taken during the voyage.[40] A second voyage was considerably more profitable for the corsairs and ended with Niño being greeted with great enthusiasm by the King who, of course, received a half share of the proceeds. His third voyage in 1405 was undertaken to aid the French, the allies of Castile, who had asked for help. The account makes plain that the galleys were provided by the King at Santander; all were fully manned, armed and victualled at royal expense, with some of the crossbowmen being members of the royal household.[41] Some of the adventures of this expedition have been discussed in earlier chapters. The point to make here is that Castile had a much more coherent naval policy, with provisions for not only building ships (largely galleys), but maintaining them and manning them, at a time when the states of northern Europe were still largely dependent on conscripted merchant ships for any kind of naval action. In this instance Castile had absorbed and improved on its inheritance from the Moorish rulers of Andalucía and was also much influenced by the way the provision of naval defence was organised by its neighbour, the kingdom of Aragon and Catalonia.

## The Hanseatic League

England had had trading links with the major trading cities of the Baltic since at least the twelfth century. The area produced and exported many of the essential supplies needed by shipbuilders and repairers, particularly timber and the rosin needed to treat the hulls of vessels. The ubiquity of timber from eastern Europe in English shipyards is made plain in shipbuilding accounts; these include multiple entries for 'Prussian deals' (pine wood), Righolt (soft wood exported from Riga), and wainscot board (oak from the Baltic). Arms and armour from Cologne, an inland member of the Hanse, were equally valuable and important imports to England. As well as this, the vessels of the League were deeply involved in carrying salt from the Bay of Bourgneuf (near La Rochelle) back to the Baltic to preserve the herrings which were another staple of their trade. It was the custom of the merchants of the Hanse to establish houses, or *Kontors*, in the cities which were their main trading partners, where they would live a communal life and form a formidable group able to negotiate favourable terms of trade with the authorities. In London this was on the river near Dowgate and known as the Steelyard. Other major centres were at Bruges and Bergen.[42]

Relationships between the merchants of the Hanse and their trading partners were often tense and difficult, largely because of the way in which monarchs attempted to regulate trade by imposing taxes and other dues while the league, particularly the leading cities of Danzig and Lubeck, asserted their economic power to obtain privileges for their members. In England they had, for example, successfully negotiated in the fourteenth century the payment of duties on the export of cloth which were lower even than those paid by denizen merchants. These trading rights undoubtedly led to resentment in the English, resentment which became stronger and more likely to lead to aggressive action when the Hanse were exempted from the payment of tonnage and poundage in 1437 and no reciprocal concessions were made to English merchants trading in Hanseatic towns. Hanseatic trading ships, often making for east coast ports like Boston or Lynn, had long been subject to piratical attacks both from English and Flemish vessels, but something much more akin to a war conducted entirely at sea, with attacks on trading ships as its main component, developed in the North Sea between England and the League after 1470. The trigger for the conflict was the seizure of seven English ships in the Sound by the King of Denmark. The English maintained that the Hanse was implicated in this incident and orders were given for the arrest of all merchants from Hanseatic towns in England and the confiscation of their goods. Attempts at a negotiated settlement failed and by the end of 1470 the majority of the members of the league were unleashing corsairs on English shipping.[43]

The precise nature of the bonds between the cities who were members of the league were hard to define and in many ways deliberately vague. As the league responded to Edward IV in 1469, it was a mere alliance between cities, in no way a company or any other legal body as defined in civil law. It aim was to promote trade by its members including the pursuit of any pirates and brigands who might deprive them of their goods. Each town acted individually; if decrees were issued by the assembly of the league each had to be authorised by the individual seal of each city.[44] When it came to taking common action against an enemy this depended on the agreement of all and their voluntary participation in whatever action was decided upon. This was not perhaps as difficult as it might seem since power in the cities was in the hands of the leading merchants and the interests of neighbouring cities often coincided. Divisions did occur but the Hanse as a whole held together until well after our period.

This is well demonstrated in the action taken by the league against the *Vitalienbrüder*. This ferocious group of sea rovers had come into being when the duchy of Mecklenburg launched a *kaperkreig*, or privateers' war, against Denmark. An appeal was issued to any 'who wished to try his luck as freebooter at his own expense to harm the realms of Norway and Denmark.' The appeal was only too successful, with the result that seaborne commerce became very nearly impossible in the Baltic. The scourge was finally eliminated in 1398 by a force sent by the Teutonic Knights against the pirates' base on Gotland; a much earlier scheme to put together a similar force, inspired by Lubeck, got nowhere because individual cities hesitated about contributing the necessary ships. The *Vitalienbrüder* retreated to Frisia after their defeat, but in early 1400 were attacked by a fleet raised by Hamburg and Lubeck and driven from this sanctuary. The final blow was struck by 'the men of Hamburg' in a battle off Heligoland.[45] The fleets used in these encounters were made up of ships from the merchant marine of each participating city acting strictly in their own interests. The notes of a diet (meeting) of the Prussian towns who were members of the league held in 1384 summarise this attitude neatly. The question was asked: should the towns continue to arm warships? The answer was: it is a good idea to arm ships and bring peace on the seas as soon as possible and to beg members to take action on this as they have done before. Persuasion and recognition of a common interest was what held a fleet together.[46]

*Hostilities with England in the 1470s*

In the same way, the 'war' against England in the 1470s largely consisted of individual attacks on commercial shipping by privateers licensed by individual towns. The most celebrated engagement, in fact, well illustrates the pitfalls in this kind of warfare. A large ship, originally French, the *St Pierre de la Rochelle*, had been abandoned in Danzig harbour as unseaworthy in 1462. In 1470 the city authorities repaired and refitted the ship as a privateer against England. She sailed the following year, commanded by one of the city councillors, but spent most of her time at anchor in the estuary of the Zwyn. In 1473 she was bought by three other councillors and sent to sea under the command of Paul Beneke, the most effective of the privateering captains. He attacked two galleys under the Burgundian flag, sailing from Bruges to Florence with a cargo of luxuries including an altarpiece by Hans Memling intended for a Florentine church. His excuse was that the vessels also carried a cargo of alum intended for an English port. One of the galleys was captured and eventually taken into Danzig where his coup was not popular, since the Hanseatic towns had no wish to antagonise the Duke of Burgundy.[47] War waged in this fashion brought many unexpected consequences; privateering captains could not be easily controlled, while the need to offer them large rewards for their enterprise did not make it without cost to the promoters.

The Hanseatic warehouse in King's Lynn; it was adjacent to the quay where the ships from the Baltic tied up, very often bringing in ropes, spars, timber and other naval supplies.

(AUTHOR'S COLLECTION)

The English at sea in our period were faced with forces raised and organised in a variety of different ways. In all realms there existed some sort of obligation on shipowners and seamen to aid their ruler in time of war. The details regarding the way in which this obligation was expressed and implemented varied. In France and Iberia it was either part of feudal service or of the overall power of the monarch. In the cities of the Hanseatic League it was a mixture of civic duty and self-interest. Beyond this basic obligation rulers might attempt to establish their own fleet of ships supported by royal arsenals and dockyards and more or less elaborate systems of administration. Another expedient was to turn for aid to other allied powers and to hire their vessels and their crews. No one method seems to have been outstandingly more successful than the others. Both Aragon and Castile had learnt from and adapted the methods of the leading maritime powers of the Mediterranean. In both realms the organisation and methods of the shipyards benefitted greatly from the expertise of Genoese shipwrights. Crews on their galleys were made up of seafarers from all the neighbouring coasts. These crews had much experience of fighting in the endemic corsair warfare of the region. It is no wonder that the French turned to the Castilians and the Genoese themselves when the need for fighting ships was urgent. Conditions in the Channel and the Western Approaches did not, however, really suit the operation of galley fleets in the southern model. It could be argued that there was a growing awareness among the states that bordered these waters of the need for some more permanent form of naval defence, but that none had found an entirely satisfactory solution to the problem by the middle of the fifteenth century.

OPPOSITE PAGE:
The port of Hamburg showing how important seaborne trade was to this Hanseatic city. A crane is unloading barrels from a lighter while on the right merchants discuss their business.

(HAMBURG STAATSARCHIV)

## CHAPTER 10

# The Legacy to Henry VIII

THERE IS NO DOUBT THAT defence at sea presented a major problem for any medieval government. The clear good sense of Fortescue's remark that it was too late to put together a force of ships when the enemy was already at sea was well understood not only by monarchs but by their subjects. Apart from a lingering fear of an invasion from overseas among the population at large, those affected frequently voiced their demands in English parliaments for adequate protection from sea-raiders for their homes and their livelihoods. A standing navy was, however, almost impossibly expensive for medieval governments, except in special circumstances. The republic of Venice, for example, could bear the burden since seaborne trade was the lifeblood of the state, but even a kingdom like England with its long coastline faced no such urgent imperative. Moreover, in England there was no tradition or expectation of a state enterprise on such a scale. Land armies were raised ad hoc; once peace prevailed there was no continuing need for expenditure on men and equipment. Ships had to be cared for and maintained whether they went to sea or not, or whether any naval encounter was imminent or not. It was hard to make the case for the existence of even a small squadron of royal ships when taxation, as in England, needed parliamentary consent and taxation itself was seen not as an inevitable part of life but something extraordinary, only necessary in an emergency. There was little hope, therefore, of the fulfilment of Fortescue's scheme for at least a semi-permanent force of royal ships until the problems of both administration and finance had been, at least partially, solved.

## Administration

English medieval monarchs had the support of both a relatively efficient financial system in the Exchequer and Treasury, and an effective 'secretariat' in the Chancery. Historians have benefited greatly from their well-kept records. The organisation of a 'department of state' to control royal ships and naval operations was much slower to develop, and for most of our period there was little in the way of a coherent or carefully devised system.

### Clerks of the King's Ships c.1340–1452

Nothing like the *Siete Partidas* or the *Ordinaciones* issued by the rulers of Aragon and Castile covering the operation of royal ships existed in England, or had ever been contemplated by English monarchs. By the reign of Edward III, as we have seen, officials called Clerks of the King's Ships were appointed, but few if any had any kind of maritime expertise. Their skills lay in the purchase of stores and in keeping, as far as was possible, accurate

The Water Gate, Southampton; this was used as his office by William Soper Clerk of the King's Ships, 1421–27; he also collected customs there for the Crown and organised his personal trading interests. The Water Gate opened directly on to the town quay.

**(AUTHOR'S COLLECTION)**

financial records. They had no responsibilities for operational matters or in formulating policy. Thomas de Snetesham and Matthew de Torksey, two of the longest-employed in this reign, were typical royal clerks, in holy orders, but in fact what a later period would call 'career civil servants'. By the fifteenth century the post was held by laymen.

William Catton, who was Clerk of the King's Ships from 1413–20, the period of the rapid expansion of royal naval forces under Henry V, was a royal yeoman in the service of the King. He was clearly competent but there is no indication of why he was chosen for this particular post, apart from the fact that he was already bailiff of Winchelsea, and thus would have had personal contacts in the important maritime community of Sussex and Kent.[1]

He was succeeded by William Soper who had already been involved in shipbuilding for the Crown in Southampton since 1416. Soper came from a very different background. He had probably arrived in Southampton as a young man eager to make his way as a merchant. This he had done with enough success to hold office in the corporation (he was appointed as steward in 1410) and to be frequently chosen as an MP for the town, on the first occasion in the parliament of May 1413. In London that summer he must have caught the attention of someone with influence because in the autumn of the same year he was appointed to collect the customs revenue in Southampton with a colleague, John Esgaston. From this point he continued to act as a merchant on his own account (strictly speaking illegal for a customer), and to hold official positions, principally in the customs and in connection with the increasing number of royal ships based in the town. He was well paid for his duties (at the rate of £40 per annum) as Clerk of the King's Ships, the position he took over from Catton shortly before the death of Henry V. He died a wealthy man, owning a considerable amount of property and a comfortable country house in the New Forest.[2]

His surviving accounts show that he was a careful and competent administrator who devoted much care and attention to the royal ships. He was at home in a maritime environment with an office in the Water Gate of Southampton, opening onto the Town Quay. He had close connections with the Florentine galley captains who visited the town, and himself owned and operated trading vessels. He was not, however, a seaman nor did he have any personal experience of war. He certainly had at least one clerk to assist him, and worked with master shipwrights and the other carpenters and shipkeepers needed for his work on the King's ships. Most of these men, however, were employed for a particular job; in no sense was a permanent base for the King's ships established at Southampton. When he finally relinquished the office in 1442, his work consisted in little more than looking after a miscellany of old naval stores, selling off a few bits and pieces when occasion offered, a process which was continued by his successor, Richard Cliveden, a royal official like Catton.[3] When Cliveden left office in 1452 no further permanent appointments were made until Thomas Roger, a former royal mariner, was made Clerk of the King's Ships in 1480.

### Clerks of the King's Ships 1480–1509

This appointment has been hailed as a clear sign that Edward IV appreciated the need for a reinvigorated naval administration. The King, it is claimed, also understood that relying on privately owned vessels and a very few royal ships, with maintenance the responsibility of their masters, was no longer an efficient or effective way of providing forces to fight at sea; Roger's appointment and the use made of ships in the Scots war of 1481/2 showed that England was once more a naval power.[4]

However, this is debatable since his appointment was on terms which were more comparable to those used by Edward III at the very beginning of the office, than those which had been current during the peak of royal interest in ships in the reign of Henry V. Roger's pay was only 12d per day with 6d for a clerk; he was not involved in shipbuilding, which was handled by two men of much higher status than Roger. It is true that Roger remained in office throughout the upheavals of the 1480s, successfully being reappointed first by Richard III and then by Henry VII, but this may be more an indication of his relative unimportance than anything else. His surviving accounts were made up by his widow and cover the years 1485–88.[5] Although they are in English rather than in Latin, as was the case with earlier accounts, their format and content is very similar to those from the fourteenth and fifteenth centuries. There is little sign of any change or reform in the procedures and responsibilities of the office.

Little is known about his immediate successor, William Commersall, who held office

The Antony Roll picture of the *Mary Rose*, the best known of Henry VIII's ships because of the recovery of her wreck from the Solent off Portsmouth. The contents of the vessel give a remarkably complete picture of life at sea at the time.

(PEPYS LIBRARY)

from 1488–95; he was then replaced by Robert Brygandyne whose accounts survive for the period 1495–97.[6] Brygandyne was a Yeoman of the Crown, a member of the royal household who had already been granted an annuity of £10 by the King. There are suggestions that he regarded the office of Clerk of the King's Ships as a sinecure, and all the work was done by a deputy, but there is no clear evidence that this was the case.[7] The office operated during his time as clerk in the reign of Henry VII much as it had always done. His one surviving set of accounts from 1495–97 show him being involved in some important projects, including the building of 'the dokke for the kynges Shippes at Portsmouth'. He was also in charge of the refits of the *Sovereign* and the *Regent*; both these vessels were originally built in 1487, the first under the supervision of Sir Reginald Bray, and the other under that of Sir Richard Guildford. Both men were close companions of the King, of sufficiently high status to be made Knights of the Garter. Brygandyne himself took charge of the building of the little barks, the *Sweepstake* and the *Fortune*.

It is clear, however, from the accounts of both Roger and Brygandyne, supported by some other evidence, that the role of Clerk of the King's Ships was as ill-defined as it had been in the fourteenth century. Roger had no involvement in shipbuilding, but was competent to undertake a major refit, that of the *Gracedieu*. He paid shipkeepers and workmen. He supplied cannon and powder and other stores to ships 'reteyned in the Kynges service upon the See', and paid 'wages of Warre' to other shipmasters. Payments can, however, also be found direct to other shipmasters in other sources, while his widow specifically asked to be exonerated from a sum of £40 for the 'new makyng' of the *Sovereign*. This was the responsibility of one Henry Palmer as he 'yet kepith the wole accompt and rekinnyng' of the building of this ship.[8] Roger's duties included renting a storehouse at Greenwich but in no sense was he comparable to, for example, the master of the arsenal at Seville.

Thomas Roger had, very briefly, had about eight ships in his charge when he first took office. The *Martin Garsya*, however, was given to Richard Guildford within days of Roger taking office; the *Governor* was also probably given to two London merchants in the following year. The *Fawcon* and *Trinity* disappear from the records with no note made of their fate. The *Mary of the Tower* was sent on a trading voyage to Lombardy and returned in bad repair. The old *Gracedieu*, built originally for one John Taverner in 1446,[9] was broken up and some timbers reused for the new *Sovereign*. The final tally of royal ships when Roger died in 1488 was just three, the new *Sovereign* and *Regent*, and the somewhat battered *Mary of the Tower*.[10]

In Brygandyne's case the majority of the money he received in 1495–97 came via the treasurer for war; the funds were intended for the 'dokke hedde and gates' at Portsmouth, expenses incurred on the *Sovereign* and the *Regent*, and the building of the two barks. He paid wages, for supplies and for transport costs. He also supplied stores including armaments to ships arrested for the Scottish campaign. The force of royal ships in his charge at the time of these accounts consisted of the new great ships, the *Sovereign* and the *Regent*, a purchase, the *Carvel of Ewe*, also known as the *Mary and John*, the *Sweepstake* and the *Mary Fortune*. This was hardly an impressive force even when augmented by a prize taken in 1490, the *Margaret of Dieppe*.

## Henry VII's policy regarding the King's ships

Is there then any reason to go beyond the judgements made by Oppenheim as long ago as 1896 that 'it was Henry's [VII] aim to form a reserve on which a navy could be built and which would be co-extensive with the whole maritime strength of the kingdom'; in other words that the King had a very traditional view of naval power?[11] Or to disagree with the view expressed in 1918 that 'the condition of affairs in Europe and the policy of Henry VII rendered it unnecessary for that monarch to maintain a powerful navy'?[12]

A careful look at some aspects of Henry VII's naval affairs leads to a rather different interpretation. It is true that the administration of the royal ships changed very little from the model used in earlier reigns; the Clerk of the King's Ships remained the only permanent official with ill-defined duties. It is also true that the squadron of royal ships was hardly impressive and that, as before, reliance was placed on impressed merchant ships for the logistical support of armies. This was the case in 1492 when Henry VII led a fleet of five hundred ships to France. The campaign was intended at least in part to counter the possible threat to English trade and shipping in the Channel posed by the marriage of Duchess Anne of Brittany to Charles VIII of France in the previous year, since this brought all the Breton ports and their formidable corsairs within the ambit of France.[13]

More important for future progress was the development of Portsmouth into something like a permanent base for the royal ships. Roger's group of royal ships moved from anchorage to anchorage with little evidence of permanent facilities being in existence. The *Mary of the Tower* was refitted at Southampton, moved to Bursledon, and finally docked at Erith. The *Gracedieu* was also anchored at Southampton but later docked near Netley Abbey. The *Governor* was moved from Southampton to Bursledon since it was much cheaper to 'keep' a ship there than at Southampton. Roger also hired storehouses on the Thames, one for the 'Kynges stuff and takle and ordnaunce' at Greenwich, rented for at least four years, and the other in London itself for a short time only, for cables from Genoa, confiscated from the *Mary of the Tower* after a trading voyage, as the owners had not paid the customs due.

Brygandyne, on the other hand, was in charge of the major project at Portsmouth which included the building of a dock. This was quite a substantial undertaking with the work lasting from mid June to the end of November and then restarting in the spring from early February till mid April. It was on the site of what became no. 1 basin in the modern dockyard. It was lined with timber strengthened with two tons of iron wrought into the required 'boltes barres fforlokes rynges clampes spykes staples and other necessaries'. It was closed off with gates at the dock head which were treated with pitch; there is, however, no sign of any lock mechanism in the accounts and a large quantity of rocks and stones and gravel were procured for 'ffortyfying the Dooke hedde'. The total cost of all the work on the dock was £193 0s 0¾d. The site at Portsmouth had already been fortified in 1494 with a tower and other protection at a cost of around £2070. Probably at much the same time a forge was built at which the ironwork for the dock was produced. This was well-equipped with bellows and great block pulleys 'for raysing of mastes', and something called 'thengyne to draw water at the dokke', perhaps a large pump. On the site there was also at least one store house and something called the 'Kynges Blokkehousse' in which cannon and their chambers were stored.

The dockyard was soon put to good use by Brygandyne. Both the *Sovereign* and the *Regent* underwent thorough refits on the stocks in the dock, the *Sovereign* being brought round from Erith for this purpose. The *Regent* spent some time moored off the dock basin, 'betwyxt the Towre and the dokke', on the Gosport side of the harbour before being eased into the dock. This was clearly a delicate business since sixty men beside her crew were needed to bring her across from her mooring, and to wait 'tyle time that Gode sent wynde and wedyr'. A total of ninety were needed beside the crew to get her into the dock and onto the stocks. All this cost, including victuals for the workmen, £7 6s 1d, and took at least three days. The costs of taking the *Regent* out of the dock are not recorded, but it apparently took twenty men working over a four-week period to shift the material placed between the gates of the dock, so that the *Sovereign* might leave; the total cost, again including the men's victuals, was £12 8s 2d.

With costs like these (as a comparison the total cost of building the bark *Sweepstake*, also at Portsmouth, was £120 3s 2d), it would seem that it must have been the case that the use of the dock allowed great ships to be refitted in ways not really practicable before. Brygandyne had established a shipbuilding and ship repair yard at Portsmouth which was defensible and provided the kind of base that the King's ships had never had before. Shipbuilding might still go on in other places; the *Mary Fortune* was built on the Rother at Smallhythe and work might also be done at Erith or elsewhere on the Thames, but Portsmouth had facilities lacking at the other sites.[14]

It is also the case that the four ships with detailed entries in Brygandyne's accounts, the *Sovereign* (*c.*450 tuns), *Regent* (*c.*600 tuns), *Sweepstake* and *Mary Fortune* represent a new generation of vessels. We have no details of the design of any of these ships but it is more than likely that the hulls of the two larger ships resembled the vessels depicted in the Beauchamp Pageant.[15] Both were carvel-built:[16] this is clear from the type of nails bought to repair the hulls.[17] They were both rigged, however, in a rather more elaborate way than those shown in the pageant. The method used seems to anticipate the rigging of sixteenth century ships, especially those depicted in the Antony Roll in some respects.[18] Both had four masts; a main, foremast, mizzen and bonaventure mizzen. There was also certainly a main topmast and sail while the bowsprit carried a spritsail. These details

The modern replica caravel the *Lisa von Lubeck* under sail. She has a carvel built hull, a lateen-rigged mizzen and timber fenders incorporated into the hull at her waist.

(BURKHARD BANGE)

come from the inventory sections of the accounts and therefore, while the existence of these masts and sails is quite clear, some details of the rig are lacking, and it is hard to be sure whether some masts carried lateen sails. The mainmast carried a square sail with bonnets provided for reefing in a style which originated in the fourteenth century. This rig differs from that of the Portuguese caravels, three-masted with a lateen mizzen and no spritsail. It is difficult to estimate how effective this new-style rig was. A replica of a caravel, the *Lisa von Lubeck*, rigged like this was built in 2004, but presented the modern crew with some problems in turning the vessel; it is possible that the rig of the *Sovereign* and the *Regent* was designed to overcome something of this nature.[19]

The *Sovereign*'s 'grete bote and Jolywat' were clinker-built in the old tradition, as were the much smaller *Sweepstake* and *Mary Fortune*; the 'Ruff' [roves] and 'clynche' [clench nails] needed for this style of building a hull were bought in quantity for all these vessels.[20] The two barks seem to have been rigged in very much the same fashion as their much larger contemporaries but were also provided with 'long ores' (that is to row the ship itself not a boat), sixty in the case of the *Sweepstake* and eighty in the case of the *Mary Fortune*. The design of these two ships was, perhaps, developed from that of the balingers of Henry V's navy and similar to that of Henry VIII's rowbarges, although these were much smaller vessels.

Attention has also been drawn to the armament carried by the two large ships. Both were provided with large numbers of guns, specifically serpentines. These were breech-loaders weighing around 227kg which could be made of either iron or occasionally a copper alloy; they fired lead balls or 'dyce' and were used on land as well as at sea. They were fired by fixing a powder chamber to the rear of the gun barrel.[21] In the inventories multiple chambers were provided (about three per gun), so that rapid fire was possible to some extent. The *Regent* carried 225 of these guns, but no details are given of their deployment on the ship since all were listed as being in the ship's storehouse. On the *Sovereign* the guns were deployed as follows: sixteen on the forecastle 'above the deck'; twenty-four on the forecastle 'alowe the deck'; twenty-four 'stone guns' in the waist;

One of Henry VIII's rowbarges from the Antony Roll. These were small, only about 20 tuns capacity, and the rowing system is not clear. They could be useful in a fight in a confined space or in adverse winds, but were no match for Mediterranean galleys.

(PEPYS LIBRARY)

twenty iron serpentines and one brass on the 'somercastel'; eleven stone guns on the 'somercastel'; four serpentines on the stern; twenty-five serpentines on the deck over the 'somercastel' and twenty on the poop. Stone guns would have fired stone balls rather than the lead 'dyce' that the other guns projected. Both ships were equipped with the necessary moulds and other things to make these pellets. There was not a gun deck or gun ports in the hull, as later understood, although the guns on the forecastle, and perhaps those at the stern, may have fired through openings of some kind. These were not ship-killing weapons like the later broadside, though a lucky shot might cause considerable damage to upper works and rigging. They could wreak great damage on the crew, especially if men had gathered on the deck ready to board the enemy. Both ships also were equipped with longbows, spears and other personal weapons with the clear assumption that boarding continued to be the usual final act of an engagement at sea.

The armament of the two smaller barks was almost entirely personal weapons, spears and billhooks, and longbows. However, both carried a small amount of gunpowder, lead pellets and tampions. There is no sign in the inventories of a weapon to use these items, even though they are listed as 'perused broken wasted lost and spent' in the Scottish campaign. Guns were, however, now accepted as weapons with a part to play in sea warfare beyond the causing of terror by the noise of their discharge. The cost of such armaments and their ammunition was in the reach of royal ships backed up by the Royal Ordnance at the Tower of London. Merchants might find it more difficult to equip their ships in the same manner.

There is also evidence that the way the crew was organised on a royal ship had become more complex and more sophisticated since the days of the master at 6d per day, the mariners at 3d per day and the ship's boys at 1½d per day of the fourteenth and fifteenth centuries. The crews on the great majority of earlier ships had shown little differentiation between specialists and ordinary crewmen. Occasionally, a carpenter might be on board or a pilot; some larger ships might have a clerk, although it is not clear he went to sea, being perhaps more a quartermaster at the home port; a constable was sometimes included, paid the same as the master, but his function is not clear. In the 1490s, however, the *Regent* had, while at anchor not on active service, a master, a purser, a boatswain, a steward and a gunner. The *Sovereign*, in rather similar circumstances, had a master, a purser, a boatswain, two quartermasters, a steward, a cook and a gunner. These men not only had different duties, but their pay was carefully graded from 3s 4d per week for the master, down to 1s 3d to 1s 6d for the steward and the cook, with a sum for victuals in addition.

It is arguable that this was the beginning of a process of establishing a hierarchy on board ship with linked rates of pay which can be seen completed in the 1582 Scale of Pay and Complement.[22] This sets out the pay rates for twenty-nine different ranks going from the master to the seaman, but including a surgeon, drummer and trumpeter, as well as the ranks mentioned on Henry VII's ships. It is also the case that away from the small group of royal ships, merchant ships, which, of course, made up by far the greater part of the navy of England, had also benefited from the changes in design we have seen with the royal ships. Their crews had also become more adventurous or more experienced navigators, more aware of the improvements in navigation that had been pioneered by the Portuguese and the Genoese. The somewhat mysterious voyages from Bristol out into the Atlantic, apparently to find the semi-mythical island of Brasil, took place in 1480/1 just as Roger took on responsibility for the King's ships. The voyage of Cabot to Newfoundland in 1496/7 occurred a year after the period to which Brygandyne's published accounts relate.[23] On a more prosaic note, the Bristol Customs Accounts for 1504 record that six Bristol ships successfully made voyages to Andalusia in that year, returning with large cargoes, mainly of wine and olive oil.[24] Voyages of this length and duration had become routine.

Brygandyne, therefore, had in his care a small group of ships which were potentially the nucleus of a powerful squadron. Their design represented an advance on that of the carracks and balingers of the early fifteenth century. Their armament was more powerful and marked a clear progression from that of earlier periods; it showed a better understanding of the use of gunpowder weapons at sea, even if the old weapons still had their place in close combat. The way the men on board were deployed revealed an appreciation of the different skills needed on a successful fighting ship. Moreover, the royal ships had at Portsmouth a base with better facilities than those along the Thames at Greenwich or Erith, which still had a makeshift impermanent air about them. English merchant shipping, a maritime resource which was essential to the King, was also in good heart. His own office, however, and the administration of the King's ships had barely changed since the earliest days of the King's ships. His title, Clerk of the King's Ships, was the same as that held by Thomas Snetesham in the 1340s, and his duties were no better defined than they had been in those early days. Brygandyne finally retired in 1523; his duties and other matters concerning the royal ships were divided among a number of officials and it was not until March 1545 that the 'kinges majesties counseall of the marine', or the Navy Board as it was generally known in later years, came into being. It was this administrative body which ensured the permanence of the Royal Navy, as the King's ships could now justifiably be known.[25]

## Henry VIII

It has been denied that Henry VIII had 'an instinctive appreciation of the importance of sea power and a precocious determination to build up a great navy'. He may have been more strongly motivated at the outset of his reign by the need to outdo his northern neighbour, James IV of Scotland, who had invested a high proportion of his resources in large ships carrying heavy guns. By the end of his reign, however, there had been a decisive change in maritime policy by the Crown. Merchant ships would still be called on to serve the realm in time of need, but a permanent and effective royal navy, in truth justifiably 'the navy of England', had come into being. Some of the first signs of this change are visible in the reign of his father and the work of both Thomas Roger and Robert Brygandyne. There is much truth in the statement that the Tudors 'created a modern navy out of the King's ships'.[26] It is also arguable that this the process first became visible in the final years of the first Tudor, Henry VII.

# Conclusion

MUCH OF THE WRITING about England's medieval navy has started from the unspoken assumption that the creation of a Royal Navy, either for England or for the whole kingdom of Great Britain and Ireland on the model of that which has existed from the seventeenth century till the present day, was the natural end to which earlier developments were leading. Sir Nicholas Harris Nicolas called his history, of which only the first two volumes were completed, *A History of the Royal Navy from the earliest times to the wars of the French Revolution*; since he was writing in 1847 that meant to within his own lifetime. Laird Clowes gave his seven-volume work published at the very end of the nineteenth century the same title.[1] Rodger writing in 1997 pointed out the anomalies in such an approach since, in his view, no Royal Navy existed before the sixteenth century in any part of the British Isles. He explained the various other ways in which naval warfare might be carried on without the expense and administrative burden of a state-funded navy, and saw *The Safeguard of the Sea* as a 'history of naval warfare as an aspect of national history'.[2]

In this work the phrase 'the navy of England' has been interpreted in the way it was usually understood in medieval times as meaning all the vessels in the realm from the humblest fishing boat to the grandest and most imposing of the great ships owned by the Crown. We have seen how a credible and effective defence force could be put together from this heterogeneous mass of craft at times of need as, for example, in aid of Edward I's Scottish campaigns, at the time of the battle of Sluys, and during Henry V's invasion of France. We have also seen how the changing relations between states on both sides of the English Channel and further afield along the coasts of Brittany and the Bay of Biscay had much influence on the ways rulers regarded this 'navy' which was potentially at their disposal, and whether it should be strengthened by a core of royal ships.

We have also looked at the uncertain and sometimes violent world of the seaman, at the way ships were built and designed, and how they were armed for battles at sea. The changes from the ships shown so vividly in the Bayeux Tapestry to the cogs and carracks of the fourteenth and fifteenth centuries cannot be credited to any named individuals; they were the result of the interchange of ideas between mariners in southern and northern waters, and of patient, pragmatic experiment. The ships built at the very end of the fifteenth century were more seaworthy and more manoeuvrable under sail than their predecessors. They also required greater skills in their crews; the task of handling a single square sail like that of an early cog cannot easily be compared with that of handling the rig of a vessel with four masts and perhaps as many as seven sails.[3] Advances in the

techniques of astral navigation and the wide diffusion of experience of long sea voyages among the maritime community also served to raise the profile of seagoing and to make it attractive to men of enterprise. A new-found land was no longer the stuff of the tales of old salts but a reality which might produce enormous profits.

All these factors undoubtedly impacted on the 'navy of England' at the end of the fifteenth century. They were as relevant to merchant ships as to those in the ownership of the King. Also very notable at this period were developments in the use of cannon and other gunpowder weapons on board ship. We have seen the extent to which weapons of this kind were carried on the *Regent* and the *Sovereign*. Armaments of this kind had the potential to change the nature of war at sea and tip the balance clearly in favour of a Royal Navy; the presence of a gunner among the crews of these two ships clearly indicates the increasing importance of ordnance at sea.

In April 1513 an English fleet with a high proportion of King's ships prepared to face French forces near Brest. The French had fortified the port with cannons deployed in the forts and on the cliffs overlooking the Rade de Brest. The English fleet was anchored in the bay of Bertheaume when the French squadron of galleys under Prégent de Bidoux made ready to attack; the wind had dropped so that the English fleet could not easily manoeuvre. The French galleys came on under oars and, according to the report later made by Prégent, gave the English such a hard time with a bombardment by artillery, crossbows and arrows that one large ship was sunk at once and three others were lost later in the night. The French galleys then withdrew to Whitesand Bay, where three days later the English mounted another attack; this ended in the death of the English commander, Edward Howard, and the retreat of the English to Plymouth. The report of Thomas Howard to the King on 7 May argued forcefully that the English had no alternative but to retreat: 'they [the French] should not a fayled to have sonk' the English ships because of their ordnance, 'which ordnance if it be such as they report is a thynge marvellous.'[4] The ordnance on the French galleys would most probably have been mounted in the usual Mediterranean fashion on the prow; in this position it could only be aimed by turning the whole vessel, but against a fleet of sailing ships hampered by adverse winds it was very effective. This relatively minor engagement which had little effect on the overall outcome of the war nevertheless was a portent for the future; a future of professional fighting navies using new tactics and ever more powerful weapons.

England's medieval navy had in many ways served the people well. In times of peace, it ensured that trade was healthy and profitable. In times of war, the ruler, in fact, depended on the support of the whole maritime community. When that was forthcoming, strengthened by the King's own ships, this navy could both defend the realm and carry the war to the enemy. The future lay in fact with the development of a greatly enlarged professional royal navy armed with the latest weapons. The medieval navy of England, however, should not be decried or seen as somehow inadequate and unable to cope with the country's needs. The widely-held but erroneous belief that England was never in real danger of invasion after the Norman Conquest is perhaps a tribute to its success.

# FURTHER READING

This list is not a full bibliography of the topic but a list of the books and other sources which have particular relevance to the subject of this book. References to more specialised works will be found in the notes.

## Primary sources

*The British Library*
Add. MSS 17364. Accounts of the building of Galleys at Bayonne for Edward II; printed in Susan Rose, ed, 'The Bayonne galleys', in Michael Duffy, ed (2003), *Naval Miscellany VI*, Aldershot: Ashgate for the Navy Records Society.
Add MSS 7966A The Wardrobe Book for 1300–01.

*The National Archives at Kew*
The archives at Kew contain the medieval accounts and other documents which are the principal primary sources for the administration of the king's ships in this period. The relevant accounts will be found in two sets of enrolled accounts, the Pipe Rolls (E372) and the Rolls of Foreign Accounts (E364). Many of the Pipe Rolls have been printed by the Pipe Roll Society.

Much material is also to be found in the series known as Exchequer Accounts Various (E101); this series has been fully described in *Lists and Indexes XXXV* 1912. Some items have been transcribed and printed and these will be found listed below.

The most important royal orders and writs will be found summarised in the volumes of the Calendars of Close, Patent and Fine Rolls.

*National Maritime Museum*
Phillipps MS 4102. The Account book of William Soper. The major part of the text is printed in translation in Susan Rose, ed (1982), *The Navy of the Lancastrian Kings*, London: Allen and Unwin for the Navy Records Society.

*Printed sources*
Bréard, Charles, ed (1893), 'le Compte du Clos des gales de Rouen au xiv Siècle 1382–1384', in *Documents Deuxième Serie, Société de la Historie de Normandie*, Rouen.
Brereton, Geoffrey, ed and trans (1968), *Froissart's Chronicles*, London: Penguin.
Christensen, Arne Emil and Wolfgang Steusloff (2012), *The Ebersdorf Ship Model of 1400. An Authentic Example of Late Medieval Shipbuilding in Northern Europe*, Bremerhaven.
Conlon, Joseph, ed (1972), *Li Romans de Witasse le Moine*, Chapel Hill: University of North Carolina Press.
Coxe, O, ed (1841), *Roger of Wendover, Chronica sive Flores Historiarum*, London: English Historical Society.
Crawford, Anne, intro (1992), *Howard Household Books*, Stroud: Alan Sutton for the Richard III and Yorkist History Trust.
Evans, Joan (1928), *The Unconquered Knight: a chronicle of the deeds of Don Pero Niño*, London: Routledge.
Gardiner, Dorothy M (1976), *A Calendar of Early Chancery Proceedings relating to West Country Shipping 1388–1493*, Torquay: Devon and Cornwall Record Society.
Garmonsway, G N (1972), *The Anglo-Saxon Chronicle*, London: Dent.
Given-Wilson, Chris, ed (2005), *The Parliament Rolls of Medieval England*, Leicester: Scholarly Digital Editions.
Hanham, Alison, ed (1975), *The Cely Letters, 1472–1488,* London: Early English Text Society.
Hattendorf, John B and others, eds, *British Naval Documents 1204–1960,* Aldershot: Scolar Press for the Navy Records Society.
Kingsford, Charles Lethbridge (1905), *Chronicles of London*, Oxford: Oxford University Press.
Knighton, C S and D M Loades (2000), *The Anthony Roll of Henry VIII's Navy*, Aldershot: Ashgate for the Navy Records Society.
Lockwood, Shelley (1997), *Sir John Fortescue on the Laws and Governance of England*, Cambridge: Cambridge University Press.
Marx, William (2003), *An English Chronicle 1377–1461*, Woodbridge: Boydell.
Merlin-Chazelas, Anne, ed (1977–80), *Documents Relatifs au Clos des Galées de Rouen,* Paris: Bibliothèque Nationale.
Meyer, P, ed (1891–1901), *L'Histoire de Guillaume le Maréchal,* Paris: Société de l'Histoire de France.
Myers, A R, ed (1969), *English Historical Documents, 1327–1485,* London: Eyre and Spottiswoode.
Oppenheim, M (1896), *Naval Accounts and Inventories of the reign of Henry VII 1485–6 and 1495–7*, London: The Navy Records Society.
Riley, Henry T (1853), *The Annals of Roger de Hoveden*, London: Bohm.
Sinclair, Alexandra, ed (2003), *The Beauchamp Pageant*, Donington: Paul Watkins for the Richard III and Yorkist History Trust.
Taylor, Frank and John S Roskell, eds (1975), *Gesta Henrici Quinti*, Oxford: Clarendon Press.
Thompson, Edward Maunde (1889), *Adae Murimuth Continuatio Chronicarum; Robertus de Avesbury De Gestis Miribilibus Regis Edwardi tertii*, London: Rolls Series.
Thorpe, Lewis (1973), *The Bayeux Tapestry and the Norman Invasion*, London: The Folio Society.
Twiss, Sir Travers (1871), *The Black Book of the Admiralty*, London: Rolls Series.
Warner, Sir George (1926), *The Libelle of Englyshe Polycye: a poem on the use of Sea Power 1436*, Oxford: Clarendon Press.

## Secondary sources

Bennett, Jenny, ed (2009), *Sailing into the Past: learning from replica ships*, Barnsley: Seaforth.
Bork, Robert and Andrea Kann, eds (2008), *Art Science and Technology of Medieval Travel*, Aldershot: Ashgate.

Bouet, Pierre et Veronique Gazeau (2002), *La Normandie et l'Angleterre au Moyen Age*, Caen: CRAHM.

Bourel de la Roncière, Charles (1899), *Histoire de la Marine Française*, Paris: Librarie Plon.

Brooks, F W (1932), *The English Naval Forces 1199–1272*, London: A Brown.

Burwash, Dorothy (1969), *English Merchant Shipping 1460–1540*, Newton Abbot: David and Charles.

Cushway, Graham (2011), *Edward III and the War at Sea: the English navy, 1327–1377,* Woodbridge: Boydell.

Dollinger, Phillipe (1964), *La Hanse (xii–xvii siècles)*, Paris: Aubier.

Duff, Michael, and others, eds (1992), *The New Maritime History of Devon, vol I From the earliest times to the eighteenth century*, London: Conway for the University of Exeter.

Eddison, Jill (2000), *Romney Marsh: survival on a frontier*, Stroud: Tempus.

Flatman, Joe (2009), *Ships and Shipping in Medieval Manuscripts*, London: British Museum Press.

Friel, Ian (1995), *The Good Ship*, London: British Museum Press.

Fudge, John D (1995), *Cargoes, Embargoes and Emissaries: the commercial and political interaction of England and the German Hanse, 1450–1510*, Toronto: University of Toronto Press.

Gardiner, Robert, ed (1994), *Cogs, Caravels and Galleons: the sailing ship 1000–1650*, London: Conway.

Gorski, Richard, ed (2012), *The Roles of the Sea in Medieval England*, Woodbridge: Boydell.

Hattendorf, John B, and others, eds (2003), *War at Sea in the Middle Ages and Renaissance*, Woodbridge: Boydell.

Hewitt, H J (1966), *The Organisation of War under Edward III*, Manchester: Manchester University Press.

Hicks, Michael (2002), *Warwick the Kingmaker*, Oxford: Blackwell.

Hutchinson, Gillian (1994), *Medieval Ships and Shipping*, London: Leicester University Press.

Kingsford, C L (1925), *Prejudice and Promise in XV Century England*, Oxford: Clarendon Press.

Lambert, Craig L (2011), *Shipping the Medieval Military: English maritime logistics in the fourteenth century*, Woodbridge: Boydell.

Lloyd, T H (1991), *England and the German Hanse 1157–1611: a study of their trade and commercial diplomacy,* Cambridge: Cambridge University Press.

Loades, David (1992), *The Tudor Navy: an administrative, political and military history*, Aldershot: Scolar Press.

Marcus, G L (1980), *The Conquest of the North Atlantic*, Woodbridge: Boydell.

Martin, David and Barbara (2004), *New Winchelsea Sussex: a medieval port town*, London: English Heritage.

Meier, Dirk (2006), *Seafarers, Merchants and Pirates in the Middle Ages*, Woodbridge: Boydell.

Mott, Laurence V (2003), *Sea Power in the Medieval Mediterranean: the Catalan-Aragonese Fleet in the War of the Sicilian Vespers*, Tallahassee: University of Florida Press.

Nicolas, Sir Nicholas Harris (1847), *A History of the Royal Navy from the earliest times to the wars of the French Revolution*, 2 vols, London.

Oppenheim, M (1896), *A History of the Administration of the Royal Navy and of Merchant Shipping in relation to the Navy from MDIX to MDCLX with an Introduction treating of the preceding period*, London: The Bodley Head.

Platt, Colin (1973), *Medieval Southampton: the port and trading community AD 1000–1600*, London: Routledge.

Pryor, John H (1988), *Geography, Technology and War: studies in the maritime history of the Mediterranean 649–1571*, Cambridge: Cambridge University Press.

Richmond, Colin (1998–9), 'The Earl of Warwick's Domination of the Channel and the Naval Dimension to the Wars of the Roses, 1456–60', *Southern History*, 20/21.

Rodger, N A M (1997), *The Safeguard of the Sea, vol I of A Naval History of Britain*, London: Harper Collins.

Rose, Susan (1998), *Southampton and the Navy in the Age of Henry V*, Winchester: Hampshire County Council.

—— (2002), *Medieval Naval Warfare*, London: Routledge.

—— (2007), *The Medieval Sea*, London; Continuum.

——, ed (2008), *Medieval Ships and Warfare*, Aldershot: Ashgate. A collection of some of the most important articles on this topic.

Russell, P E (1955), *The English Intervention in Spain and Portugal in the Time of Edward III and Richard II*, Oxford: Oxford University Press.

Russon, Marc (2004), *Les Côtes Guerrières: mer, guerre et pouvoirs au Moyen Age, France-Façade océanique xiii-xv siècle*, Rennes: Presse Universitaire de Rennes.

Sherborne, James, ed Anthony Tuck (1994), *War, Politics and Culture in Fourteenth Century England*, London: Hambledon.

Smith, Robert Douglas and Kelly de Vries (2005), *The Artillery of the Dukes of Burgundy 1363–1477*, Woodbridge: Boydell.

Sumption, Jonathan (1990–2009), *The Hundred Years War*, 3 vols, Philadelphia: University of Pennsylvania Press.

Taylor, E G R (1956), *The Haven-Finding Art: a history of navigation from Odysseus to Captain Cook*, London: Hollis and Carter.

Terrier de Lorcy, Le Marquis (1877), *Jean de Vienne Amiral de France, 1341–1396*, Paris: Librarie de la Société Bibliographique.

Ward, Robin (2009), *The World of the Medieval Shipmaster: Law, Business and the Sea, c.1350–1450*, Woodbridge: Boydell.

Waters, David W (1958), *The Art of Navigation in England in Elizabethan and Early Stuart Times*, London: Hollis and Carter.

# TIMELINE

## Notable Dates

| | |
|---|---|
| 789 | First recorded landing of Danish ships in English territory. |
| 793 | Destruction of Lindisfarne Abbey by raiders called 'heathen' (Danes). Period of frequent raids by Norsemen called variously Vikings and Danes follows. |
| 865 | Danish settlements in eastern England begin. |
| 871–96 | Alfred the Great's campaigns against the Danes including actions against ships in estuaries and near the shore. |
| 896 | Alfred orders warships to be built to meet the Danish ships |
| 899 | Death of Alfred. |
| 991 | Resumption of Danish raids; defeat of the English at Maldon. |
| 1013 | King Swein Forkbeard of Denmark accepted as King of England. |
| 1016 | Cnut becomes King of England, now part of a northern empire. |
| 1042 | Edward the Confessor, a descendant of Alfred, becomes King of England. |
| 1064 | Harold Godwinson, Earl of Wessex shipwrecked at Ponthieu and captured by the Count. Later handed over to William, Duke of Normandy whose claim to the throne of England he may have sworn to support. |
| 1066 | Death of Edward the Confessor; Harold becomes king. William prepares a fleet to invade England. Complete victory on 14 October 14 at Hastings; Harold slain. |
| 1087 | Succession of William Rufus. |
| 1100 | Succession of Henry I. |
| 1120 | Disastrous wreck of the White Ship off Barfleur. |
| 1135 | Death of Henry I. Succession disputed between Stephen and Matilda; intermittent civil war. |
| 1152 | Henry of Anjou, later Henry II, marries Eleanor of Aquitaine, former wife of Louis VII of France. |
| 1154 | Accession of Henry II; Angevin Empire extends from Scottish borders to the Pyrenees. |
| 1189 | Death of Henry II; succession of Richard I. |
| 1190–92 | Participation of Richard in the Third Crusade. |
| 1199 | Death of Richard; accession of John. War with France ruled by Philip II Augustus. |

| | |
|---|---|
| 1204 | John loses his territories in Northern France including Normandy. |
| 1213 | Battle of Damme. |
| 1214 | Battle of Bouvines; Philip completes defeat of John. |
| 1215 | Baronial rebellion against John; Magna Carta agreed. The Dauphin Louis invades England in support of the rebels. |
| 1216 | Death of John; accession of Henry III. |
| 1217 | Battle of Dover; killing of Eustace the Monk. |
| 1224 | French take La Rochelle and Poitou. |
| 1272 | Death of Henry III; accession of Edward I. |
| 1277 1282/3 | Edward's campaigns in Wales. |
| 1295 | Philip IV of France sets up his galley yard at Rouen. Edward orders galleys to be built by English towns. |
| 1296 | First campaign in Scotland; war continued intermittently till Edward's death in 1307. Both the Welsh and the Scots wars required the extensive logistical support of English shipping. |
| 1293 | Conflict off Breton coast between Normans and Gascons. |
| 1307 | Accession of Edward II; war with Scotland continued until Scots victory at Bannockburn in 1314. |
| 1324 | French attacks on English Gascony. |
| 1326/7 | Edward II deposed; Edward III becomes king. |
| 1337 | Philip IV confiscates English Gascony. |
| 1338 | French raids on English coastal towns including Portsmouth and Southampton; English royal ships captured at Middelburg. |
| 1339 | Further French raids. |
| 1340 | English raid on Boulogne; battle of Sluys. |
| 1346 | Edward III lands at St Vaast la Hogue prior to battle of Crécy; opening of siege of Calais. |
| 1347 | Fall of Calais to the English. |
| 1348 | The Black Death; plague epidemics returned at intervals notably in 1361/2, 1369, 1375. |
| 1350 | Les Espagnols sur Mer, or the battle of Winchelsea. |
| 1356 | English capture John of France at the battle of Poitiers. |
| 1360 | French sack Winchelsea. |
| 1369 | Formal resumption of war with France. |

| | |
|---|---|
| 1372 | Battle of La Rochelle; French capture of the Earl of Pembroke. |
| 1377 | French raids all along the south coast; death of Edward III. Accession of Richard II. |
| 1381 | The Peasants' Revolt. |
| 1385/6 | French prepare for invasion of England. |
| 1399 | Henry of Lancaster deposes Richard II, becomes king as Henry IV. |
| 1401–5 | Rise in attacks on shipping in the Channel; Castilian galleys raiding English ports |
| 1410 | Death of Henry IV; accession of Henry V. |
| 1415 | Agincourt campaign; English take Harfleur. |
| 1416 | Duke of Bedford raises French siege of Harfleur; captures three Genoese carracks. |
| 1417 | English conquest of Normandy; *Clos des galées* at Rouen burnt. Regular naval patrols in the Channel till 1420. |
| 1421 | Treaty of Troyes with Charles VI of France; Henry V recognised as his heir. |
| 1422 | Henry V dies; accession of Henry VI, as King of England and France. Sale of Henry V's ships in accordance with his will. |
| 1435 | French take Dieppe. |
| 1436 | Abortive Burgundian siege of Calais. |
| 1450 | Normandy reconquered by the French. |
| 1453 | Battle of Castillon; loss of Gascony by the English. |
| 1455 | Civil conflict in England till accession of Edward IV in 1461. |
| 1457 | French raid on Sandwich; the Earl of Warwick Captain of Calais. |
| 1461 | Accession of Edward IV. |
| 1470 | The Earl of Warwick supports the re-adoption of Henry VI. |
| 1471 | Death of Warwick at the battle of Barnet; Edward IV restored to the throne. |
| 1482 | Campaign in Scotland. |
| 1483 | Death of Edward IV; brief reign of Edward V; seizure of the throne by Richard III. |
| 1485 | Battle of Bosworth; death in battle of Richard III; Henry VII becomes king. |
| 1509 | Death of Henry VII; accession of Henry VIII. |
| 1512/3 | War of the Holy League; battles off Brittany. |

# NOTES

## INTRO

[1] Shakespeare, *Richard II*, Act 2 sc 1.

[2] *The Anglo-Saxon Chronicle*, trans G N Garmonsway (1972), London: Dent, 55.

[3] *The Anglo-Saxon Chronicle*, 73.

[4] N A M Rodger (1997), *The Safeguard of the Sea: a naval history of Great Britain*, vol I, 660–1649, London: Harper Collins, 49.

## CHAPTER 1

[1] Sir Nicholas Harris Nicolas (1847, reprinted 2005), *A History of the Royal Navy*, vol I, Cranbury NJ: The Scholar's Bookshelf, xi.

[2] Henry Rothwell, ed (1975), *English Historical Documents 1189–1327*, London: Eyre and Spottiswoode, 'The "History of William the Marshal" for the years 1216–19', 92–4.

[3] John B Hattendorf et al, eds (1993), *British Naval Documents 1204–1960*, Aldershot: Scolar Press for the Navy Records Society, item 9, 18–9.

[4] The most recent Spanish edition of this book is Rafael Beltrán Llavador, ed (1997), *El Victorial*, Salamanca: Salamanca University Press. A translation of the incident discussed can be found in John B Hattendorf et al, eds (1993), *British Naval Documents*, Aldershot: Scolar Press/Navy Records Society, 26–9.

[5] John B Hattendorf et al, eds (1993), *British Naval Documents*, item 17, 26–9.

[6] Class E (Exchequer) 364 at TNA.

[7] Class E101 at TNA; listed in *Lists and Indexes XXXV*.

[8] National Maritime Museum, Phillipps MS 4102. The account book has been edited by Susan Rose in (1982), *The Navy of the Lancastrian Kings*, London: George Allen and Unwin for the Navy Records Society.

[9] TNA Class E 36; listed in *Lists and Indexes XXXV*.

[10] These are BL Add MSS 43491 ff.7 and 42. They are printed in John B Hattendorf et al, eds, *British Naval Documents*, 30–2.

[11] Alison Hanham (1985), *The Celys and their World*, Cambridge: Cambridge University Press, 361–97.

[12] *The Household Books of John Howard, Duke of Norfolk, 1462–71 and 1471–3*, Anne Crawford, intro (1992), Stroud: Alan Sutton for the Yorkist History Trust.

[13] Sir G Warner, ed (1926), *The Libelle of Englyshe Polycye*. The section quoted is printed in John B Hattendorf, *British Naval Documents*, 11–13.

[14] Bibliothèque Nationale de France, MS français 2643.

[15] The whole MS has been produced in a printed version: Alexandra Sinclair, ed (2003), *The Beauchamp Pageant*, Donington: Paul Watkins for the Yorkist History Trust.

[16] Joe Flatman (2009), *Ships and Shipping in Medieval Manuscripts*, London: The British Library, 37.

[17] A good example is the vessel from the Luttrell Psalter reproduced in Joe Flatman, *Ships and Shipping in Medieval Manuscripts*, 77.

[18] Pamela O Long, David McGee and Alan M Stahl (2009), *The Book of Michael of Rhodes*, vol I facsimile, 310–13.

[19] Pepys MS 2820, Magdalene College, Cambridge.

[20] These pictures are reproduced in Michael Duffy et al, eds (1992), *The New Maritime History of Devon*, vol I, Exeter: Exeter University and Conway Maritime Press, 76–7.

[21] Joe Flatman discusses the iconographical evidence for the hulk in *Ships and Shipping in Medieval Manuscripts*, 87–8.

[22] Gillian Hutchinson (1994), *Medieval Ships and Shipping*, Leicester: Leicester University Press, 191–8; the London entries are 193–4.

[23] Olaf Olsen and Ole Crumlin-Pedersen (1978), *Five Viking Ships from Roskilde Fjord*, Roskilde: Vikingeskipshallen.

[24] A full discussion of the creation of replica ships and the value of experimental archaeology of this type can be found in Jenny Bennett, ed (2009), *Sailing into the Past: learning from replica ships*, Barnsley: Seaforth Publishing, 16–23.

## CHAPTER 2

[1] Lewis Thorpe (1973), *The Bayeux Tapestry and the Norman Invasion*, London: The Folio Society, 9. This was the theory put forward by William of Jumièges and William of Poitiers, both writing from the Norman point of view.

[2] Lewis Thorpe, *The Bayeux Tapestry*, frames 2–7.

[3] Lewis Thorpe, *The Bayeux Tapestry*, frames 40–6.

[4] There is a full discussion of Norse ships, their design and building in Angelo Forte, Richard Oram and Frederik Pedersen (2005), *Viking Empires*, Cambridge: Cambridge University Press, 118–69.

[5] Jenny Bennett, ed (2009), *Sailing into the past: learning from replica ships*, Barnsley: Seaforth, 54–69.

[6] An example of this kind of engagement is that in 896 between King Alfred's ships and a Danish squadron beached in an estuary not far from the Isle of Wight, perhaps in the Beaulieu river. N A M Rodger (1997), *The Safeguard of the Sea*, London: Harper Collins, 16–17.

[7] The details of Anglo-Saxon methods of putting together a fleet to defend the country can be found in Nicholas Hooper (1992), 'Some observations on the navy in late Anglo-Saxon England', in Matthew Strickland, ed, *Anglo-Norman Warfare: studies in late Anglo-Saxon and Anglo-Norman military organisation and warfare*, Woodbridge: Boydell Press, 17–27.

[8] G N Garmonsway, trans (1972), *The Anglo-Saxon Chronicle*, Dent: London, 196.

[9] William's tactics for the crossing of the Channel are discussed in C M Gillmor (1984), 'Naval Logistics of the Cross-Channel Operation 1066', in *Anglo-Norman Studies VII*, 105–31, and in Christine Grainge and Gerald Grainge (1993), 'The Pevensey expedition: brilliantly executed plan or near disaster?', *Mariner's Mirror; 79*, 261–73.

[10] Rodger, *Safeguard of the Sea*, 49.

[11] F W Brooks (1930), 'The battle of Damme 1213', in *MM* 16, 263–71.

[12] The battle is described in the verse biography of William Marshal, Earl of Pembroke and in his entry in ODNB; also see below.

[13] *Froissart's Chronicles*, 113–19.

[14] A list of chronicles, from both English and French sources, which mention this battle in some detail can be found in Rodger, *Safeguard of the Sea*, n29, 528; also see below.

[15] Jonathan Sumption (2009), *The Hundred Years War, III, Divided Houses*, Philadelphia: University of Pennsylvania Press, 551–7.

[16] Geoffrey Brereton, ed (1968), *Froissart Chronicles*, London: Penguin, 304–7.

[17] Jonathan Sumption (2009), *The Hundred Years War III*, 592.

[18] Colin Platt (1973), *Medieval Southampton: the port and trading community AD1000–1600*, London: Routledge and Kegan Paul, 36–8.

[19] *Froissart Chronicles*, ed Geoffrey Brereton, 60–1.

[20] Platt, *Medieval Southampton*, 107–12.

[21] Rodger, *Safeguard of the Sea*, 111.

[22] One London chronicle recorded the event in blunt words. 'In this yere Sandwich was robbid and dispoilid by Frenssheman.' As a result there was 'gret watch in London and al the gates kept every nyght and ii aldermen watchynge'. *A Chronicle of London from 1089 to 1483*, reprint 1995, Felinfach: Llanerch, 139.

[23] *Parliament Rolls of Medieval England*, eds C Given-Wilson et al (2005), Leicester: Scholarly Digital editions, Parliament of October 1377.

[24] *Parliament Rolls of Medieval England, 1378*, item 41.

[25] Marc Russon (2004), *Les Côtes guerrières: mer, guerre et pouvoirs au Moyen Age; France – façade océanique xiii–xv siècle*, Rennes: Presse Universitaire de Rennes, 83–99.

[26] ODNB entry John Hawley.

[27] Dorothy M Gardiner, ed (1976), *A Calendar of Early Chancery proceedings relating to West Country Shipping 1388–1493*, Devon and Cornwall Record Society, new series vol 21, items 9, 11, 14, 15, 16, 24, 25.

[28] This is discussed in C J Ford, 'Piracy or Policy: the Crisis in the Channel, 1400–1403', reprinted in S Rose, ed (2008), *Medieval Ships and Warfare*, Aldershot: Ashgate, 105–19.

[29] *Parliament Rolls of Medieval England*, Parliament of March 1406, item 19.

[30] Susan Rose (1982), *The Navy of the Lancastrian Kings*, London: Allen and Unwin for the Navy Records Society, 48–52.

[31] George Warner (1926), *The Libelle of Englyshe Polycye: a poem on the use of sea-power 1436*, Oxford: Clarendon Press, 1, 50–1.

[32] George Warner (1926), *The Libelle of Englyshe Polycye*, 54.

[33] *Parliament Rolls of Medieval England*, Parliament of January 1442, item 30.

[34] Marcus Pitcaithly, 'Piracy and Anglo-Hanseatic Relations, 1385–1420', in R Gorski, ed (2012), *Roles of the Sea in Medieval England*, Woodbridge: Boydell, 125–45.

[35] Off Barfleur. Chroniclers embroider the story by stating that the crew and most of the passengers were drunk.

[36] Henry T Riley, ed (1853), *The Annals of Roger de Hoveden*, London: H G Bohn, 350.

[37] Nicholas Harris Nicolas (1847, reprint 2005), *A History of the Royal Navy from the earliest times to the wars of the French Revolution*, vol I, 106–15. Nicolas' account is closely based on that of various medieval chronicles, principally that of Hoveden.

[38] F W Brooks published a series of articles on naval affairs in this period including 'William de Wrotham and the office of the Keeper of the King's Ports and Galleys' (1925), *EHR*, 40, 570–9; 'The King's Ships and Galleys, mainly under John and Henry III' (1928), *MM*, 14, 115–31; 'Naval Administration and the raising of fleets under John and Henry III' (1929), *MM*, 15, 351–90. He also published *The English Naval Forces 1199–1272*, London: A Brown and Sons.

[39] Rodger, *The Safeguard of the Sea*, 53.

[40] Nicolas, *Royal Navy*, vol I, 195–206.

[41] Rodger, *The Safeguard of the Sea*, 77–8.

[42] W Stanford Reid (1960), 'Sea-power in the Anglo-Scottish war 1296–1328', *MM*, 46, 7–23, provides an overview of the Scots wars.

[43] Susan Rose (2008), 'The provision of ships for Edward I's campaigns in Scotland, 1300–1306: barges and merchantmen', in Susan Rose, ed (2008), *The Naval Miscellany VII*, Aldershot: Ashgate for the Navy Record Society, 1–5.

[44] TNA E101/10 /30, printed in *Naval Miscellany VII*.

[45] BL, ADD MSS 7966A.

[46] H C B Rogers (1957), 'The siege of Caerlaverock Castle', *The Army Quarterly*, 73, 257.

[47] Document 4, TNA E101/11/28 in Susan Rose, 'The provision of ships for Edward I's campaigns in Scotland'.

[48] Froissart, *Chronicles*, 51.

[49] At this date, the term 'tun' signified a large wooden barrel, usually of the capacity of the Bordeaux wine tun, not a measure of weight.

[50] Craig L Lambert (2011), *Shipping the Medieval Military, English Maritime Logistics in the Fourteenth Century*, Woodbridge: Boydell. Lambert provides a detailed and thorough analysis of this aspect of the use of ships by the Crown from 1320–60. The figures referred to above come from tables on 72 (2.3 and 2.30), 151 (3.2) and 154 (3.3). A full list of all the ships in the fleet raised in 1345 to take Henry of Lancaster's army to Bordeaux can be found at H J Hewitt (1966), *The Organisation of War under Edward III 1338–62*, Manchester: Manchester University Press, 182–6.

[51] The account for the expedition is TNA E101/40/19; a list of ships can be found at TNA E101/42/18; the expedition is discussed by P E Russell (1955), *The English Intervention in Spain and Portugal in the time of Edward III and Richard II*, Oxford: Clarendon Press,

411–21.

52 Frank Taylor and John S Rosskell, eds (1975), *Gesta Henrici Quinti, the Deeds of Henry V*, Oxford: Clarendon Press, 20–1.

53 J Stevenson, ed (1864), *Letters and Papers illustrative of the wars of the English in France during the reign of Henry VI, King of England*, London: Rolls Series, 588.

54 J Stevenson, ed (1864), 597.

55 TNA E101/54/14. Most of these ships came from West Country ports on this occasion.

56 N A M Rodger, *The Safeguard of the Sea*, 47.

57 P E Russell (1955), *The English Intervention in Spain and Portugal in the time of Edward II and Richard II*, Oxford: Clarendon Press, 229.

58 Graham Cushway (2011), *Edward III and the war at sea: the English Navy 1327–1377*, Woodbridge: Boydell, 217–8.

59 Sir John Fortescue, ed Shelley Lockwood (1997), *On the Laws and Governance of England*, Cambridge: Cambridge University Press, 96–7.

CHAPTER 3
1 Samson Wascelin's ship.
2 To repair the King's *esnecca*. Nicolas, *History of the Royal Navy*, vol I, 432–4 has a note on the *Esnecca* which suggests that references to a royal ship described like this can be found in the reign of Henry I.
3 The references to payments to shipmasters or owners can be found in various volumes among the Pipe Rolls Society's publication. They are as follows: vol 22 for 21 Henry II (1175); vol 24 for 22 Henry II (1167); vol 26 for 23 Henry II (1177); vol 27 for 24 Henry II (1178); vol 33 for 30 Henry II (1184); vol 37 for 33 Henry II (1187).
4 N H Nicolas, *History of the Royal Navy I*, 127.
5 ODNB articles on Wrotham, William of, and Cornhill, Gervase de.
6 See chapter 1, sources.
7 The introduction to the published Pipe Roll for 7 John details these payments and also the orders assembling the fleet and the necessary supplies. Pipe Roll Society, vol lvii, N.S. 1, Pipe Roll for 7 John (1205), 1941, xii–xxi.
8 John Gillingham (1997), 'Richard I, Galley-warfare and Portsmouth: the Beginning of the Royal Navy', in Michael Prestwich, ed, *Thirteenth Century England VI*, Woodbridge: Boydell, 6–8.
9 *Oeuvres de Ricord et de Guillaume le Breton*, ed H F Delaborde (1882), vol II *Philippidos*, vii, ll. 173–4.
10 Pipe Roll Society, vol xli, N.S. 3, 1927, Pipe Roll for 5 Richard I (1193), 150.
11 Pipe Roll Society vol xliv, N.S. 6, 1929, Pipe Roll for 7 Richard I (1195), 113.
12 Pipe Roll Society, vol xxxix, N.S. 1, 1925, Pipe Roll for 2 Richard II (1190), 131.
13 CCR, Henry III, vol 1, August 1229, 248–50, online at http://www.british-history.ac.uk, accessed 1 May 2012.
14 Keeper of the great ship and the galleys.

15 The 'great ship' is not identified elsewhere. CCR, Henry III, vol 1, 1227–31, 170–80, online at http://www.british-history.ac.uk, accessed 1 May 2012.
16 CCR, Henry III, vol 4, 1237–42, 465–72, online at http://www.british-history.ac.uk, accessed 1 May 2012.
17 *British Naval Documents*, 43, item 31.
18 CCR, Henry III, May 1248, vol 6, 1247–61, 42–55, online at http://www.british-history.ac.uk, accessed 1 May 2012.
19 CCR, May 1257, Henry III, vol 10, 1256–59, 50–60, online at http://www.british-history.ac.uk, accessed 1 May 2012.
20 CCR, July 1264, Henry III, vol 12, 1261–64, 347–52, online at http://www.british-history.ac.uk, accessed 1 May 2012.
21 Susan Rose (2008), 'The provision of ships for Edward I's campaigns in Scotland 1300–1306; barges and merchantmen', in Susan Rose, ed, *Naval Miscellany VII*, Aldershot: Ashgate for the Navy Records Society, 1–56. This contains a translation of the building accounts for these vessels as well as an introduction explaining the background.
22 J T Tinniswood (1949), 'English Galleys 1272–1377', *The Mariner's Mirror*, 35, 276–7.
23 CCR Edward II 1312.
24 CCR Edward II 1315.
25 CPR Edward II, vol I, 502.
26 The cog ships were the *Cog St Marie of Westminster, Cog St Piere, Cog John, Cog Notre Dame*.
27 CPR Edward II, vol 5, 278. Andrew Rosekyn ordered to recruit sixty men for the King's galley *Marie*.
28 TNA C131/2/2
29 Susan Rose, ed (2003), 'The Bayonne Galleys', in M Duffy, ed, *The Naval Miscellany VI*, Aldershot: Ashgate for the Navy Records Society, 1–36. This contains a translation of the accounts of the building of the galleys as well as an introduction which details what is known of their careers.
30 Graham Cushway (2011), *Edward III and the War at Sea: the English navy 1327–1377*, Woodbridge: Boydell, 225–35.
31 Clewere's particulars of account are to be found in TNA E101/25/14, a bundle which includes various individual pieces or rotulets. These accounts are pieces nos 3, 5, 10.
32 TNA E372/203. These accounts have been transcribed and translated by Susan Rose and will appear in *Naval Miscellany VIII*, The Navy Records Society, forthcoming.
33 TNA E101/29/39.
34 Alan Moore (1920), 'A barge of Edward III', in *Mariner's Mirror*, 6, 229–42.
35 John Chamberlain enrolled accounts; TNA Exchequer Lord Treasurer's Remembrancer, E364/39 and 43. The surviving particulars are Exchequer Accounts Various, E101/42/39, E101/43/2 and E101/43/6.
36 TNA E364/46.

37 TNA E101/44/23.

38 TNA E364/54.

39 Frank Taylor and John S Roskill, eds (1975), *Gesta Henrici Quinti; the deeds of Henry V*, Oxford: Clarendon Press, 20.

40 Account of Robert Berde, TNA E364/57.

41 Susan Rose, ed (1982), *The Navy of the Lancastrian Kings: Accounts and inventories of William Soper. Keeper of the King's Ships, 1422–27*, London: Allen and Unwin for the Navy Records Society, 34–9. Catton's final account is TNA E364/59. Soper's enrolled accounts for his first years in office are TNA E364/61, membrane G (repair of the *Holy Ghost* and *Gabriel*) and membrane D et seq for the years 1418–22.

42 Susan Rose, ed (1982), *The Navy of the Lancastrian Kings*, 52–55.

43 David Loades (1992), *The Tudor Navy: an administrative, political and military history*, Aldershot: Scolar Press, 27–31.

44 M Oppenheim (1896), *Naval Accounts and Inventories of the reign of Henry VII 1485–8 and 1495–7*, London: Navy Records Society, 3–81.

45 M Oppenheim (1896), *Naval Accounts and Inventories*, 135–344.

46 Susan Rose (2012), 'The value of the Cinque Ports to the Crown 1200–1500', in Richard Gorski, ed, *Roles of the Sea in Medieval England*, Woodbridge: The Boydell Press, 41–4.

47 J Topham, ed (1787), *Liber Quotidianus Contrarotulatoris garderobae 1299–1300*, London, 271–9. Also see Susan Rose, ed (2012), 'The value of the Cinque Ports', 49–50.

48 Craig L Lambert (2012), 'The Contribution of the Cinque Ports to the wars of Edward II and Edward III: new methodologies and estimates', in Richard Gorski, ed, *The Roles of the Sea*, 59–78.

49 Helen Clarke (2012), *Discover Medieval Sandwich: a guide to its history and buildings*, Oxford: Oxbow Books, 1–6.

50 *Calendar of Fine Rolls 1337–47*, 238.

51 David and Barbara Martin (2004), *New Winchelsea, a medieval port town*, London: Institute of Archaeology, University College London, 1–6.

52 See the illustration on page 73 and also Joe Flatman (2009), *Ships and Shipping in Medieval Manuscripts*, London: British Library, 77–9, and Gillian Hutchinson (1994), *Medieval Ships and Shipping*, London: Leicester University Press, 153.

53 Lewis Thorpe (1973), *The Bayeux Tapestry and the Norman Invasion*, London: Folio Society, frames 43–46.

54 James Lydon (1981), 'Edward I and the war in Scotland, 1303–4', in James Lydon, ed, *England and Ireland in the later middle ages: essays in honour of Jocelyn Otway-Ruthven*, Blackrock, 43–61. Details of the preparation of the ships to take horses on board are 48–9.

55 The account is printed in H J Hewitt (1966), *The Organisation of War under Edward III 1338–62*, Manchester: Manchester University Press,

56 Craig L Lambert (2011), *Shipping the Medieval Military: English Maritime Logistics in the Fourteenth Century*, Woodbridge: Boydell Press, 93–100.

57 The account in TNA E101/10/30. It has been transcribed and translated in Susan Rose (2008), *The Naval Miscellany VII*, Aldershot: Ashgate for the Navy Records Society, 37–47 and the Introduction, 4–5.

58 TNA E101/54/4.

59 The most easily accessible version of the so-called 'Roll of Calais' is in N H Nicolas (1847, reprinted 2005), *A History of the Royal Navy*, II, 507–10. The various versions are discussed in Craig Lambert, *Shipping the Medieval Military*, 136–40.

60 Craig Lambert, *Shipping the Medieval Military*, 145–50.

61 Frank Taylor and John S Roskill, eds (1975), *Gesta Henrici Quinti*, Oxford: Clarendon Press, 20–1.

62 Christopher Allmand (1992), *Henry V*, London: Methuen, 78–9.

63 Robin Ward (2009), *The World of the Medieval Shipmaster*, Woodbridge: Boydell, 107–8.

64 The best known ration scale is that of the crews of the Venetian galleys, Susan Rose (2007), *The Medieval Sea*, 88.

65 N A M Rodger (1997), *The Safeguard of the Sea*, 119.

66 N A M Rodger (1997), *The Safeguard of the Sea*, 122.

67 TNA E101/10/21, a file of writs; the text has been transcribed and translated in Susan Rose, ed (2008), *The Naval Miscellany VII*, Aldershot: Ashgate for the Navy Records Society, 30–7.

68 Full details of the campaign in Brittany and its naval component are in Graham Cushway (2011), *Edward III and the War at Sea*, 110–13. This desertion from the royal fleet is also discussed in Craig Lambert (2011), *Shipping the Medieval Military*, 129–34.

69 Chris Given-Wilson, ed (2005), *The Parliament Rolls of Medieval England*, Leicester: Scholarly Digital Editions, Edward III, January 1348, ii, 172.

70 *Parliament Rolls of Medieval England*, Edward III, February 1371, ii, 307.

71 *Parliament Rolls of Medieval England*, Richard II, October 1385, iii, 212.

72 *Parliament Rolls of Medieval England*, Henry IV, October 1404, iii, 554.

73 *Parliament Rolls of Medieval England*, Henry V, March, 1416, iv, 79.

## CHAPTER 4

1 C S Knightom and D M Loades, eds (2000), *The Antony Roll*, Aldershot: Ashgate for the Navy Records Society. This contains reproductions of all the ships on the Roll of which the original MS is now split into three sections in three different collections.

2 Susan Rose (1982), *The Navy of the Lancastrian Kings*, 41.

[3] Gillian Hutchinson (1994), *Medieval Ships and Shipping*, l, London: Leicester University Press, 191–8.

[4] H Lovegrove (1964), 'Remains of two old vessels found at Rye, Sussex', in *Mariner's Mirror*, 50, 115–22.

[5] Gustav Milne (2004), 'The Fourteenth Century Merchant Ship from Sandwich: a study in medieval maritime archaeology', in *Archaeologia Cantiana*, 124, 227–63.

[6] Ian Friel (1993), 'Henry V's *Gracedieu* and the wreck in the R Hamble near Bursledon, Hampshire', in *The International Journal of Nautical Archaeology*, 22, 3–19; Richard Clarke et al (1993), 'Recent work on the R Hamble wreck near Bursledon, Hampshire', in *The International Journal of Nautical Archaeology*, 22, 21–44.

[7] J Kate Howell and Richard Trett (2008), 'The Newport Medieval Ship', in *Gwent County History*, 2, Cardiff: Cardiff University Press, 163–6; Richard Trett, (2005), 'The Newport Medieval Ship; historical background', in *The Monmouthshire Antiquary*, 21, 103–6.

[8] Rikke Johansen, 'The Viking ships of Skuldelev', 54–69; Wolf-Dieter Hoheisel, 'The Hanseatic Cog', 72–83, in Jenny Bennett, ed (2009), *Sailing into the Past: learning from replica ships*, Barnsley: Seaforth.

[9] J W van Nouhuys (1931), 'The Model of a Spanish Caravel of the beginning of the Fifteenth Century', in *Mariner's Mirror*, 17; Clinton A Edwards (1992), 'Design and Construction of fifteenth century Iberian ships : a review', *Mariner's Mirror*, 78, 419–32.

[10] Wolfgang Steusloff (1983), 'das Ebersdorfer Koggenmodell von 1400: ein Beitrag zum nordeuropaischen Schiffbau des spatlen Mittlelalters', in *Deutsches Schiffahrtsarchiv*, 6, 189–207.

[11] J W van Nouhuys (1931), 'The Model of a Spanish Caravel of the beginning of the Fifteenth Century', *Mariner's Mirror*, 17.

[12] TNA E101/24/14 and enrolled accounts of Thomas Snetesham for 1353–58.

[13] It has been suggested, probably erroneously, that 'balingers', in French *baleinier*, are so-called because they were developed originally on the French coast around Bayonne for the hunting of whales, *baleines*, in the Bay of Biscay; J Bernard (1968), *Navires et gens de mer á Bordeaux*, I, 247.

[14] R J Whitwell and C Johnson (1926), 'The "Newcastle" galley AD 1294', in *Archaeologis Aeliana*, fourth series, II, 142–93. This article has an introduction to the accounts and a full summary in English followed by a transcription of the Latin text from TNA E101/5/20.

[15] The earliest text with details of the building of galleys and other vessels in Venice and some drawings is by Michael of Rhodes. It has been published in Pamela O Long, David McGee and Alan M Stahl, eds (2009), *The Book of Michael of Rhodes: a fifteenth century maritime manuscript*, Cambridge, Mass: MIT Press, 4 vols. The English text is 'Fragments of Shipwrightry', *c*.1586, by Matthew Baker in the Pepys Library at Magdalene College, Cambridge; Pepys MS 2820.

[16] R J Whitwell and C Johnson (1926), 'The "Newcastle" galley AD 1294', 160.

[17] Ian Friel (1986), 'The Building of the Lyme galley, 1294–6', in *Dorset Natural History and Archaeological Society Proceedings*, 108, 41–4.

[18] There is an overview and comparison of 'galleys' built in the fourteenth century in J T Tinniswood (1949), 'English galleys 1272–1377', *Mariner's Mirror*, 35, 276–315.

[19] This account has been published in S Rose, ed (2003), 'The Bayonne galleys', in M Duffy, ed, *Naval Miscellany VI*, Aldershot: Ashgate for the Navy Records Society, 1–36.

[20] John Bennell (2000), 'The Oared Vessels', in Knighton and Loades, *The Antony Roll of Henry VIII's Navy*, 34–8.

[21] James Sherborne (1977), 'English Barges and Balingers of the Late Fourteenth Century', originally published in *MM*, 63, 1977, reprinted in Anthony Tuck, ed (1994), *War, Politics and Culture in Fourteenth Century England*, London: Hambledon Press, 71–6.

[22] Details of the *Paul* can be found in the City of London Letter Book G f.304 in H T Riley (1868), *Memorials of London and London Life in the xiii, xiv and xv centuries*, London: Rolls Series.

[23] Graham Cushway (2011), *Edward III and the War at Sea*, 203.

[24] Susan Rose, ed (1982), *The Navy of the Lancastrian Kings*, London: Allen and Unwin for the Navy Records Society, 222–8.

[25] Susan Rose (1982), *The Navy of the Lancastrian Kings*, 42–3.

[26] Frank Taylor and John S Roskill (1975), *Gesta Henrici Quinti*, Chapter 24, 160–7.

[27] NNAS, shelf 2 no 6, printed in *The Household Books of John Howard, Duke of Norfolk, 1462–71, 1481–83*, Stroud: Alan Sutton for the Richard III and Yorkist History Trust, xliv.

[28] *The Household Books of John Howard, Duke of Norfolk, 1462–71, 1481–83*, Stroud: Alan Sutton for the Yorkist History Trust, I, 197–213. Howard's carvel was called the *Edward*.

[29] Dorothy Burwash (reprint 1969), *English Merchant Shipping 1460–1540*, Newton Abbot: David and Charles, 194–7.

[30] Susan Rose (1982), *The Navy of the Lancastrian Kings*, 189–205, inventories and appendix 4, 245.

[31] Gillian Hutchinson (1994), *Medieval Ships and Shipping*, 27–31.

[32] Michael E Mallett (1967), *The Florentine Galleys in the Fifteenth Century*, Oxford: Clarendon Press, 258–9.

[33] '*Unser Stad Siegel ghenomed den kogghen*', quoted in Detlev Ellmers (1994), 'The Cog as cargo carrier', in Robert Gardiner, ed, *Cogs, Caravels and Galleons*,

London: Conway Maritime Press, 29.

[34] J Topham, ed (1787), *Liber Quotidianus Contrarotulatoris Garderobae 1299–1300i*, London.

[35] TNA E101/10/29.

[36] Graham Cushway (2011), *Edward III and the War at Sea*, appendix 3.

[37] Susan Rose (1982), *The Navy of the Lancastrian Kings*, 249.

[38] Dorothy Burwash (reprint 1969), *English Merchant Shipping 1460–1540*, 192–3.

[39] Ian Friel (1995), *The Good Ship: ships, shipbuilding and technology in England 1200–1520*, London: British Museum Press, 35–8.

[40] Detlev Elmers (1994), 'The cog as cargo carrier', in Robert Gardiner, ed, *Cogs, Caravels and Galleons*, 44–6.

## CHAPTER 5

[1] R J Whitwell and C Johnson (1926), 'The Newcastle galley, AD 1294', *Archaeologia Aeliana*, 162.

[2] N A M Rodger, *The Safeguard of the Sea*, 53.

[3] R C Anderson (1928), 'English galleys in 1295', *Mariner's Mirror*, 14, 223.

[4] J T Tinniswood (1949), 'English Galleys, 1272–1377', *Mariner's Mirror*, 35, 280; C Johnson (1927), 'London shipbuilding AD 1295', *Antiquaries Journal*, 7, 424–5.

[5] Gillian Hutchinson (1994), *Medieval Ships and Shipping*, 110.

[6] Susan Rose (2004), 'Royal Ships on the Thames before 1450', in Roger Owen, ed, *Shipbuilding on the Thames and Thames-built Ships*, West Wickham: J R Owen, 11–19.

[7] TNA E364/59.

[8] The accounts relating to the building of these ships are to be found in TNA E364/57 Berd's Account for the *Gracedieu* and her companion ships. Soper's first account is TNA E364/61 which includes the costs of the building of the *Holighost de la Tour*.

[9] Fragmentary accounts of work on these ships appear in Appendices 1 and 2 in Susan Rose, ed (1982), *The Navy of the Lancastrian Kings*.

[10] *Ad modus unius gallee* TNA E364/59; entry under the ship's name.

[11] Peter S Bellamy and Gustav Milne (2003), 'An Archaeological Evaluation of the Medieval Shipyard Facilities at Small Hythe', *Archaeologia Cantiana*, 353–82.

[12] Susan Rose (1982), *The Navy of the Lancastrian Kings*, 39.

[13] Susan Rose (1998), *Southampton and the Navy in the Age of Henry V*, Winchester: Hampshire County Council, 5.

[14] Susan Rose (1982), *The Navy of the Lancastrian Kings*, 39, 69.

[15] L A Burgess, ed (1976), *The Southampton Terrier of 1454*, London: HMSO, entry 276, 85.

[16] TNA E101/53/11. An investigation of the supposed site in Bursledon by the *Time Team* television programme found one or two possible ship nails, but was stymied by the fact that the most likely position for a shipbuilding dock was under the station car park.

[17] The accounts of the building of the dock at Portsmouth and the *Sweepstake* and the *Mary Fortune* can be found in M Oppenheim, ed (1896), *Naval Accounts and Inventories of the Reign of Henry VII*, London: Naval Records Society. This edition also includes details of the repair of the *Sovereign* and the *Regent*.

[18] C.P.R. 1422-9, 460.

[19] Ian Friel (1993), 'Henry V's *Gracedieu* and the wreck in the R Hamble near Bursledon, Hampshire', *The International Journal of Nautical Archaeology*, 22, 5.

[20] Ian Friel (1993), loc cit.

[21] Susan Rose (1998), *Southampton and the Navy in the Age of Henry V*, Winchester: Hampshire County Council, 6.

[22] Ian Friel (1986), 'The Building of the Lyme galley, 1294–5', 41.

[23] R C Anderson (1928), 'English galleys in 1295', *Mariner's Mirror*, 230.

[24] Charles Johnson (1927), 'London Shipbuilding, AD 1295', 431.

[25] M E Mallett (1967), *The Florentine Galleys in the Fifteenth Century*, 258–9.

[26] TNA E364/61.

[27] Susan Rose (1982), *The Navy of the Lancastrian Kings*, 211–12.

[28] M Oppenheim (1896), *Naval Accounts and Inventories*, 294.

[29] Inventories for many of Henry V's ships can be found in Susan Rose (1982), *The Navy of the Lancastrian Kings*. The later ones for the reign of Henry VII are in M Oppenheim (1896), *Naval Accounts and Inventories*, details of flags on 273.

[30] R J Whitwell and C Johnson (1926), 'The Newcastle galley, AD 1294', 161–87.

[31] Ian Friel (1986), 'The Building of the Lyme galley, 1294–5', 41.

[32] R C Anderson (1928), 'English galleys in 1295', *Mariner's Mirror*, 225.

[33] Ian Friel (2012), '1295 and all that: the English galley-building accounts revisited', forthcoming.

[34] Susan Rose, ed (2008), 'The provision of Ships for Edward I's campaign in Scotland 1300–1306, barges and merchantmen', *Naval Miscellany VII*, 12–22.

[35] Susan Rose (1998), *Southampton and the Navy in the Age of Henry V*, Winchester: Hampshire County Council, 11.

[36] M Oppenheim (1896), *Naval Accounts and Inventories*, 178–81, Wages of Shipwrights and Caulkers working on the *Sovereign*.

[37] N A M Rodger (1997), *The Safeguard of the Sea*, 119.

[38] Ian Friel (1993), 'Henry V's *Gracedieu* and the wreck in the R Hamble near Bursledon, Hampshire', 4.

[39] A R Myers, ed (1969), *English Historical Documents IV*, 516–22.

40 The total costs of building these ships can be found in Ian Friel (1986), 'The building of the Lyme galley', 42. Costs for Henry VII's ships in M Oppenheim's *Naval Accounts and Inventories*, 299, 325.

41 R C Anderson, (1928), 'English galleys in 1295', *Mariner's Mirror*, 220–41

42 TNA C47/2/49/item 14.

43 Susan Rose (1982), *The Navy of the Lancastrian Kings*, 176–7 and 135.

44 Susan Rose (1982), *The Navy of the Lancastrian Kings*, 200.

45 David Childs (2009), *Tudor Sea Power: the Foundation of Greatness*, Barnsley: Seaforth Publishing, 167.

CHAPTER 6

1 Matthew Paris, ed Henry R Luard (1872–83), *Chronica Majora*, London: Longman and Co, Rolls Series, V, 270, 272.

2 Jill Eddison (2004), 'The Origins of Winchelsea', in David and Barbara Martin, eds, *New Winchelsea, Sussex: a medieval port town*, London: Institute of Archaeology, University College, 1–5. Also see Jill Eddison (2000), *Romney Marsh, Survival on a Frontier*, Stroud: Tempus, 77–9.

3 Jill Eddison (2000), *Romney Marsh, Survival on a Frontier*, 79–80.

4 *Gervase Opera* (1880), ed William Stubbs, London: Longman and Co, Rolls Series, II, 292.

5 Jill Eddison (2004), 'The Origins of Winchelsea', in David and Barbara Martin, eds, *New Winchelsea, Sussex: a medieval port town*, 6.

6 Helen Clark (2012), *Discover Medieval Sandwich: a guide to its history and buildings*, Oxford: Oxbow Books, 1–6.

7 Helen Clark (2012), *Discover Medieval Sandwich*, 100.

8 Robin Ward (2004), 'The Earliest Known Sailing Directions in English: transcription and analysis', *Deutsches Schiffahrtsarchiv*, 27, 78.

9 Reginald of Durham, 'Life of St Goderic', in G C Coulton (1918), *Social Life in Britain from the Conquest to the Reformation*, Cambridge: Cambridge University Press, 415–20.

10 Robin Ward (2009), *The World of the Medieval Shipmaster: Law, Business and the Sea c.1350–c.1450*, Woodbridge: Boydell, Appendix 1, 183–205.

11 Robin Ward (2009), *The World of the Medieval Shipmaster*, 191–2.

12 TNA, Kew, Exchequer Accounts Various, E101/44/29. Particulars of the Accounts of William Catton.

13 Susan Rose (1977), 'Henry V's *Gracedieu* and mutiny at sea: some new evidence', *MM*, 3–5.

14 Robin Ward (2009), *The World of the Medieval Shipmaster: Law, Business and the Sea c.1350–1450*, Woodbridge: Boydell, 95–7.

15 *Pearl*, lines 152–60 modernised; quoted in Robin Ward (2009), op cit, 97.

16 Susan Rose (2002), *Medieval Naval Warfare*, London: Routledge, 20.

17 TNA, Kew, Exchequer Accounts Various, E101/24/7.

18 Susan Rose (1982), *The Navy of the Lancastrian Kings*, 129–30.

19 TNA Kew, E372/203.

20 Lucy Toulmin Smith, ed (1894), *Expeditions to Prussia and the Holy Land made by Henry Earl of Derby (afterwards King Henry IV) in the Years 1390–91 and 1392–93*, London: Camden Society, 157–8.

21 Robin Ward (2009), *The World of the Medieval Shipmaster*, 203.

22 Alison Hanham (1985), *The Celys and their World: an English merchant family of the fifteenth century*, Cambridge: Cambridge University Press, 390–1.

23 These tubs are listed in the inventories of royal ships in the fifteenth century. Susan Rose, (1982), *The Navy of the Lancastrian Kings*, 169, 173, 175, 176.

24 Susan Rose (2007), *The Medieval Sea*, London: Hambledon/Continuum, 103–4.

25 Craig Lambert (2011), *Shipping the Medieval Military: English Maritime Logistics in the Fourteenth Century*, Woodbridge: Boydell, 187.

26 Susan Rose (1982), *The Navy of the Lancastrian Kings*, 241.

27 Susan Rose (1982), *The Navy of the Lancastrian Kings*, 245.

28 Søren Thirslund (nd), *Viking Navigation: sun compass guided Norsemen first to America*, Humlebaek, Denmark.

29 M Bound and J Monaghan (2001), *A ship cast away about Alderney: investigations of an Elizabethan Shipwreck*, Alderney: Alderney Maritime Trust.

30 Guy Ropars and others (2011), 'A depolarizer as a possible precise sunstone for Viking navigation by polarised sunlight', *Proceedings of the Royal Society A: Mathematical, Physical and Engineering Science*, published online 2/11/2011.

31 E G R Taylor (1956), *The Haven-Finding Art: a History of Navigation from Odysseus to Captain Cook*, London: Hollis and Carter, 81–4.

32 David W Waters (1958), *The Art of Navigation in England in Elizabethan and Early Stuart Times*, London: Hollis and Carter, 31.

33 Alan M Stahl (2009), *The Book of Michael of Rhodes: a fifteenth century manuscript*, vol II, Cambridge, Mass: MIT Press, 365–73.

34 A printed Breton tide set of tide tables from the sixteenth century shows an English flag flying over Bordeaux, although it was captured by the French in 1453. E G R Taylor (1956), *The Haven-Finding Art*, 170–1.

35 There is a full discussion of early navigation in Richard A Paselk, 'Medieval Tools of Navigation: an overview', in *Art, Science and Technology*.

36 A Moore (1914), 'Accounts and Inventories of John Starlyng', *MM*, 168.

37 TNA E101/25/7. An extract from this document including this passage is included in Susan Rose, ed, 'Accounts from the early days of the office of the Clerk of the King's Ships: Thomas de Snetesham's

Accounts for 1344–5 and 1350–54', in Brian Vale, ed, *The Naval Miscellany VIII*, The Navy Records Society, forthcoming.

38 *The Cely Papers*, 177.

39 Robin Ward (2004), 'The earliest known Sailing Directions in English: transcription and analysis', *Deutsches Schiffahrtsarchiv*, 27, 49–92.

40 E Galili, B Rosen, D Zneily (2009), *IJNA*, 38.

41 Robin Ward (2004), 'The earliest known sailing directions in English', *Deutsches Schiffahrtsarchiv*, 27, Transcription of the Hastings MS rutter, 83.

42 E G R Taylor (1956), *The Haven-Finding Art*, 159.

43 Richard A Paselk fully describes early navigational instruments in 'Medieval Tools of Navigation: an Overview'.

44 A fuller discussion of the advance of scientific navigation in sixteenth century England can be found in Susan Rose (2004), 'Mathematics and the Art of Navigation: the advance of scientific seamanship in Elizabethan England', *Transactions of the Royal Historical Society*, sixth series xiv, 175–84.

45 Frederick J Furnivall, ed (1867), *The Stacions of Rome and the Pilgrim's Sea Voyage*, London: Early English Text Society, vol 25, 37–40.

46 R C Anderson (1962), *Oared Fighting Ships from Classical Times to the Coming of Steam*, London: Percival Marshall, chapters 5–8.

47 Graham Cushway (2011), *Edward III and the War at Sea*, 85; N A M Rodger (1997), *The Safeguard of the Sea*, 138–9.

48 Nicholas Rodger (1997), *The Safeguard of the Sea*.

49 Wolf-Dieter Hoheisel (2009), 'The Hanseatic Cog', in Jenny Bennett, ed, *Sailing into the Past: Learning from Replica Ships*, Barnsley: Seaforth, 70–98.

50 Susan Rose (2007), *The Medieval Sea*, London: Continuum, 17. The MS is discussed in R C Anderson (1925), *The Mariner's Mirror*, 11.

51 Wolf-Dieter Hoheisel (2009), 'The Hanseatic Cog', in Jenny Bennett, ed, *Sailing into the Past: Learning from Replica Ships*, 70–83.

52 Philippe Dollinger (1964), *La Hanse, xii–xvii siécles*, Paris: Aubier, 182.

53 John H Hattendorf and others, eds (1993), *British Naval Documents, 1204–1960*, London: The Scolar Press for the Navy Records Society, 18–19. The account has been taken from the *Chronica Majora* of Matthew Paris.

54 From *El Victorial*, the life of Dom Pero Niño by his standard bearer; the translation used is that in *British Naval Documents, 1204–1960*, 26–29.

55 Robin Ward (2009), *The World of the Medieval Shipmaster*, 24, 228.

## CHAPTER 7

1 C T Allmand, ed (1973), *Society at War: the experience of England and France during the Hundred Years War*, Edinburgh: Oliver and Boyd, 17–18.

2 G W Coopland (1949), *The Tree of Battles of Honoré Bonet*, Liverpool: Liverpool University Press, 143–4, 190.

3 Sir Travers Twiss (1871), *The Black Book of the Admiralty*, vol I, London: the Rolls Series, 25. In Travers Twiss's book the articles are printed in the original Norman French with a translation into English made by Thomas Bedford, the Registrar of the Admiralty Court in the reign of James II (Travers Twiss, vol I, lxxii). Quotations are from this translation.

4 Travers Twiss (1871), *The Black Book of the Admiralty*, 21, 23. The term *gaillioters* probably means nothing more than 'galleymen'; that is, the crew of many of the vessels in the State navies of Mediterranean powers.

5 Christopher Allmand (2011), *The De Re Militari of Vegetius: reception, transmission and legacy of a Roman text in the Middle Ages*, Cambridge: Cambridge University Press, 322–9.

6 Travers Twiss (1871), *The Black Book of the Admiralty*, 13.

7 Graham Cushway (2011), *Edward III and the War at Sea*, 85.

8 Robert Douglas Smith and Kelly DeVries (2005), *The Artillery of the Dukes of Burgundy, 1363–1477*, Woodbridge: Boydell, 11.

9 Susan Rose (1982), *The Navy of the Lancastrian Kings*, 141, 151. The *Graunt Marie* had three cannon and the *Thomas* four.

10 Gillian Hutchinson (1994), *Medieval Ships and Shipping*, 160.

11 Robert Douglas Smith and Kelly DeVries (2005), *The Artillery of the Dukes of Burgundy, 1363–1477*, 239–41; pictures of early guns, 263–5.

12 Gillian Hutchinson (1994), *Medieval Ships and Shipping*, 156–8.

13 Ian Friel (2003), 'Oars, Sails and Guns: the English and war at sea, c.1200-1500', in John B Hattendorf and Richard W Unger, *War at Sea in the Middle Ages and the Renaissance*, Woodbridge: Boydell, 73.

14 Alexandra Sinclair, ed (2003), *The Beauchamp Pageant*, Donnington: Paul Watkins, XXXVI [f.18v].

15 M Oppenheim, ed (1886), *Naval Accounts and Inventories of the Reign of Henry VII*. London: Navy Records Society, 194–6, 274, 277–9.

16 Henry T Riley, trans (1853), *The Annals of Roger de Hoveden comprising the History of England and of other countries of Europe from AD 732 to AD 1201*, vol II, London: Bohn, 206.

17 Sir Nicholas Harris Nicolas (1847), *A History of the Royal Navy*, 106–22.

18 Carole Hillenbrand (1999), *The Crusades: Islamic Perspectives*, Edinburgh: Edinburgh University Press, 565–6.

19 J A Giles (1849), *Roger of Wendover's Flowers of History*, vol 2, London: Bohn, 271–3.

20 There is a full biography of the Earl in ODNB. The verse biography is to be found in P Meyer, ed (1891–1901), *L'Historie de Guillaume le Maréchal*, 3 vols, Paris.

21 Eustace's career can be found in *Li Romans di Witasse le Moine*, Denis Joseph Conlon, ed (1972), Chapel

Hill: University of North Carolina.

22 Squirrel fur.

23 The battle and its aftermath are described in verses 17216–17528 of the verse biography of the Marshal; 258–69 in vol III.

24 Matthew Paris, largely following Roger of Wendover, describes the battle in *Historia Anglorum*, 219–21.

25 N A M Rodger (1997), *The Safeguard of the Sea*, 93.

26 N A M Rodger (1997), *The Safeguard of the Sea*, 96.

27 Geoffrey Brereton, ed (1968), *Froissart Chronicles*, 61.

28 Colin Platt (1973), *Medieval Southampton: the port and trading community AD 1000–1600*, London: Routledge, 111.

29 Edward Maunde Thompson, ed (1889), *Adae Murimuth Continuatio Chronicarum*, 103–4.

30 Sir Nicholas Harris Nicolas gives a full account both of the preliminaries and the battle itself in his *History of the Royal Navy*, vol II, 44–64. A clear account of the meeting with the Chancellor will be found in Edward Maunde Thompson, ed (1889), *Robertus de Avesbury De gestis Edwardi Tertii*, 310–12.

31 John B Hattendorf et al, eds (1993), *British Naval Documents 1204–1960*, Aldershot: Scolar Press for the Navy Records Society, 22.

32 Edward Maunde Thompson, ed (1889), *Chronicon Galfridus le Baker*, Oxford.

33 Kelly DeVries, 'God, Leadership, Flemings and Archery: contemporary perceptions of victory and defeat at the battle of Sluys 1340', printed in S Rose, ed (2008), *Medieval Ships and Warfare*, Aldershot: Ashgate, 131–50, gives an overview of reactions to the battle. Graham Cushway (2011), *Edward III and the War at Sea*, 90–100, also looks at the battle in detail.

34 Edward Maunde Thompson, ed (1889), *Robetrus de Avesbury De Gestis Edwardi Tertii*, 412.

35 Geoffrey Brereton, ed (1968), *Froissart Chronicles*, 113–9.

36 Edward Maunde Thompson, ed (1889), *Chronicon Galfridus le Baker*, Oxford, 109–11.

37 James Sherborne (1994), 'The Battle of la Rochelle and the War at Sea, 1372–75', in Anthony Tuck, ed, *War Politics and Culture in Fourteenth Century England*, 41–53.

38 V H Galbraith, ed (1927), *The Anonimale Chronicle 1333–1381*, 71.

39 S Luce, ed (1862), *Chronique des quatre premiers Valois*, Paris: Societé de l'Histoire de France, 232–4.

40 James Sherborne (1994), 'The Battle of la Rochelle and the War at Sea, 1372–75', 41.

41 Graham Cushway (2011), *Edward III and the War at Sea*, 202.

42 Tony K Moore, 'The Cost-benefit Analysis of a Fourteenth Century Naval Campaign: Margate/Cadzand, 1387', in Richard Gorski, ed (2012), *Roles of the Sea in Medieval England*, Woodford: Boydell, 103–24.

43 Susan Rose (1982), *The Navy of the Lancastrian Kings*, 48–9.

44 Frank Taylor and John S Roskell (1975), *Gesta Henrici Quinti: the deeds of Henry V*, Oxford: Clarendon Press, 145–7.

45 Frank Taylor and John S Roskell (1975), *Gesta Henrici Quinti*, 149.

46 Charles Lethbridge Kingsford, ed (1905), *Chronicles of London*, 71.

47 Frank Taylor and John S Roskell (1975), *Gesta Henrici Quinti*, 161–7.

48 Susan Rose (1982), *The Navy of the Lancastrian Kings*, 49–51.

49 Susan Rose (1977), 'Henry V's *Gracedieu* and mutiny at sea: some new evidence', *MM*, 63.

CHAPTER 8

1 Michel Mollat (1975), 'De la piraterie sauvage á la course réglementée (xiv-xv siècles)' in *Course et Piraterie: Commission Internationale d'Histoire Maritime*, San Francisco, 162–84.

2 David J Starkey (2011), 'Voluntaries and sea robbers: a review of the academic literature on privateering, corsairing, buccaneering and piracy', in *MM*, 97, 127–47; R G Marsden (1909), 'Early Prize Jurisdiction and Prize Law in England', in *EHR*, 24, 675–97.

3 Jacques Paviot (1994), 'Le problème de la sûreté sur la Manche et la Mer du Nord au début du xv siècle', in *Les Champs Relationnel en Europe du Nord et du Nord-Ouest des origines à la fin du Première Empire; 1ère Colloque Historique de Calais*, Calais: np, 171–6.

4 R G Marsden (1909), 'Early Prize Jurisdiction', 678, 681–2.

5 Graphs in E M Carus-Wilson and Olive Coleman, eds (1963), *England's Export Trade 1275–1547*, Oxford: Clarendon Press, give a clear view of the trends in total exports for wool on 122–3, and for cloth on 138–9.

6 Glyn S Burgess (1997), *Two Medieval Outlaws: Eustace the Monk and Fouke Fitzwaryn*, Woodbridge: D S Brewer, 78. From the translation of *Li Romans de Witasse le Moine*.

7 This is a translation from the rhyming chronicle of Lodewijk Van Velthem, *Voortzetting van de Spieghel Historiael*, translated by Henry S Lucas (1945), in 'John Crabbe: Flemish Pirate, Merchant and Adventurer', in *Speculum*, 20, 341–2.

8 Henry S Lucas (1945), 'John Crabbe: Flemish Pirate, Merchant and Adventurer', in *Speculum*, 20, 334–50.

9 Joan Evans, ed (1928), *The Unconquered Knight; a chronicle of the deeds of Don Pero Niño*, London: Routledge, 122–4.

10 C L Kingsford (1925), 'West Country Piracy: the School of English Seamen', in *Prejudice and Promise in XVth century England*, Oxford: Clarendon Press, 82–3.

11 There are several accounts of his career and that of his son. See Dorothy A Gardiner (1966/7), 'John Hawley of Dartmouth', in *Devonshire Association Report and Transactions*, 98–9, 173–206; Stephen P Pistono (1979), 'Henry IV and John Hawley, privateer, 1399–1408', in *Devonshire Association*

Report and Transactions, 111, 145–63.

[12] Dorothy A Gardiner (1976), *A Calendar of Early Chancery Proceedings Relating to West Country Shipping 1388–1493*, Torquay: Devon and Cornwall Record Society, 9, 11, 8–9, 12–13.

[13] Dorothy A Gardiner (1976), *A Calendar of Early Chancery Proceedings Relating to West Country Shipping 1388–1493*, Torquay: Devon and Cornwall Record Society, 14 a to c, 15–16.

[14] Stephen P Pistono (1975), 'Henry IV and the English privateers', in *EHR*, 90, 322–30.

[15] C J Ford (1979), 'Piracy or Policy: the Crisis in the Channel, 1400–1403', in *TRHS*, 5th series, 29, 53–78.

[16] Dorothy A Gardiner (1976), *A Calendar of Early Chancery Proceedings Relating to West Country Shipping 1388–1493*, Torquay: Devon and Cornwall Record Society, 36–7.

[17] C L Kingsford (1925), 'The School of English Seamen', in *Prejudice and Promise in XVth Century England*, Oxford: Clarendon Press, 78–106.

[18] Dirk Meier (2006), *Seafarers, Merchants and Pirates in the Middle Ages*, Woodbridge: Boydell, 146–59.

[19] Lists of admirals can be found in Graham Cushway, *Edward III and the War at Sea*, 219–24 and N A M Rodger, *The Safeguard of the Sea*, 504–7.

[20] Travers Twiss (1871), *The Black Book of the Admiralty, I*, London: Rolls Series, 69. Travers Twiss collated a number of different MSS to produce his edition and printed seventeenth century English translations, where these existed, of the documents in Norman French. Those in Latin are left untranslated. Where possible quotations are taken from Twiss's printed translations.

[21] Robin Ward (2009), *The World of the Medieval Shipmaster*, 28–36.

[22] Travers Twiss (1871), *The Black Book of the Admiralty*, 27.

[23] David and Barbara Martin (2004), *New Winchelsea, a medieval port town*, London: Institute of Archaeology, 79.

[24] TNA E101/10/30, printed in *Naval Miscellany VII*, ed Susan Rose, Aldershot: Ashgate for the Navy Records Society, 40. BL ADD MSS 7966A.

[25] TNA SC8/10/471 (petitions to the Crown), consulted online on 19/12/12.

[26] CPR 1301–7, 469.

[27] Graham Cushway (2011), *Edward III and the War at Sea*, 95. Also ODNB Walter Manny.

[28] Jonathan Sumption (1990), *The Hundred Years War: Trial by Battle*, Philadelphia: University of Pennsylvania Press, 264.

[29] Graham Cushway, *Edward III and the War at Sea*, 75.

[30] Graham Cushway, *Edward III and the War at Sea*, 77.

[31] ODNB Robert Morley.

[32] Graham Cushway, *Edward III and the War at Sea*, 77–9.

[33] Edward Maunde Thompson, ed (1889), *Robertus de Avesburt, De Gestis Mirabilibus Regis Edwardi tertii*, London: Rolls Series, 310–11.

[34] Edward Maunde Thompson, ed (1889), *Adae Murimuth Coninuatio Chronicarum*, 107.

[35] Graham Cushway, *Edward III and the War at Sea*, 170–2.

[36] Susan Rose (1982), *The Navy of the Lancastrian Kings*, 49.

[37] The first part of this petition is printed in English in John Hattendorf et al (1993), *British Naval Documents 1204–1660*, 13. The whole petition can be found in *Rotuli Parliamentorum*, V, 59.

[38] C F Richmond (1964), 'The Keeping of the Seas in the Hundred Years War', in *History*, 167, 283–98. Also see Susan Rose (2002), *Medieval Naval Warfare*, London: Routledge, 88–90.

[39] C F Richmond (1971), 'The War at Sea', in Kenneth Fowler, ed, *The Hundred Years War*, 116.

[40] A R Myers (1969), *English Historical Documents IV 1327–1485*, London: Eyre and Spottiswoode, 267.

[41] Anne Crawford (1992), introduction to *The Household Books of John Howard, Duke of Norfolk, 1462–71, 1481–83*, Stroud: Alan Sutton for the Richard III and Yorkist History Trust, xxii–xxiii, I, 197–213.

[42] Warwick's career as a shipowner and as Captain of Calais are covered in Michael Hicks, (2002), *Warwick the Kingmaker*, Oxford: Blackwell, 142–8.

[43] Colin F Richmond (1998/9), 'The Earl of Warwick's Domination of the Channel and the Naval Dimension to the Wars of the Roses, 1456–1460', *Southern History*, 6.

[44] Norman Davus, ed, *Paston Letters*, II, 340–1. A version in modern English is in *British Naval Documents*, 31–2.

[45] Quoted in Colin F Richmond (1998/9), 'The Earl of Warwick's Domination of the Channel and the Naval Dimension to the wars of the Roses, 1456–1460', 2. The quote comes from John Bales's Chronicle printed in Ralph Flenley, ed, *Six Town Chronicles of England*, Oxford: Oxford University Press, 147.

[46] William Marx, ed (2003), *An English Chronicle 1377–1461*, Woodbridge: Boydell, 82. The details of the events of 1459/60 can be found in R A Griffiths (1998), *The Reign of King Henry VI*, Stroud: Alan Sutton, 817–29.

[47] Michael Hicks, *Warwick the Kingmaker*, 176.

[48] William Marx, *An English Chronicle*, 82; C L Kingsford, ed (1905), *Chronicles of London*, Oxford: Clarendon Press, 171.

[49] R C Anderson (1919), 'The *Grace de Dieu* of 1446–86', in *EHR*, 34, 584–6.

[50] Michael Hicks (2002), *Warwick the Kingmaker*, 250.

[51] G V Scammell (1962), 'Shipowning in England c.1450–1550', in *TRHS* fifth series 12, calls his 'piracies', 'the most flagrant and familiar', and comments on his 'bold if irresponsible handling of seapower.'

[52] Michael Hicks (2002), *Warwick the Kingmaker*, 313.

[53] Shelley Lockwood, ed (1997), *Sir John Fortescue, On the Laws and Governance of England*, Cambridge: Cambridge University Press, 96–7.

[54] *Howard Household Books* II, 3–4.

[55] Anne Crawford (1992), Introduction, *Howard Household Books*, xxiv–xxv.

CHAPTER 9

[1] Quoted in Marc Russon (2004), *Les Côtes Guerrières: mer, guerre et pouvoirs au Moyen Age; France-Façade Océanique xiii–xv siècle*, Rennes: Presses Universitaires, 24.

[2] Marc Russon (2004), *Les Côtes Guerrières: Mer, Guerre et Pouvoirs au Moyen Age, France-Façade océanique xiii–xv siècle*, Rennes: Presses Universitaires, 201–14.

[3] The political aspects of this conflict can be followed in David Abulafia (1997), *The Western Mediterranean Kingdoms, 1200–1500: the struggle for dominion*, London: Longman. The naval aspects can be found in Susan Rose (2002), *Medieval Naval Warfare*, London: Routledge, 44–51.

[4] Full details of the galleys built for the house of Anjou can be found in J H Pryor (1993), 'The galleys of Charles I of Anjou, King of Sicily: ca.1269–84', in *Studies in Medieval and Renaissance History*, 14, 34–103.

[5] Anne Merlin-Chazelas (1977/8), *Documents Relatifs au Clos de Galées de Rouen*, Paris: Bibliothèque Nationale, vol I, 29.

[6] Anne Merlin-Chazelas (1977/8), *Documents Relatifs au Clos de Galées de Rouen*, vol I, 103.

[7] Anne Merlin-Chazelas (1977/8), *Documents Relatifs au Clos de Galées de Rouen*, vol II, item XXXVII, 144.

[8] Charles Bréard (1893), 'Le Compte du Clos des Galées de Rouen au xiv siècle 1382–84', in Blanquart, Bouquet, Bréard, de Circourt, Regnier Sauvage, eds, *Documents, Deuxième Serie*, Rouen: Société de la Historie de Normandie, 90–154.

[9] Anne Merlin-Chazelas (1977/8), *Documents Relatifs au Clos de Galées de Rouen*, vol II, item LXXII, 176–178.

[10] Anne Merlin-Chazelas (1977/8), *Documents Relatifs au Clos de Galées de Rouen*, vol II, 205.

[11] Anne Merlin-Chazelas (1977/8), *Documents Relatifs au Clos de Galées de Rouen*, vol I, 103–4.

[12] Some English commentators are also very impressed by the *Clos*. See Graham Cushway, (2011), *Edward III and the War at Sea*, 52.

[13] Marc Russon (2004), *Les Côtes guerrières: mer, guerre et pouvoirs au Moyen Age; France-Façade océanique xiii–xv siècle*, Rennes: Presses Universitaires, 352–5.

[14] Sir Travers Twiss, *The Black Book of the Admiralty*, vol 1, 426–9.

[15] Charles Bourel de la Roncière (1899), *Histoire de la Marine Française*, Paris: Librarie Plon, vol I, 399.

[16] Susan Rose (2002), *Medieval Naval Warfare*, London: Routledge, 64. The accounts of the 'army of the sea' and a list of the ships involved can be found in Anne Merlin-Chazelas (1977/8), *Documents Relatifs au Clos de Galées de Rouen*, vol II, 33–49, 67–142.

[17] Charles Bourel de la Roncière (1897), 'La Marine au Siège de Calais', in *Bibliothèque de l'école de chartes*, 556–9.

[18] Charles Bourel de la Roncière (1897), 'La Marine au Siège de Calais', in *Bibliothèque de l'école des chartes*, 58, 554–78, 566.

[19] Marc Russon (2004), *Les Côtes guerrières*, 359.

[20] Anne Merlin-Chazelas (1977/8), *Documents Relatifs au Clos de Galées de Rouen*, Document LVIII, 157–8.

[21] Terrier de Lorcy (1877), *Jean de Vienne, Amiral de France*, Paris: Librarie de la Société Bibliographique, Piéces Justicatives, 71, lxi–lxv.

[22] Léopold Pannier and Paul Meyer, eds (1877), *Le Débat des Hérauts de France et d'Angleterre suivi de The Debate between the Heralds of England and France by John Coke*, Paris: Didot, Société des Anciens Textes Français.

[23] This translates freely as: 'I pray to God that he will give the king of France the heart and courage to fight you [the English] at sea because these are the rods with which he can chastise you and cool your courage and that of your neighbours whenever it pleases him to do so.' Léopold Pannier and Paul Meyer, eds (1877), *Le Débat des Hérauts de France et d'Angleterre*, 34.

[24] Philippe Contamine (2003), 'A l'abordage! Pierre de Brézé, grand seneschal de Normandie, et la guerre de course (1452–1458)', in Pierre Bouet et Veronique Gazeau, *La Normandie et l'Angleterre au Moyen Age*, Caen: CRAHM, 307–58.

[25] Philippe Contamine (2003), 'A l'abordage! Pierre de Brézé, grand seneschal de Normandie, et la guerre de course (1452–1458)', 349. The sum is in the French currency *livres tournois*; the rate of exchange was usually four *livres tournois* to the pound sterling.

[26] Lauria has acquired a great reputation as a leader of galleys in battle; accounts of his exploits can be found in J H Pryor (1983), 'The naval battles of Roger of Lauria', *Journal of Medieval History*, 9.

[27] Lawrence V Mott (2003), *Sea Power in the Medieval Mediterranean: the Catalan-Aragonese Fleet in the War of the Sicilian Vespers*, Gainesville et al: University Press of Florida, 82–95.

[28] Lawrence V Mott (2003), *Sea Power in the Medieval Mediterranean*, 210–24.

[29] Lawrence V Mott (2003), *Sea Power in the Medieval Mediterranean*, 146–50.

[30] Lawrence V Mott (2003), *Sea Power in the Medieval Mediterranean*, 143–85.

[31] Galleys with an opening at the poop.

[32] Lawrence V Mott (2003), *Sea Power in the Medieval Mediterranean*, 155–75.

[33] Lawrence V Mott (2003), 'Iberian Naval Power, 100–1650', in John B Hattendorf and Richard W Unger, eds, *War at Sea in the Middle Ages and the Renaissance*, Woodbridge: Boydell, 108.

[34] Wendy R Childs (1978), *Anglo-Castilian Trade in the Later Middle Ages*, Manchester: Manchester University Press, 13.

[35] Florentino Pérez-Embid (1969), 'La marina real castellana en el siglo xiii', in *Annuario de estudios medievales*, 10, 141–55.

[36] Lawrence V Mott (2003), *Sea Power in the Medieval*

*Mediterranean*, 82–3. The Almohad dynasty held power in Andalucia from the mid twelfth century. Its authority was greatly diminished after its forces were defeated by the Christians at the battle of Las Navas de Tolosa in 1212.

[37] Florentino Pérez-Embid (1969), 'La marina real castellana en el siglo xiii', 154–7.

[38] Soft soap was recommended by Vegetius to make decks slippery; it would have been projected by a form of ballista in jars. Its actual use in an engagement is seldom met with.

[39] Florentino Pérez-Embid (1969), 'La marina real castellana en el siglo xiii', 157–66.

[40] Joan Evans (1928), *The Unconquered Knight: a chronicle of the deeds of Don Pero Niño*, London: Routledge, 51–2.

[41] Joan Evans (1928), *The Unconquered Knight*, 100–101. Also see Carlos Martinez-Valverde (1985), 'La nota marinera en la Cronica de Don Pero Niño', *Revista de Historia Naval*, 8, 15–43.

[42] Philippe Dollinger (1964), *La Hanse (xii-xvii siècles)*, Paris: Aubier, is a general history of the League.

[43] T H Lloyd (1991), *England and the German Hanse 1157–1611: a study of their trade and commercial diplomacy*, Cambridge: Cambridge University Press, 173–216.

[44] Philippe Dollinger (1964), *La Hanse (xii-xvii siècles)*, 500–502. Text of the note sent to Edward IV following the arrest of Hanseatic merchants in London in 1469.

[45] Dirk Meier (2006), *Seafarers, Merchants and Pirates in the Middle Ages*, Woodbridge: Boydell, 146–59.

[46] Philippe Dollinger (1964), *La Hanse (xii-xvii siècles)*, 495–6.

[47] John D Fudge (1995), *Cargoes, Embargoes and Emissaries: the commercial and political interaction of England and the German Hanse 1450–1510*, Toronto: University of Toronto Press, 71–3.

## CHAPTER 10

[1] William Catton's accounts as Clerk are TNA E364/54 and 59.

[2] Susan Rose (1982), *The Navy of the Lancastrian Kings*, 6–27.

[3] Susan Rose (1982), *The Navy of the Lancastrian Kings*, 37–40.

[4] Colin Richmond (1967), 'English Naval Power in the Fifteenth Century', *History*, 52, 10.

[5] M Oppenheim, ed (1896), *Naval Accounts and inventories of the Reign of Henry VII, 1485–8 and 1495–7*, London: Navy Records Society, 3–81.

[6] M Oppenheim, ed (1896), *Naval Accounts and inventories of the Reign of Henry VII, 1485–8 and 1495–7*, 135–344.

[7] N A M Rodger (1997), *The Safeguard of the Sea*, 159.

[8] M Oppenheim ( 1896), *Naval Accounts and Inventories*, 34–5.

[9] R C Anderson (1919), 'The *Grace Dieu* of 1446–86', in *EHR*, 136, 584–6.

[10] David Loades (1992), *The Tudor Navy*, 36–8.

[11] M Oppenheim, ed (1896), *Naval Accounts and Inventories of the Reign of Henry VII*, ix.

[12] C S Goldingham, (1918), 'The navy under Henry VII', in *EHR*, 33, 472.

[13] David Loades (1992), *The Tudor Navy: an administrative, political and military history*, Aldershot: The Scolar Press, 42–5.

[14] M Oppenheim (1896), *Accounts and Inventories*, Brygandynes' Account for 1495–7, passim.

[15] Alexandra Sinclair, ed (2003), *The Beauchamp Pageant*, plates ix, xv, xxv, xxvi, xxxvi, xlix, l.

[16] David Loades states that they were clinker-built, but this would have been very unusual for English ships of this size by the 1480s. When repaired in 1495–97 the accounts printed by Oppenheim make clear that both had carvel-built hulls. David Loades (1992), *The Tudor Navy*, 39.

[17] M Oppenheim (1896), *Naval Accounts and Inventories*, 181–2, 228–9.

[18] C S Knighton and D M Loades, eds (2000), *The Anthony Roll of Henry VIII's Navy*, Aldershot: Ashgate for the Navy Records Society.

[19] Burkhard Bange (2009), 'The caravel', in Jenny Bennett, ed, *Sailing into the Past*, Barnsley: Seaforth, 95–8.

[20] M Oppenheim (1896), *Naval Accounts and Inventories*, 181, 293, 313.

[21] Robert Douglas Smith and Kelly DeVries (2005), *The Artillery of the Duke of Burgundy 1363–1477*, Woodbridge: Boydell, 227–30.

[22] N A M Rodger (1997), *The Safeguard of the Sea*, 500–1.

[23] Details for the Bristol voyages and supporting documents can be found online at www.bris.ac.uk/Depts/History/Maritime/Sources/1 498ayala.htm, consulted on 14/02/13.

[24] Susan Flavin and Evan T Jones, eds (2009), *Bristol's Trade with Ireland and the Continent, 1503–1601*, Dublin: Four Courts Press for the Bristol Record Society, 24–6, 71–2, 78.

[25] N A M Rodger (1997), *The Safeguard of the Sea*, 222–5; David Loades (1992), *The Tudor Navy*, 81–3.

[26] David Loades (1992), *The Tudor Navy*, 9.

## CONCLUSION

[1] William Laird Clowes (1897–1903), *The Royal Navy: A History from the Earliest Times to the Present*, 7 vols, London: Sampson Low, Marston.

[2] N A M Rodger (1997), *The Safeguard of the Sea*, xxv.

[3] The illustration of the rig of a galleon dated 1555 may be similar to that of the *Regent*. The rig of the *Santa Clara* from an inventory of 1498 does not show either a main topmast and sail or a sprit sail which were certainly carried by the *Regent*. R Gardiner, ed (1994), *Cogs, Caravels and Galleons*, London: Conway, 96, 101.

[4] Alfred Spont (1897), *Letters and Papers relating to the war with France 1512–13*, London: Navy Records Society, 155.

# INDEX

# ACKNOWLEDGEMENTS

The format of this book was suggested to me by Julian Mannering, the guiding spirit of Seaforth Publishing, and my first thanks must be to him. Without his constant support and encouragement it would probably never have seen the light of day. I have also shamelessly trespassed on the goodwill of my friend Shoshanna Hoffman who translated for me, from German, material relating to the Ebersdorf ship model. This involved getting to grips with many technical terms relating to medieval shipbuilding and was a formidable task undertaken with enormous patience and goodwill.

The staff at the British Library and The National Archives at Kew have also smoothed my path in many ways and I am very grateful for their help. My husband accompanied me on our enjoyable trips taking photographs of fortifications and ports, some of which can be seen in the book. His support was, as ever, unstinting and invaluable, contributing greatly to the completion of the project. I am, of course, responsible for any errors or omissions but I hope that readers will enjoy the book as much as I have enjoyed putting it together.

SUSAN ROSE
*Highgate, 2013*